GOD OF THE POOR

Praxis - transforming action

Victorio Araya

GOD OF THE POOR

THE MYSTERY OF GOD
IN LATIN AMERICAN LIBERATION THEOLOGY

Translated from the Spanish by
Robert R. Barr

ORBIS ✪ BOOKS

Maryknoll, New York 10545

The Catholic Foreign Mission Society of America (Maryknoll) recruits and trains people for overseas missionary service. Through Orbis Books Maryknoll aims to foster the international dialogue that is essential to mission. The books published, however, reflect the opinions of their authors and are not meant to represent the official position of the society.

First published as *El Dios de los pobres: El misterio de Dios en la teología de la liberación*, by Departamento Ecuménico de Investigaciones (DEI), Apdo. 339, San Pedro de Montes de Oca, San José, Costa Rica, and Ediciones SEBILA, Apdo. 901, San José, Costa Rica

© 1983 by Victorio Araya Guillén and Departamento Ecuménico de Investigaciones

English translation © 1987 by Orbis Books, Maryknoll, NY 10545
Manufactured in the United States of America

Manuscript editor: William E. Jerman

Library of Congress Cataloging-in-Publication Data
Araya, Victorio, 1945-
  God of the poor.

  Translation of: El Dios de los pobres.
  Bibliography: p.
  1. Liberation theology.   I. Title.
BT83.57A713   1987   230   87-7808
ISBN 0-88344-566-2
ISBN 0-88344-565-4 (pbk.)

To the memory of my parents,
Rosa and José María

For Noel Vargas Castro,
Protestant minister and religious educator,
murdered October 19, 1983,
in Pantasma (in the north of Nicaragua)
for his fidelity to the God of the poor
in the service of the least
of his brothers and sisters (John 15:13)

The universality of God's love is inseparably linked with the preferential option for the poor. . . . The ultimate reason for our making this option is in the God in whom we believe. I have called it the *ultimate* foundation of Christian discipleship because there can be, and are, other valid motives: the situation of the poor today, the results of socio-political analysis, the evangelizing potential of the poor, and so on. But when all is said and done, the reason for solidarity with the poor—with their life and with their death—is anchored in our faith in God, the God of life. This is a theo-centric option, centered in God.

GUSTAVO GUTIÉRREZ,
El Dios de la vida

The very reality of a crucified people poses—in its most radical form, to my way of thinking—the question of the ultimacy of reality and the reality of the divine. . . . The very reality, the historical reality, of a crucified people cries out to God even before its groans are made the object of thought. If we would know "where" the question of God is posited, it is here. Faced with the alternatives of life/death, liberation/oppression, salvation/condemnation, sin/grace, we are faced with the paramount question of God—in history.

JON SOBRINO,
Jesús en América Latina

Contents

PREFACE   **xiii**

ACRONYMS   **xv**

INTRODUCTION   **1**
The Theme of this Study: Scope and Limits   1
   The Mystery of God   *1*
   Latin American Theology of Liberation as Concrete Framework   *1*
   Thematic Delimitations   *2*
Sources   3
   Works of Gustavo Gutiérrez   *3*
   Works of Jon Sobrino   *4*
   Other Theological Works   *6*
Presuppositions   7
   Epistemological Locus   *7*
   Theological Locus   *7*
Methodology   11
   A Monographic-Bibliographic Study   *11*
   Development: Steps to Be Followed   *11*

CHAPTER 1
LIBERATIVE THEO-LOGY: MEANING PARADIGM   **13**
Liberation Process and Liberative Theology   15
   Negative Definition of Liberation Theology   *15*
   Positive Definition of Liberation Theology   *16*
Liberative Theo-logy and the Outlook of the Poor   20
   The Poor as Locus Theologicus   *20*
   A New Conception of the Political   *23*
Outlook of the Poor and Theo-logy: Modality of Liberative
        Theo-logical Reflection   24
   Believing   *25*
   Responsible   *25*
   Historical   *28*
   Dialectical   *29*
   Praxic   *31*
   Evangelical   *32*

Liberative Theo-logy and the Mystery of God   33
   A Basic "Thesis Text" ("Primordial Intuition")   *33*
   Reading Keys: Hermeneutic Keys   *34*
Excursus I: Historico-Prophetic Religion—Theistic Hermeneutics
          of History   40
   Historico-Prophetic Religions   *40*
   Elements of a Religion of History   *41*
   The Religion of Israel   *42*
   Israel's Theo-logical Vision   *43*

CHAPTER 2
LIBERATIVE THEO-LOGY: DOGMATIC ARTICULATION   **46**
The Mystery of God: Ongoing Manifestation   46
   Self-Manifestation (Autophany)   *46*
   God's Manifestation in Jesus of Nazareth   *48*
The Mystery of God: In Hidden Solidarity   50
   A God Hidden . . .   *51*
   "You Are the God of the Poor"   *52*
   God: Suffering Love   *58*
The Mystery of God: Salvific Praxis   67
   The Liberator God: The Exodus Experience   *68*
   God as Go'el: *Vindicator*   *69*
   The God of Life "Who Vanquishes Death and Re-creates Life"   *70*
Conclusion: The God of the Kingdom   75

CHAPTER 3
LIBERATIVE THEO-LOGY AS THEO-PRAXIS   **77**
Gratuity/Exigency: Constitutive Dialectic of the Faith-Life   79
   The Meaning of "Praxis secundum Deum*" (Theo-praxis)*   *79*
   Theo-praxis: Conversion and Mission   *80*
Levels of "Correspondence to God"   83
   Love of God and Love of Neighbor: One Love   *83*
   Anti-Idolatry Praxis: Faith in God against the Idols of
             Oppression   *91*
Excursus II: Historical Praxis, Sin, and the Reign of God   104
   Human History and Sin (Mysterium Iniquitatis)   *104*
   Personal Commitment and Kingdom (Mysterium Liberationis)   *106*

CHAPTER 4
LIBERATIVE THEO-LOGY: AN EVALUATION   **108**
Theo-logical Overview   108
Value Judgment   111
   "Dialogical Openness" to Liberation Theology   *111*
   The Outlook of the Poor: Key to the Understanding and Evaluation
             of Liberation Theology   *112*
   Theological Method   *119*

The Mystery of God   125
The Poor as Theo-phanic Locus   125
Theo-phanic Value of Praxis from a Point of Departure in the
                    Poor   126
The God of the Poor   129
Theo-praxis and Ecclesiology   136
Theo-praxis: A Way of Corresponding to God   137
Theo-praxis in Solidarity with the Poor   138
Negative Moment (via negativa) *of Denunciation and Exposé   141*
Positive Moment (via positiva) *of Affirmation, Accompaniment,*
                    Proclamation, and Celebration   142
Ecumenical Dimension of an Ecclesial Praxis in Solidarity with the
                    Poor   143
Prospective Reflection   144
Final Reflection   146
Discerning the Signs of the Times   146
Open History   146
Wagering on Humankind   148
Room to Be Persons   149
Living according to the Spirit   151
Conclusion   152

NOTES   **153**

REFERENCE BIBLIOGRAPHY   **193**

Preface

The commitment to the defense of the fundamental right to a full life for the impoverished majorities of the Third World (which contains two-thirds of the world's population) has meant for many persons a new and profound encounter with the God of the Bible, who was revealed in Jesus Christ, who "made himself poor though he was rich" (2 Cor. 8:9).

Insofar as it is an "understanding of the faith," the theology of liberation is a reflection on the historico-salvific manifestation of God (*Mysterium Liberationis*), a salvation that in the first place is offered as good and joyful news to the poor (Luke 4:18). And that reflection has led many to listen as never before very clearly to the word of God through the lacerating cry of millions of the poor—truly the condemned of the earth.

From an incarnation in the world of the poor ("the underside of history"), the essential role of Latin American liberation theology has been to explain and to locate concretely in history the fact that the Mystery of God has manifested itself as the *God of the poor.* The God of the poor is the God of the Bible. The God of the Bible is the God who unconditionally and passionately takes the side of the poor and oppressed on behalf of their life and liberation, and who juxtaposes their lives to the justice of the kingdom of God.

The present work, as its title indicates, seeks to offer, in the perspective of faith, a reflection on the Mystery of God; it is a quest for a deeper understanding of God who is as *Mysterium Liberationis* at the heart of our concrete history of oppression (a history of sin) and struggle for a liberation to the justice of the kingdom (a history of grace); it is a quest that takes its point of departure in God's loving, constitutive partiality to the poor and oppressed of the earth.

This work is divided into four chapters. Chapter 1 establishes and elucidates the *hermeneutic key*—the "meaning paradigm"—founding and governing a view of the Mystery of God from the "antihistory of the downtrodden."

Chapter 2 is a "dogmatic" treatment of my theme, with a point of departure in three "moments": (1) God's *manifestation* to history in order to save and fulfill it in Jesus Christ; (2) the Mystery of God as *hidden* in suffering, loving solidarity; and (3) the Mystery of God as *salvific praxis*—as a liberating love that establishes justice and the rights of the poor and oppressed—the Mystery of God as giver of life, of the God to whom we draw near in the reign of God.

Chapter 3 is a discussion of the demands of faith in God in a liberating perspective—response to God along a path of discipleship and historical obedience, in a "praxis according to God," a praxis of love, a praxis of justice, and an "anti-idolatry praxis."

Chapter 4 seeks to identify the basic content of the view of God as God of the poor, and to single out the reasons for its statements, evaluations, and pursuits.

The present work, under the title, "The Mystery of God in the Theology of Liberation: Study of a Theo-logical Vision from the 'Underside of History,' " was presented and successfully defended as a dissertation in partial fulfillment of the requirements for the degree of doctor of theology in the Faculty of Theology of the Pontifical University of Salamanca, Spain.

I wish to express my gratitude to the Rev. Dr. Xabier Pikaza Ibarrondo, O.M., professor of biblical exegesis and dogmatic theology at the University of Salamanca, for his warm collaboration and precious assistance and encouragement in the development of this study.

My thanks are due as well to others—to too many friends to list them all—who have accompanied me in various ways, to the great advantage of my work.

Finally, I wish to thank the Seminario Bíblico Latinoamericano, the Departamento Ecuménico de Investigaciones, and Orbis Books, thanks to whose efforts and contributions it was possible to offer this work in book form to a wider public. From the beginning, I had intended it to be an instrument in the service of a liberative ecclesial praxis—that is, in the service of a church seeking to be faithful to the demands of the reign of God in the service of the poor majorities of our Indo-Afro-Hispanic American peoples, who are teaching us, as Archbishop Romero put it, "what is scandalous in the Mystery of God."

Acronyms

ASET, Asociación Ecuménica de Teólogos del Tercer Mundo (= EATWOT)
BAC, Biblioteca de Autores Cristianos (Madrid)
CELAM, Consejo Episcopal Latinoamericano
CEP, Centro de Estudios y Publicaciones (Lima)
CIIR, Catholic Institute for International Relations (London)
CLAR, Conferencia Latinoamericana de Religiosos
CRT, Centro de Reflexión Teológica (Mexico City)
DEI, Departamento Ecuménico de Investigaciones (San José, Costa Rica)
EATWOT, Ecumenical Association of Third World Theologians
ECA, *Estudios Centroamericanos* (San Salvador)
IECT, International Ecumenical Congress of Theology (São Paulo, 1980)
IHC, Instituto Histórico Centroamericano (Managua)
REB, *Revista Eclesiástica Brasileira* (Petrópolis)
UCA, Universidad Centroamericana (San Salvador)

All references to *Concilium* are to the Spanish edition (Madrid). All references to *Christus* are to the journal published in Mexico City. Similarly: *Cristianismo y Sociedad* (Buenos Aires); *Diakonía* (Managua); *Misión Abierta* (Madrid); *Selecciones de Teología* (Barcelona); *Servir* (Mexico City).

GOD OF THE POOR

Introduction

THE THEME OF THIS STUDY: SCOPE AND LIMITS

The Mystery of God

The present work is situated within the specific ambit of *theo-logical* reflection.[1] That is, it pertains to the *logos* (reflection, intelligence, understanding, reasoned word, discourse) on God *(Theos)*.

I propose to investigate the meaning of the manifestation of the mystery of God in history—in a conflictual history, a history of oppression and struggle for liberation, at whose innermost core, in a manner ever novel and concrete, God is revealed as Mystery: *Mysterium Liberationis.*

Latin American Theology of Liberation as Concrete Framework

In view of the breadth and complexity of the thematic of the mystery of God, this study takes as its concrete framework the theology of liberation, in its Latin American expression.

I understand the theology of liberation as theo-logical reflection "from the underside of history."[2] The "underside of history" is history from the perspective of the poor.[3]

Without in any way denying that liberation theology is deeply rooted in the reality and history of Latin America, we must reject any Latin American chauvinism that distorts that theology by presenting it as an "exotic" or "folkloric" product of Latin America. As Leonardo Boff has stressed, the theology of liberation seeks to be a universal theology:

> In spite of its contextual, hence relative and limited, character, the theology of liberation entertains a pretension to universality. Without exception, any theology seeking to be genuine theology—articulating, on a theoretical level, the concrete presence of God and the Risen One in various human situations—must be contextual and historical. The presence of God and of the Risen One is always a *concrete universal.* Consequently, theology too must be a concrete universal. In whatever corner of the earth, theology will have to meditate this concretion on the part of God and the Risen One, with the living, vital attitudes that this

1

concretion implies for human beings. This is a norm that theology must always observe; it must be contextual. Were it to prescind from its contextuality, theology would run the risk of reflecting on the image of God projected by the ideology of the dominant class, rather than on the image of the God of Abraham, Isaac, and Jacob, the God of all the prophets [*Teología,* 5–6].

Theology of liberation, enriched by encounter and dialogue with other Third World theologians, has gone beyond the boundaries of Latin America. New theological perspectives—under the impulse of the urgency of liberation—are developing in Africa and Asia (Torres, "Teología"; Torres and Fabella, *Gospel*).[4] They are emerging also in "Third World pockets" in developed countries, so that there is, for example, a black theology of liberation in North America.[5] Theological congresses on theology and poverty have been held in Madrid.[6]

Liberation theology, as an effort of reflection nurtured by faith, has maintained the dimension of mystery from its very beginning.[7] Its particular approach to its own identity as "theo-logy" has not been to develop the subject of God as a new theme, or to work out a new way of talking about God (see Gutiérrez, *A Theology,* 15). The theology of liberation seeks to be a theological methodology for the discernment of the presence or absence of God in history, and a response to God's contemporary, ever new manifestation at the heart of reality (Richard, "Razón," 49–50).

Thematic Delimitations

I shall not attempt to offer a view of all the most frequently occurring axes of theological explicitation in the theology of liberation. Were I to attempt to do so, I should be obliged either to construct a much lengthier synthesis or, worse, sketch out an incomplete, and therefore faulty, summary.[8]

With reluctance, I must forgo the attempt to offer a historical survey of the social and ecclesial processes that have made it possible for the theology of liberation to come into being and to thrive.[9] Nevertheless, it is important to keep the historical matrix of liberation theology in mind, in order to avoid an abstract understanding (or confrontation) that might arise from a purely conceptual discourse devoid of any praxic content.

I shall not attempt to locate and explicitate the theme of this study within the rich, complex ambit of Latin American popular piety, with its practices, rites, and symbols. Such an investigation would require a monograph of its own. The need for such a study is becoming more and more urgent. And it will require a methodology suitable for socio-religious investigation.[10]

Neither will it be possible for me to analyze the broad, rich spectrum of occasional materials—liturgical celebrations, popular manifestos, the results of regional or national meetings and seminars held by various church or lay groups the entire length and breadth of Latin America.[11]

These delimitations will permit me to give closer, more exclusive attention to a properly theo-logical study. Even so, I cannot, of course, undertake a detailed analysis of each and every problem in this so very pregnant, rich, and highly complex theme. My undertaking is a more modest one. Furthermore, to be sure, the creativity of liberation theology, as historically situated reflection, is characterized by an ongoing openness, so that this theology is still growing, diversifying, and maturing. And the spirit of God is still speaking, with depth and novelty.

SOURCES

Two authors have especially commanded my attention: Gustavo Gutiérrez and Jon Sobrino. I have felt that, in view of the large number of authors, as well as the rich, extensive bibliography available in and upon the theology of liberation, realism dictated selectivity.

The theological writings of Gutiérrez and Sobrino—the product, *actu secundo,* of their solidarity with popular Christian communities in Peru and El Salvador, respectively—constitute two of the most *systematic* and *influential* contributions in and from Latin America. (For the notion of "second act" see Gutiérrez, *Power,* vi, xi, 46–47, 103). Their theological production, then, is not something strictly personal. It is the expression of the faith of a real people simultaneously oppressed and believing. We must keep in mind the central fact and raison d'être of the theology of liberation: the historical irruption of the poor in society and the church. "The poor are not theologians, but they are the ultimate source of any originality the theology of liberation may have" (Sobrino, *True Church,* 113; see Gutiérrez, *A Theology,* 302; idem, *Power,* 90–91, 202).

I propose to take up, analyze, and evaluate the theo-logical contributions of Gutiérrez and Sobrino "synchronously." It is possible and legitimate to distinguish between these authors' particular emphases or preferences. For example, Sobrino is particularly exegetico-christological, whereas Gutiérrez is particularly historico-pastoral. But on the whole, their theo-logical contributions show a remarkable unity, a fertile diversity.

My treatment will place special emphasis on the properly *dogmatic* or systematic aspect of my theme. It is my judgment that this will be the point of departure from which I can best extract the fundamental and foundational elements of a view of God proper to the theology of liberation.

Works of Gustavo Gutiérrez

Gustavo Gutiérrez is the best known, most representative, and most influential of the liberation theologians.[12] His name has been linked with the theology of liberation from its inception; he is the "dean" of liberation theologians. Edward Schillebeeckx, renowned European theologian, has pointed to Gutiérrez as "the first person in modern history to reactivate the great themes of

Christian theology from a point of departure in the basic option for the poor"
(Schillebeeckx, "Presentación," 464). It is not so much that Gutiérrez adds a
new subject or a new chapter to the old theology, but that he introduces a new
manner of doing theology: he does theology "from the underside of history."
He writes:

> Our only task is to live saturated with the Christian message pure and
> simple, but in a determinate context—the context of a poor, politically
> and economically oppressed people. We seek to read the Bible and the
> whole tradition of Christian experience with the eyes of an enslaved
> population that has been deliberately kept in poverty for centuries [cited
> by Schillebeeckx, ibid., 465; cf. Gutiérrez, *Power,* 90–91].

I concentrate on two major works by Gutiérrez. One is the now classic *A
Theology of Liberation.*[13] The other is *The Power of the Poor in History,* a
collection of eight relatively short pieces written (with one exception) between
1972 and 1979.[14] I have consulted these two works in conjunction with a great
number of other articles and addresses, especially *El Dios de la vida.*[15]

The first sketch of what was to become his classic *A Theology of Liberation*
was presented by Gutiérrez in an address to a national meeting of the ONIS
Sacerdotal Movement in July 1968 in Chimbote, Peru.[16] Here he speaks clearly
on fundamental matters for himself and his work:

> We encounter the Lord in our encounters with men and women. An
> option for the human being is an option for the God of the Christian
> faith, an option for the incarnate God—the God who became a human
> being—an option for Christ.
>
> Today, as we have observed, this neighbor of ours is not only the
> human being taken individually, but whole peoples, especially those that
> suffer misery and oppression ["Apuntes," 18; cf. *A Theology,* 190–94].

In *El Dios de la vida* Gutiérrez emphasizes the importance of theo-logical
reflection. When we speak of God, we speak of the basic element of our faith,
our being, and what gives sense to our life:

> In speaking of God, we "touch bottom." We stand before the ultimate
> foundation of our faith and our being. We face our options of every
> sort—personal, evangelical, spiritual, political, and so on. In speaking of
> God we are speaking of what gives meaning to the whole of our personal
> and collective life [p. 5].[17]

Works of Jon Sobrino

Jon Sobrino has made the Central American republic of El Salvador his
home ever since his arrival there from his Basque homeland in 1957.[18] He lives

at the heart of a systematically persecuted, martyr church.[19] Sobrino has been deepening and broadening a rich theo-logical vision, and his work is perhaps the most systematic treatment of theo-logical themes from the "underside of history":

> No reflection with pretentions to being theological can run on for long without treating of God. If it hopes to be theology, and theology that will be effective for the church and for historical processes, it must come to the subject of God. From start to finish, theology involves a tautology. "Theo-logy" comes from *theos,* "God." Whatever be the concrete themes of which theology treats—church, sacraments, justice, hope, Christ, and so on—unless it periodically makes God its explicit object, unless it returns to its original tautology, it will see its theological content weakened. To turn to God in theology is not, it seems to me, a sterile tautology, but an effective one, and basically the most effective one—provided, of course, God always be spoken of adequately, and it is this that I shall now attempt to do, with a certain fear and trembling ["Dios y los procesos revolucionarios," 106].

Sobrino absolutely insists on a theo-logical reflection that will adopt as its hermeneutic locus the historical alternatives of life and death, the de facto reality of a "crucified people."[20] Hence his approach to the mystery of God— the ultimacy of the reality of God—from God's partisan, sides-taking self-manifestation to the poor, and God's absolute demand that the poor have a life genuinely worthy of human beings:

> In its Christian fullness, "God" is a far from empty term. It is far from a remote, passive abstraction. Quite the opposite. God is the prime source of all life, justice, love, and truth, and the ultimate horizon to which all these reach out. It is God who lays upon us the absolute demand that we live our lives in a way truly worthy of human beings, that we strive always to make ourselves more human by continually ridding ourselves of that which makes us less than human ["Theologian's View," 22–23].

Does God really contribute anything to the solution of the concrete problems of history? Is a discourse on God in our history and in the liberation processes "good for" anything? Sobrino answers with precision: "I believe that a discourse on God [*explicitar a Dios*] is, in one sense, 'good for' *nothing,* and, in another sense, 'good for' *everything"* ("Dios," 108; emphasis added).

It is that simple, and that complicated. A discourse on God does *not* involve introducing into the analysis of history an additional element that will explain all problems. We do not know many more concrete things about history by reason of our discourse on God. God is of no use as a concrete recipe for planning a national economy or for the organizing of a people.

On the other hand, God is "good for" everything. God "primes" historical realities by drawing them toward the maximal realization of their possibilities for good:

> God is the real utopic principle par excellence. As *utopic* reality, God can never be adequately historicized. Only on the last day will God be fully historicized—will be all in all, as Paul says. In history, God will always remain u-topic—that is, without a place. But as utopic *principle,* God can give "principiation" to historical realities, giving them an ultimate direction, exigency, and meaning. Christian faith consists precisely in believing that this possibility is always a part of reality.
>
> [God's] principiation of historical realities consists in this that history give more of itself, precisely where the temptation to stagnation appears. . . . A discourse on God brings it about that the concrete historical never be simply what it is, but that it set out in the direction of the God of this discourse. Faith in God is basically only the tireless giving of historical form, however limited and imperfect that form must always be, to God's utopia. But in the historical phenomenon of giving historical form to utopia, God becomes present in history. God is "good for" this: for drawing history to the best it can be—for drawing it to the godhead ["Dios," 109].

Significantly, Sobrino grounds his reflections on the mystery of God the "ever greater"—*Dios siempre Major*—on two theological axes crucial for liberative theology: the *christological* and the *ecclesiological*.[21]

In the historical discipleship of Jesus as it is found among the poor, faith is faced with the ultimate reality of the God proclaimed by Jesus. The church of the poor offers us the "neccessary channel and epistemology for belief in God to have sense—a determinate sense" (Sobrino, "Fe de la Iglesia," 146).

Other Theological Works

My concentration on the writings of Gustavo Gutiérrez and Jon Sobrino by no means entails an exclusive reference to them. To be sure, the "logic" of my study and its "conceptual infrastructure" are very much determined by their contributions. At the same time, depending on the specific subject matter under consideration, I judge it opportune to open up and complement their perspectives with material from other authors within the framework of Latin American liberation theology.[22] I consider important the works of Rubem Alves and Juan Luís Segundo.[23] They deserve attention here in spite of their being in a certain sense "antecedent" to the theology of liberation. Surely they play an important "beachhead" role with respect to a theological discourse "in a liberative key." Also important is the work of José Porfirio Miranda, Leonardo Boff, and José Míguez Bonino.[24] I also make considerable use of three works of multiple authorship: "Jesucristo, centro de la historia"; Pablo Richard et al., *The Idols of Death and the God of Life;* and the "Final

Document" and "Letters of the International Ecumenical Congress of Theology" (IECT), São Paulo, 1980.[25]

PRESUPPOSITIONS

An increasing number of concrete cases makes it evident that (a) every formulation of a problem is made possible only by a previous actual human experience which involves such a problem; (b) in selection from the multiplicity of data there is involved an act of will on the part of the knower; and (c) forces arising out of living experience are significant in the direction which the treatment of the problem follows.

—Karl Mannheim[26]

Epistemological Locus

All investigation involves *presuppositions.* My work is no exception. Presuppositions may be defined as the constituents of the theoretical framework with which one defines, analyzes, and endows with meaning the theme with which one is concerned. It is a basic principle of hermeneutics that there is no such thing as a totally neutral reading of a text. Every reading is done in the light of certain antecedent presuppositions—is done from a point of departure in a context of interpretation, a field of meaning (Pikaza, *Experiencia,* 17, 66, 134).

This theoretical or categoric framework is precisely what has enabled me to select my theme, prioritize certain authors rather than others, and, as I have indicated, study and evaluate these authors.

Theological Locus

I single out three presuppositions: a decision for belief, a desire for liberation, and a spirit of ecumenism.

A Decision for Belief

One point of departure for me is the decision for belief, which may be defined, in the words of Xabier Pikaza, as "the interpretive a priori of the vision of faith" (*Experiencia,* 18).

Faith—acceptance *of* and response *to* God's love—is a manner of existing, a fundamental attitude. It is living in the light of the reality of the mystery that is God. It is discovering the deep meaning of life, of the world, of history, from the ultimate meaning of God.[27] Having faith does not mean that we possess Mystery. It does not mean that faith gives us a key to the manipulation of Mystery. We journey toward God. We never possess God totally, either in our orthodoxy (ortho-logy) or in our worship (ortho-latry). God is the *ever greater.*

Having faith in God means seeking God, ever leading our life against a horizon of renewed, ceaseless openness to God, being "open to the radical word of God" in the knowledge that we may be summoned by God. Faith supposes a personal *encounter* with God, called conversion. It means a trusting surrender to God, in obedience (Gutiérrez, *Power,* 19–20). Faith is the acceptance of God's plan of life for human beings, and acceptance of communion with our fellow human beings. Faith involves a demand that we be at the service of what God is doing for human beings—the reign of God—by being at the service of human beings. Faith is being not only hearers but doers of God's word. But the obedience of faith is never the expression of servile submission, of sickly kowtowing. Faith cannot entail the humiliation of human beings, for they are the creative subjects of history (Metz, *La fe,* 68).[28]

Being a believer is not another way, a religious way, of sidestepping history and commitment to its transformation, commitment to making a world according to God's plan. On the contrary, being a believer is the believing way of bestowing ultimacy and radicality on history.

A Desire for Liberation

Liberation is the most profound, most human, most Christian, most Latin American struggle in Latin America [Richard, *Iglesia,* 18].

Our Christian, Latin American experience has led us to the conviction that, for us, the history of *today*—the real context of the life of faith, the "kairological today," the "today" of God's salvific manifestation in behalf of human beings—is the history of oppression and struggles for liberation. It is the history of a re-creation of a life in justice and interhuman fellowship in the "chronological today." The kairological today can be lived only in the chronological today (L. Boff, *Periferia,* 10–14).[29]

Faith and liberative commitment, far from excluding each other, demand, complement, and enrich each other. In José María González Ruiz's celebrated phrase, "to believe is to be committed" *(Creer es comprometerse* [Barcelona, Fontanella, 1967]). Not that faith and liberative commitment are the same. Each will preserve its distinct identity. Faith does not automatically spring from praxis. There are many men and women of profound, authentic liberative commitment who do not explain or justify that commitment from a faith vision. Faith involves a "more" that transcends the properly historical, transcends what liberative commitment bestows of itself. (Sobrino, *True Church,* 156–59). But faith cannot be lived outside a liberative commitment. Faith must pass by way of just such a commitment.

To have faith is to emerge from oneself, to commit oneself to God and human beings. To live, profess, and celebrate the faith has no sense or value apart from a *prise de conscience* or conscientization, together with a commitment to the transformation of history through a praxis of love and justice (Míguez Bonino, *Fe en busca,* 24.) The believer is called upon to break with what Marie-Dominique Chenu has called the fraud of an atemporal, abstract, idealistic faith "coming down from above," authoritarian, and bereft of prophetic commitment ("Realidad," 44). The faith that acts through love (Gal. 5:6) will pierce to the deepest root of injustice—the breach of friendship with God, breach of fellowship among human beings.

Faith is not an ideology.[30] An ideology begets a particular political strategy. Faith is an aid offered to believers to define themselves in a determinate direction and assume a basic option in favor of the oppressed, their struggles, and their rights. Our faith would not be credible if it were merely a verification of orthodoxy as inscribed in creeds. As its witnesses, we must be capable of demonstrating it in a liberative praxis—an "orthopraxis"—without evasion, resigned inactivity, or despair. We must be capable of manifesting it in an active, concrete solidarity with the impoverished and humiliated of history.

My work of investigation takes its point of departure in what Juan Luís Segundo has called "a pretheological human commitment to change and improve the world" (*Liberation,* 39), and aspires, with all its limitations, to constitute a theoretical contribution that will be at the service of an ecclesial and social liberative praxis. It seeks to be at the service of the poor of our Indo-Afro-Hispanic America, who have taught us, as Archbishop Romero put it, "what is scandalous in the mystery of God" (cited in Sobrino, *Resurrección,* 40).[31]

A Spirit of Ecumenism

I intend my perspective to be ecumenical. That is, it does *not* seek to prefer, impose, or defend any determinate confessional viewpoint apropos of the subject with which I am concerned. I have no intention to ignore, much less deny, my own Protestant (Evangelical, Methodist, and Latin American) tradition.

From my own religious tradition, then, I hope to be able to present a treatment of my theme that will "rise above" confessional barriers in a grass-roots ecumenical spirit, and *desde los pobres*—from the viewpoint of the poor.[32]

The bulk of the liberation theology of Latin America, a continent where one-third of the Catholics of the world live, has naturally been produced by theologians writing from the theological and pastoral interior of the Catholic Church: Gustavo Gutiérrez, Jon Sobrino, Leonardo and Clodovis Boff, Juan Luís Segundo, and others. I do not deny that this "imposes" the framework and accents of a specific theological and ecclesial tradition. Any theologian, as believer, thinks from within a church community. Still, I believe that I discern, within the matrix of the liberative theological task, a fertile *ecumenical space,* arising from the Evangelical option for the poor of Latin America. The liberation process and service to the poor in solidarity with them are the sign of a real theater of ecumenical encounter, and set in relief all that Christians have in common, including, of course, their common theology (Sobrino, *True Church,* 39-40).[33]

In a society like that of Latin America, characterized by division and disunity resulting from injustice, what is really at stake is not the defense of orthodoxy (understood abstractly) or the specific accents of a Christian confession, legitimate as these may be. What is at stake is the praxis of love in the perspective of the reign of God incarnated in the world of the poor. The International Ecumenical Congress of Theology (São Paulo, 1980) expresses it as follows:

> Many Christians are rediscovering the gift of unity as they encounter the one Christ in the poor of the Third World (Matt. 25). The promotion of total liberation, the common suffering, and the sharing of the hopes and joys of the poor have put in clear relief all that we Christians hold in common.
>
> In this option for the poor and in the practice of justice, we have deepened the roots of our faith in the one Lord, the one church, the one God and Father. In the following of Jesus we confess Christ as the Son of God and the brother of all people. *In the struggle for a just life for the poor we confess the one God, Father of all.* In our ecclesial commitment we confess the church of Jesus Christ as his body in history and as sacrament of liberation ["Final Document," in Torres and Eagleson, *Challenge,* 243–44; emphasis added].

The theology of liberation, from a point of departure in its profession of the one liberator God of the poor, the Father of all, has moved ahead in its theology without posing many of the problems traditionally confronting Catholics and Protestants. Neither does my study attempt to pose them, or directly confront them. I do, however, presuppose them, and they will often be discernible in the background. In practice, they have been transcended, or at least they do not have the power of expression that they once had.

In the past, for example, there was clearly a distinct sensibility with respect to access to God, as we know from the controversy over natural theology. Liberation theology does not treat this theme directly. It does not situate the "problem" of the existence of God within the ambit of "rational" or "cosmic" proofs. Liberation theology situates this "problem" within a field of "praxis," where what is important is the prophetic word that speaks of a "knowledge of God" indivisibly uniting a profession of the one God and the practice of justice toward human beings. The locus of the encounter with God is the locus of God's own predilection—the world of the poor. The locus of the manifestation of God is our history, in a liberative praxis in solidarity with the poor and the lowly, a praxis that strives toward the justice of God's kingdom. History and praxis thus have a theo-phanic value.

In the future, when our common path of ecumenical experience will have continued and matured, it will be possible to treat these themes in a liberative key, with more depth and creativity.

METHODOLOGY

A Monographic-Bibliographic Study

My investigation is of a monographic-bibliographic nature. That is, it is conceived as the study of a specific theological theme (the mystery of God) in the theo-logical framework of Latin American liberation theology (its sources), with special reference to the contributions of Gustavo Gutiérrez and Jon Sobrino.

Inasmuch as "any reading is at bottom an interpretation of what is being read" (Pikaza, *Presupuestos,* 4), this study will attempt to combine an analytical-expository and an interpretive-evaluative approach. From a yoking of analysis (exposition) and evaluation (theological critique), I hope to contribute to a more systematic and profound understanding—in a liberative key—of the meaning of God's manifestation in history.

Chapters 1, 2, and 3 will be devoted to the moment of analysis and exposition (the level of *seeing*). Chapter 4 will pursue the interpretive-evaluative moment (the level of *judging*): here, having set forth the content of Latin American liberation theology, I shall attempt to offer a systematic reflection of my own from a point of departure in that body of thought.

Development: Steps to Be Followed

Chapter 1 explores the meaning paradigm (theoretical framework) that presides over and bases the particular view of God pursued by liberation theology. In my judgment, it will be necessary to establish and clarify, as best I can, the point *from which* the theo-logical vision in question is explicitated as a decisive viewpoint for the faith community and for society. This point is not theological *simpliciter,* but stands in relationship with an interlocutor or historical subject: *the poor.* It dynamically links ecclesial praxis, the historical, and the social. It bespeaks relationship to a social ambient, to our experience of oppression and struggle for liberation. I attempt to identify what liberative theology in general and its theo-logical reflection in particular see as the essential nature of liberation and the perspective of the poor. I propose a definition of Latin American liberation theology, and of the elements that, in my judgment, compose the perspective of the poor (the "spinal column" of this liberative theo-logy). I take up the overall attitude and disposition of liberative theological reflection (believing, responsible, historical, dialectical, praxic, evangelical), as well as its properly theo-logical hermeneutic key (its way of "seeing the Mystery"): its "primordial intuition." Finally, I treat four fundamental theo-logical presuppositions: the bipolarity of language concerning God; history as locus of revelation; access to God; the meaning of mystery.

Chapter 2 is a treatment of the theo-logical theme in its "dogmatic" specificity. I spell out three moments (more for methodological reasons of exposition and explanation) to be observed in the consideration of a theme that is very much a "seamless robe"—one in which all elements are interdependent, so that a consideration of one is *eo ipso* a consideration of the others. These moments are: (1) the mystery of God in its ongoing manifestation, its self-manifestation, in history, in order to save and fulfill that history; (2) the mystery of the *hidden God* of solidarity with the poor—the "lesser God," the *Dios Menor* who is "love that suffers," the crucified God; (3) the mystery of God as *salvific praxis* (the *Dios Mayor*), as God the Liberator, who establishes justice and right, the giver of life, the God who is approached in the reign of God.

Chapter 3 is a discussion of what I consider to be the principal exigencies or concretions (practical locus) of faith in God in a liberative perspective. The life of faith in the God of the poor is framed in a constitutive dialectic of gratuity and exigency: God is absolutely and unconditionally demanding. Hence the somewhat pretentious title I have given to this chapter: "Liberative Theo-logy as *Theo-Praxis*"—meaning, liberative theology as a response to, a "correspondence" to God along a path of discipleship and historical obedience in a "praxis according to God." I discern three "praxic" levels of "correspondence to God": a praxis of love, a praxis of justice, and a praxis of anti-idolatry.

Chapter 4 is devoted to my *evaluative judgment* (axiological level) of what will by then have been analyzed and set forth. This chapter will situate the basic content of the theo-logical vision of the Latin American theology of liberation, and identify the reasons for its affirmations, values, scope, and limits. I shall make an evaluation (a judgment) in dialogue with this theology, not in polemical confrontation with it. I shall distinguish three levels: a view of the whole, an evaluative judgment properly so-called, and a prospective reflection. By way of conclusion, chapter 4 will have something to say *ad intra,* with respect to my own ecclesial tradition.

The works that I have used in bringing this work to realization—the sources of liberation theology, studies in and upon that theology, and other theological works that have been of help—are listed in the Bibliographic References. I do not pretend to offer an exhaustive bibliography of Latin American theology of liberation.[34]

CHAPTER 1

Liberative Theo-logy: Meaning Paradigm

"Every theological viewpoint comes from a particular point of view" (L. Boff, *Teología*, 72). The Latin American theology of liberation is no exception. Every theology has its own central point of view, which determines its view of the whole of theology. It will therefore be appropriate, and necessary, I think, to devote a chapter to the justification of the "meaning paradigm," the "reading key," proper to theoretical articulation concerning the Mystery of God (theo-logy) from the underside of history.

What is this particular point of view? It is the *perspective of the poor.*

But it is not enough to make this general statement. All the various elements that go to make up this real, demanding outlook must be explicitated:

Liberation theology cannot be understood without an understanding of something *previous and anterior* to it: the awareness of the extreme poverty damning millions of our brothers and sisters on the Latin American continent, and the awareness that this poverty is not episodic, but epidemic [L. Boff, "Declaración," in Cabestrero, *Teólogos*, 70].

In the absence of any reference to this fundamental outlook—the "backbone" of liberation theology, as Gustavo Gutiérrez calls it—it is difficult indeed to understand the theology of liberation.[1] It will be seen abstractly as a "system of ideas." Its anchoring in the "cellars of history" will be overlooked (see Libânio Cristo, *Creo*, 117, 142, 147, etc.). Liberation theology is a theology committed to the poor of Latin America, with a view to a breach with the present situation of oppression and injustice.

But in fact, as we shall see, a consideration of the meaning paradigm of the theology of liberation, although methodologically the first moment to be rendered explicit, is not "something previous and anterior" to that theology. It is a consitutive moment of that theology, an actual step along the way of its very reflection on the Mystery of God.

Inasmuch as the liberator God chose to exist conjointly with history, in an essential relationship with history, it is impossible to name that God without

13

speaking of human beings and their concrete, step-by-step, conflictual history of oppression and liberation, of death and life. It is impossible to articulate this God's salvific manifestation, this God's "kairological today," without alluding to the historical experience of a crucified people and the mechanisms of oppression that today—the chronological today—oppose and reject God's liberative cause. Jon Sobrino expresses this notion as follows:

> Oppression is not merely one of several possible hermeneutic loci for a presentation of faith in God. It is the locus that is *de facto the most apt for the presentation of that faith in Third World situations,* and *de jure the locus that appears throughout the length and breadth of Scripture* for a grasp of the message of salvation.
>
> Any Christian theology that is to be faithful to its biblical origin, and therefore historical, must take the *signs of the times* absolutely seriously for its reflection. . . .
>
> Although these [signs] are manifold, one of them runs all through history: the "ever present sign of a crucified people, a people for whom existence has always meant crucifixion. *This crucified people* is the historical continuation of the Servant of Yahweh, hounded by the sin of the world, despoiled of everything, even life itself—*especially* life" ["Fe en el Hijo," 331, citing Ignacio Ellacuría; see also Sobrino, *Jesús*, 185].

It is to this meaning paradigm, then, this reading key for a theo-logy of liberation in tune with a historically crucified people, that this chapter is devoted.

It consists of four parts. I first explicitate my understanding of liberation theology, in whose framework, as my specific point of reference, I propose to examine the mystery of God.

The expressions *teología liberadora*, "liberative theology," or *teología de la liberación*, "theology of liberation," are used so broadly today that it is important to delimit their semantic field. Accordingly, I shall offer a "minimal definition" of what I judge liberation theology *not* to be—*via negativa*—and of what I judge it to *be*—*via positiva*—as a new way of doing theology from a starting point in the practice of a faith lived, shared, and celebrated at the heart of a liberative practice from the outlook of the poor.

In the second part of this chapter, I give special attention to the central importance of the "perspective of the poor." Over against the indeterminacy of a universalizing language about the poor, I undertake to explain just who these poor are. "Poor" is a *concrete universal*, defined in the basic, although not exclusive, sense of the real, material poor: the hungry, the exploited, the marginalized of our cultural world, whose right to life is threatened by an oppressive system.

Various elements converge in the perspective of the poor: the historical irruption of the poor, the new historical hermeneutics, the mediation of socio-analytic discourse, and a new understanding of the political. From a point of departure in poverty viewed as structural and destructive (antilife), I come to a new meaning for the traditional correlation between poverty and God.

In the third part of this chapter, in light of previous explicitations, and still within the theological framework of the theology of liberation, I describe and characterize liberative theo-logical reflection. From the underside of history, theological reflection assumes a particular tone: it is *believing* (seeking an "understanding of the faith," *intellectus fidei*), *responsible* (in the sense of being responsive to the reality around it), *historical* (founded on questions arising out of the present: the dilemma of the life and death, the oppression and liberation, of the masses), *dialectical* (in the sense that it seeks God not by analogy with the world, but by contrast with real, experienced misery), *praxic* (because its interest is not speculation or abstract truth, but the inauguration of the reign of God), and *evangelical* (it proclaims the good, glad news that in God is salvation, life, hope, and courage for the struggle).

In the fourth and last part of this chapter I explicitate the liberative theological meaning paradigm or hermeneutic key more specifically. I focus on a "thesis text"—the "Letter to Christians in Popular Christian Communities of the Poor Countries and Regions of the World," one of the final documents of the International Ecumenical Congress of Theology held in 1980. This text will serve as my starting point, and at the same time provide the axis for a cohesive articulation of my theme, for it will furnish me with certain (hermeneutic) reading keys. I lay great emphasis on the *theistic hermeneutics of history*—the view of history as a privileged "theo-phanic" locus—and on the approach to mystery that manifests itself (in a "gracious self-bestowal") when undertaken from the privileged world of the oppressed.

LIBERATION PROCESS AND LIBERATIVE THEOLOGY

> The important thing is not liberation theology, but *liberation* [L. Boff, *Teología*, 71].[2]

Negative Definition of Liberation Theology

The theology of liberation is not defined in virtue of the predominance of a new theme over others. It is not a theology of compartments, a "theology of genitives," simply treating of one theme ("liberation") among many such in the whole corpus of theology.[3] Juan Luís Segundo, in his discussion of the hermeneutics of liberation theology, says:

> The most progressive theology in Latin America is more interested in *being liberative* than in *talking about liberation*. In other words, liberation deals not so much with content as with the method used to theologize in the face of our real life-situation [*Liberation*, 9].[4]

Neither is liberation theology defined by a new theological language. Nor is its basic character defined by the fact that it "switches methodologies"—

moving from an abstract to a concrete methodology (or from a deductive to an inductive methodology), taking its point of departure in reality.[5] Nor, finally, is liberation theology defined in virtue of its originality in the utilization of the theoretical mediation provided by the social sciences.[6]

Positive Definition of Liberation Theology

I understand the theology of liberation as a theological reflection that, in recent years in Latin America, has sprung up from within numerous Christian communities out of a pastoral praxis in solidarity with the oppressed.[7] Liberation theology is a reflection that starts out from the underside of history, from the "antihistory" of the lowly and downtrodden, and assumes the outlook of the poor.

Liberation theology is *a way of doing theology*, consisting in an ecclesial reflection from a point of departure in *faith* as lived, shared, and celebrated *in practice*. Liberation theology is incomprehensible apart from its relationship with that practice. The "first act" is life, and commitment to the struggle being waged against oppression and injustice by Latin American peoples, peoples at once oppressed and believing.[8] Theology comes only afterward as "second act" (Gutiérrez, *Power*, 200):[9]

> Liberation theology . . . is merely one part, *and surely not the most important part*, of a process of intensifying identification between Latin American Christian elements and the efforts of peoples to satisfy their basic needs—for the implementation, in an adequate historical project, of *their basic human rights* [Assmann, "Tecnología," 31; emphasis added].

This struggle for basic human rights has been, and continues to be, the "matrix" of the theological elaboration that has led to Latin American liberation theology, giving rise to a new way of being a person and a believer, of living and thinking one's faith, of being called and of calling others into an *ecclesia* (Gutiérrez, *Power*, 169, 191). This is the background against which Gutiérrez's now classic formulation is to be understood:

> [Liberation] theology . . . will be a critical reflection both from within, and upon, historical praxis, in confrontation with the word of the Lord as lived and accepted in faith. . . . [It] will be a reflection in, and on, faith as liberation praxis. It will be an understanding of the faith from an option and a commitment [*Power*, 60; see also his *A Theology*, 6–15].

The theology of liberation posits its basic structure in the unitary articulation—neither facile nor mechanical—of two fundamental realities: faith and liberative praxis. It is a pistic reflection (faith is operative) and an actuating reflection (praxis is operative). It takes its point of departure in a new form of praxis of faith—a loving solidarity with the poor—in response to God's manifestation in the current signs of the times; in response to the irruption of the poor in the church and in society. From within this historical praxis—faith real-ized—liberation theology undertakes a reflection in confrontation with God's word addressed to us here and now, in order to articulate this praxis, theoretically and critically (through the use of "critical reason"), with a view to the total liberation of the human being—eschatological plenitude.

Speaking in the Theology in the Americas Conference in Detroit in 1975, Gustavo Gutiérrez gives a broad description of his understanding of historical praxis. There are three elements to be distinguished:

[a. *Transformation of history*:] What we understand by "praxis" is "transforming action," not simply any kind of action, but rather a historical transformation. Historical praxis means a transforming change, a transforming action of history. [b. *History as nature and society*:] History, in this sense, must be understood not simply as the history of groups but also as the transformation of nature. When we speak of a historical praxis we are speaking of the transforming action of history understood as transformation of nature, as the relationship of the person to nature, and as the relationship of the persons among themselves. [c. *Liberation ("praxis from below")*:] By transforming praxis we mean a transforming action by the poor and the humiliated, by the despised races and marginated cultures themselves. . . . We are talking, then, about an action and a praxis which is subversive in the double meaning that subversive might have here. In the first place, we are talking about changing history, turning it on its head (*vertir*), and secondly, we are talking about a transforming historical praxis which comes from below (*sub: subvertir*-subversive). The established order has taught us that we are to think in a pejorative way of the term "subversive." But what we would rather reject is a "superversive" (coming down from the top) way of making history ["Statement," 310–11].[10]

In view of the importance of historical praxis for the theology of liberation, I shall expand upon these observations of Gutiérrez.[11]

Transformation of History

For two centuries now, ever since the beginning of the modern revolution in various fields of activity, it has been a commonplace to say that human beings are capable of transforming the world in which they live.[12] That is, they are recognized as capable of transforming history by taking it into their own hands. The human being, as creative subjectivity, has gradually taken up the reins of history. Freedom is beginning to prevail over nature, and in social organization (Gutiérrez, *Power*, 48, 171; *A Theology*, 27–33).

History as Nature and Society

History can be grasped only if nature and society are seen in conjunction. The transformation of history entails the unavoidable and simultaneous transformation of the relationship of human beings to nature and with one another, their society. This being the case, this transformative praxis will involve more than a mere new awareness of the meaning and importance of economic and political activity. It will involve a new way of being a person in history (Gutiérrez, *Power*, 50).

Praxis of Liberation "From Below": Subversion in History

The historical process of the transformation of nature and society over the course of the last two centuries of Western history has brought the contradictions of society to a head. It has produced the deepest imaginable differences among the peoples of the earth. As a result of a process of unequal development, as evidenced in the situation of impoverishment of the greater part of humanity, it has produced the so-called third world. The existence of developed (*rich*) countries and underdeveloped (*poor*) countries, in the dialectical framework of center-and-periphery, is not the outcome of two successive stages of an abstract, mechanical process. It is the expression of a single historical movement (Dussel, "Dominación," 329–31; "Coyuntura," 204–8).

Consequently, the transformation of history from "the underside of history" becomes liberative praxis.

> We come to see something that perhaps escapes us when we view things from the standpoint of the minority of humankind that controls most of the science and technology, as well as most of the political power, in today's world. And suddenly this liberating praxis acquires *subversive* features— subversive of a social order in which the poor, society's "others," have only just begun to make their voices heard [Gutiérrez, *Power*, 50].

Historical Transformation and Liberative Love

In the *sub*versive transformation of history, what is really at stake is not primarily a greater rationality in the organization and execution of economic activity (nature), or a better social organization (society). Rather, through these secondary goals, the primary goal of justice, and real and historically effective love, is to be attained.

> The use of the terms "justice" and "love" recalls to our minds that we are speaking of real human persons, whole peoples, suffering misery and

exploitation, deprived of the most elemental human rights, scarcely aware that they are human beings at all. The praxis of liberation, therefore, inasmuch as it starts out from an authentic solidarity with the poor and the oppressed, is ultimately a praxis of love—real love, effective and concrete, for real, concrete human beings. It is a praxis of love of neighbor, and of love for Christ in the neighbor, for Christ identifies himself with the least of these human beings, our brothers and sisters. Any attempt to separate love for God and love for neighbor gives rise to attitudes that impoverish both.

It is easy to make a distinction between a heavenly and an earthly praxis—easy, but not faithful to the gospel of the Word who became a human being. It therefore would seem more authentic and profound to speak of a praxis of love as having its roots in the gratuitous and free love of the Father and as becoming concrete in solidarity with human beings—first with the poor and dispossessed, and then through them with all human beings [Gutiérrez, *Power*, 50].

An understanding of the faith from a conscious, conscientious identification and solidarity with the struggles and hopes of Latin Americans, nearly all of whom are really poor, is the expression of what Jon Sobrino has called a profound "honesty with the real" (Sobrino, "Espiritualidad," 59). It is not a matter of an arbitrary limitation to be imposed on the locus and task of theology. It is a matter of assuming the theological task from a point of departure in a demanding "concrete universal."[13] It is matter of a "situated incarnation" (Assmann, *Theology*, 54; see also 55–58). Nor is what is at stake the defense of theological originality—and still less the illegitimate pretension to a Christian message that would be exclusive, "our own private revelation" in Latin America. What is really at stake is deep, fertile fidelity to a faith experience in a world of oppression, and fidelity to the struggles of the poor for justice and life. What is really at stake is a reading of the *gospel* and of the whole of Christian *tradition* and experience in the light of the cultural, social, and political ambient of Latin America with the eyes of a poor people that for centuries has been deliberately maintained in conditions of "nonpersonhood." Liberation theology is an expression of the right of an oppressed and believing people to speak out on the subject of its faith and hope, an expression of its right to *exist* and to *think*, which is part of the exercise of its right to *life*, its right to *liberation* (see Gutiérrez, *Power*, 78–79, 90–91):

In the last instance we will have an authentic theology of liberation only when the oppressed themselves can freely raise their voice and express themselves directly and creatively in society and in the heart of the People of God, when they themselves "account for the hope" [cf. 1 Peter 3:15] which they bear, when they are the protagonists of their own liberation [Gutiérrez, *A Theology*, 307].

LIBERATIVE THEO-LOGY AND THE OUTLOOK OF THE POOR

Latin American theology gives a privileged place to the cries of the oppressed. They are a stimulus to *theo*logical thinking. This does not mean that Latin American theology fails to deal with the positive themes of theology (the love of God, hope, reconciliation, the reign of God). It does, however, mean that it adopts *a perspective of its own* in dealing with them. It does not approach these great positive themes directly and in isolation. They are always accompanied or even brought into play by some great suffering [Sobrino, *True Church*, 28; emphasis added].

The praxis and outlook of the poor are inseparable. It is not enough to say that praxis is the "first act." One must consider the historical subject of this praxis— the poor of Latin America, in the real and material sense (although not exclusively in this sense) of the word "poor." These are the oppressed, the marginalized, the hungry, those whose basic right to life is threatened.[14] From this vantage, the theology of liberation will speak of the poor as a "privileged theological locus," and will render explicit the basic content of their outlook.

The Poor as *Locus Theologicus*

It is its reference to the poor as a *locus theologicus* par excellence that enables liberation theology to situate and concretize the accents and themes of its theological discourse (Ellacuría, "Pobres"). No theological theme is left out of consideration: sin, grace, hope, the kingdom, eternal life, and so on, are all treated. But the reading key is new. Liberation theology is not a theology *of* the poor (as a new theme), or a theology *for* the poor (as addressed paternalistically to the poor), but a theology set in motion *from a point of departure* in the poor, the poor as interlocutor, as historical subject.[15]

Outlook of the Poor

The better to understand the "outlook of the poor," backbone of the theology of liberation (and hence of its theo-logy), let us turn our attention to certain constitutive elements of this outlook: the new, massive irruption of the poor in society; a new understanding of the fundamental fact of Latin American dependency and underdevelopment; the mediation of a new socio-analytic discourse; and a new conception of the political.

Historical Irruption of the Poor

Recent decades in Latin America have been stamped by an intensifying real presence of the world of the other, the world of the poor. Absent from history until now, the poor are suddenly becoming present to it. The exploited classes, oppressed cultures, and racial groupings suffering discrimination are awakening and raising their voice, shaking the yoke of their slavery from their necks with a power nurtured in history.[16] In the words of the 1980 EATWOT conference:

> The situation of suffering, misery, and exploitation of the great majority of human beings, concentrated especially but not exclusively in the so-called Third World, is as undeniable as it is unjust.
>
> Nevertheless, the most important historical process of our times has begun to be led *by these very peoples*, the truly "wretched of the earth." . . .
>
> In the context of the Third World, the emerging popular classes generate social movements; in their struggles is forged a more lucid consciousness of society as a whole as well as of themselves.
>
> These popular social movements express much more than an economic grievance. They represent a phenomenon, new in our times: *the massive irruption of the poor in every society.* These are the exploited classes, the oppressed races, people who some would like to keep anonymous or absent from human history, and who, with increasing determination, show their own faces, proclaim their word, and organize to win by their own efforts the power that will permit them to guarantee the satisfaction of their needs and the creation of authentic conditions of liberation [in Eagleson and Torres, *Challenge*, 232; emphasis added].

A New Historical Hermeneutics[17]

A new historical hermeneutics, based on a better knowledge and a more all-inclusive and structural understanding of Latin American history, has enabled us to discover the fundamental fact of our dependency and underdevelopment as a reality pervading our history, as a condition that has given shape and concrete body to what we are culturally, socially, economically, and politically.[18]

The historical process of our dependency is an old one. It has its roots in the colonial exploitation and spoliation that victimized Latin America for centuries, and that today is prolonged in our neocolonial present—a present dependent on the economic and political imperialism of transnational monopolistic capital and its political and military instruments (Gorostiaga, *Entender*, chap. 2, 4).

As Pablo Richard remarks, it is insufficient to specify the starting point of liberation theology abstractly, identifying it simply as "Latin America." The starting point of liberation theology is *dominated Latin America*:

> It is in Latin America that the theology of liberation has sprung up because it is here that imperialism and capitalism have massively unleashed the irrational might of their oppression and repression, and underdevelopment and dependence are finally becoming intolerable. If

there is a Latin American specificity in theology, it is that we have taken up the central problem of Latin America as the central problem of the theological task: the subsistence and liberation of our 250 million exploited and dominated brothers and sisters. The theology of liberation is Latin American because liberation is the most profound, most Christian, most Latin American struggle in Latin America. We have discovered our Latin American identity, for we have discovered our dependence and underdevelopment, and we see that it is generated by imperialistic and capitalistic domination. Our theology is not a priori anti-European. It is anti-imperialistic. We feel closer ties with Europeans struggling for liberation than with Latin Americans struggling to maintain capitalist domination in our great Latin American homeland [*Iglesia*, 18; emphasis added].

A New Socio-Analytic Discourse

The burden of the great masses of the poor is an unjust one. Living conditions and the quality of life are continually worsening. Life itself is threatened.[19] A perception of the wretchedness of this real-life situation has evinced the urgency of gaining a knowledge of its historical causality, of the structural mechanisms (or "objective logic") generative of an antilife poverty.[20] There are socio-analytic resources ready to hand that must inevitably constitute the mediation of the Christian option for the poor, and thus of any theological articulation with its starting point in a faith lived and pondered from this option.

This theme is central for liberation theology, but it is beyond the scope of the present work. In all brevity, then, let me sketch three levels of understanding present in the "perspective of the poor," from a point of departure in this new mediation of socio-analytic discourse.

Poverty: Destructive

Poverty is not innocent or neutral. Poverty is lethal. Material poverty is life historically menaced, thwarted, and destroyed, for the primary sources of the real life of the poor are menaced by the permanent nonsatisfaction of their basic needs: employment, food, housing, good health. Life is being annihilated, either slowly, by oppressive structures, or quickly and violently, by repressive structures (Gutiérrez, "Violencia"; Sobrino, "Dios," 111). Poverty is the expression of the true necrophiliac essence of an institutionalized system built on the death of the poor for the benefit of an elite, whose wealth is continually increasing at the expense of the increasing poverty of the masses.[21]

Out of a perception of this poverty arises, first, for the believer, an "ethical and prophetical indignation"; "God does not will poverty." "Things just can't go on like this!" "This is objective sin" (see Gutiérrez, "Violencia"; 566–68). Poverty contradicts God's creative design, for it despoils creatures of their dignity as human beings and daughters and sons of God. This is "the fruit of a great injustice that cries to heaven like the blood of Abel, murdered by Cain (Gen. 4:10)" (IECT, "Letter," 247).

Poverty: Structural

Poverty is not something "accidental" or casual—the product of an insufficiency of resources, or still more unfortunately, the result of a blind, inexorable fate. Poverty is not the result of the "laziness" or "inferiority" or "lack of education" or "lack of opportunities" of a people (Freire, *Iglesias*, 19). Poverty is historico-causal, the result of economic, social, and political structures. The poor, consequently, are the *product* of an unjust system, structured for the benefit of an elite. The poor, despoiled of the fruit of their labor, are members of a social class openly or subtly exploited by another social class (Gutiérrez, *Power*, 44–45).

The Poor: A Collective Subject

The option for the poor has made it clear that the poor cannot be materially distinguished from the social class to which they belong. There is no such thing as a poor person in isolation. The poor belong to social, racial, cultural, and sexual groupings. They constitute a collective, historically determined, subject. One of the merits of the CELAM general conference in Puebla was precisely to give the poor a concrete collective name.[22] This collective nature of the poor-as-subject is what makes the irruption of the poor harsh and conflictual. It is not enough to become aware of the reality of poverty. One must go a step further. Perception and protestation must inspire action. A life-destroying poverty is not something to be alleviated; it is something to struggle against.

A New Conception of the Political

Everything is political. But politics is not everything [Emmanuel Mournier].[23]

If poverty is a destructive, structural, material reality to be fought, and if the poor are poor not individually but as a collective subject, then the option for the poor leads unfailingly to the world of the political, and to the logic, the reasoning, peculiar to that world. This option bestows a special value on the political—not necessarily on any partisan, "sectorial" dimension of the political, but on the political globally, inasmuch as it embraces and inexorably conditions the entire collective endeavor of human realization.[24]

The political dimension of Christian love is discovered in the quest for the common good, and in the establishment of the right to life as a right of the masses of the poor.[25] Love and enthusiasm go hand in hand: "As a Christian I love the oppressed, and so I act with enthusiasm—I *do* something" (Míguez Bonino, "Compromiso," 24; see also his *Fe en busca*, 140). Love for the oppressed calls for expertise in political thinking, which will enable it, dialectically and without compromising its evangelical gratuity, to become effective in terms of both the reign of God and a political commitment.

The praxis of love translates today into a pledge to transform a social order that generates marginalization and poverty (Gutiérrez, "Praxis," 354, 356–60; *Power*, 48–50). We must question the "givenness" of the injustice and misery that crushes the vast majority of the populations of the "third world." In this historical situation, the option for the poor, in solidarity with their struggles, inevitably acquires a conflictual character. On the terrain of the political, as the political presents itself today, the option for the poor involves confrontations between human groups and social classes, with their opposing interests.[26] To love the poor collectively means to have enemies:

> This is a hard, uncomfortable truth for those who prefer not to see these conflictual situations. . . . It is equally hard for those who . . . confuse universal love with a fictitious harmony. But the gospel enjoins us to love our enemies. . . . There is no way not to have enemies. What is important is not to exclude them from our love [Gutiérrez, *Power*, 48].[27]

OUTLOOK OF THE POOR AND THEO-LOGY: MODALITY OF LIBERATIVE THEO-LOGICAL REFLECTION

The faith of the poor in the God of their deliverance seeks, from its own exigencies, to understand itself. This is the classic Anselmian *fides quaerens intellectum*. Christians have the right to think through their faith in the Lord, to think out the experience of their own liberation [Gutiérrez, *Power*, 101; St. Anselm, *Proslogion*].

Reflection on Mystery—theo-logy—is not an easy task. How may one articulate in words the "unspeakable Gift" bestowed upon us? God is *siempre Mayor*; God will always be greater than the limited words and notions that we can articulate. "The God who reveals himself in concrete history is a God who is irreducible to our manner of understanding him, irreducible to our theology and even to our faith" (ibid., 209).[28]

On the other hand, there is always the risk, once more, of taking God's name in vain.[29] In Latin America, this continent of profound Christian gestation, abuse of God's name for blessing injustices, for sacralizing inhuman policies and antilife, is such that it can at times seem supremely consistent for a believer to fall silent before Mystery (see Jiménez Limón, "Meditation," 150–51). And yet one may not, one cannot, so fall silent. "The mystery of God," Sobrino tells us, "becomes present in the very need to name God, even though we know beforehand the difficulty, and ultimately the impossibility, of naming God. Any word to be pronounced on this mystery is doomed to failure, but the failure will be even greater if we neglect the attempt" ("Dios," 121).

In the current historical and ecclesial situation in Latin America, it is more incumbent upon Christians than ever before to give an account of the presence of the God of Life, of the liberator God of the poor who bursts into history incarnate in the figure and messianic practice of Jesus.[30] If this is how God has come to manifestation, then God cannot be reduced to some abstract universal idea, above and beyond our history of oppression and struggle for a more human and just life.

This, then, is the specific modality conferred on theo-logical reflection by our living and thinking our faith in God from the universe of the "damned of the earth."[31]

Believing

Theo-logy is "believing" because it springs from the experience of faith and enriches the life of faith. A people's recognition of itself as the people of God implies the ongoing demand to pose to itself the question: Who is God for us today? (Gutiérrez, *Power*, 209).[32] In this way, a people seeks ever to renew its creative obedience to the faith in the quest and discipleship of the liberator God.

In Latin America there is a radical circularity between the option for the poor and the experience of God. The ultimate reason for this option is anchored in faith in God (see Gutiérrez, *Dios*, 87). But this option of solidarity with the poor has occasioned a deeper living experience of the encounter with God in the poor, and a better discernment of the current manifestation of the living God of Jesus in collective history and personal life.[33]

Responsible

Theo-logical is responsible, in the concrete sense—though not the exclusive sense—of *responding* to the questions of reality itself. That is, it responds to its "social locus." It does not wait upon the theologian's arbitrary decision to articulate one theme rather than another, but proceeds in accordance with the requirements of the challenges of historical and social reality itself. Theo-logy—reflection on the nucleus of God's ongoing self-manifestation—as believing and responsible, "is *ante et retro oculata*: it has two eyes. One looks back toward the past, where salvation broke in; the other looks toward the present, where salvation becomes reality here and now" (L. Boff, *Way*, viii). This twofold vision enables theo-logy to capture the meaning of the past (without turning into pure archeology), and at the same time give meaning to the present (without turning into pure phenomenology). Boff expatiates upon this theme:

> Any *theo*logy is constituted from a point of departure in two loci: the locus of faith, and the locus of the social reality within which faith is lived. The locus of faith is a given. The locus of social reality has to be identified. The fathers of the faith, in the first centuries, used to say that theology had two eyes, one before and one behind—*theologia ante et retro oculata*. With the "eye that looks backward," *theo*logy directs its view to the past, where the salvific, definitive presence of God has worked its historical irruption. . . . With the "eye that looks forward," it

gazes upon the present, detects the challenges posed by socio-historical reality, and makes an effort to articulate faith with life, love of God with political love, human hopes with the divine promises. *Theo*logical production is good when it succeeds in expressing the truth of faith discerned by the "eye that looks backward" in such wise that it engenders an existential and social sense in the present, as that present is visualized by the "eye that looks forward." Only then are we sure that our vision of reality is not distorted (the reality of our faith and that of our present time), but that we have the whole view that can be attained only by looking with both eyes [*Periferia*, 9; emphasis added].[34]

The believing *logos* is integrally bound up with church and society. As human thought, this *logos* is necessarily specified by a social and historical locus or situation. A paradigm of theological understanding is never totally neutral. However ecclesial it may be, it always has a relationship with the profane historical and social situation. The theologian occupies a social place, a social locus. Gutiérrez puts it forcefully:

All theology is in part a reflection of this or that concrete social process. Theology is not something disembodied or atemporal. On the contrary, theology is the attempt to express the word of the Lord in the language of today—in the categories of a particular time and place. Of course, I am speaking of authentic, relevant theology. No meaningful theology can be elucubrated in disconnection from concrete history, by stringing together a set of abstract ideas enjoying some manner of interior logical connection. No meaningful theology springs forth fully arrayed from the dusty tomes of yesterday. No, a meaningful theological reflection consists in an expression, and a calling into question, of broad historical processes. Only as such will theology fulfill its role as a reading of the faith from within a specific social practice.

Reflection on the faith is an effort on the part of particular believers, or groups of believers, who reflect on their belief in determinate social conditions, in order to work out interpretations and courses of action that will affect those conditions—that will play a role in the events and struggles of a given society. The theologian is not adrift in some historical limbo. His or her reflection has a precise locus, a precise point of departure. It springs up out of the material foundations of society. Like Archimedes of old, the theologian, too, needs a "place to stand" [*Power*, 90-91].[35]

Liberation theology insists on this point. Insufficient cognizance is taken of it today by a theological discourse bereft of a clear awareness of the socio-political and ideological "conditionings" of theology, a discourse in want of a clear awareness of its own social locus.[36]

Theo-logy is not carried on within the four walls of a laboratory, protected from the ideological tendencies and struggles of the present. The theologian does not waft about in thin air, but is inserted into the social conjunct. There is something very important, then, to be pointed out: "We must understand and appreciate the ideological mechanisms of established society, if theology is to take the word of God and convert it from a vague outline to a clearly worked out message. Otherwise theology will become and remain the unwitting advocate of the ideas of the ruling factions and classes" (Segundo, *Liberation*, 39).[37] Thus a grave responsibility falls on the Christian theologian's shoulders; in Jürgen Moltmann's apt phraseology:

> A *theo*logy that seeks to be *responsible* today must consider the psychic and political implications of its words, images, and symbols. . . . It must ask itself *in its whole discourse about God whether it is offering a religious opium or a real leaven of freedom* ["Crítica," 18; emphasis added].

Latin American theo-logy, as a responsible theology—one that responds to reality—claims to be an echo of the longing for historical liberation that rises up from the great masses of the poor. It claims to elaborate, from a starting point in the liberation process, a theo-logical methodology for discerning the liberative presence of God in history (as privileged theo-phanic locus). In this same measure, liberative theo-logy responsibly assumes the task of confronting and rejecting any vision of a god who fails to hear the cry of the poor or act in a preferential option in their behalf, inasmuch as such a god would bear no resemblance to the liberator God of the scriptures. Leonardo Boff states:

> Attention must be called to the existence of an image of God *ideologically bound to the system that justifies the de facto situation.*[38]
> —The capitalist system presents God as the Supreme Being who establishes classes in society as something natural. Hence, capitalism insists, there will always be rich and poor.[39]
> —It preaches a God who commands observance of the laws of nature, with use of persons, competition, and free enterprise being understood as consequences of the natural law.
> —It proclaims a God who demands obedience to the established order. It does not ask itself whether this notion may not be the fruit of the selfishness and self-interest of certain groups. The situation becomes tragic for faith when we realize that the basic concepts of Christianity itself *have been assimilated in support and justification of the system of oppression*—for example, humility, obedience, honesty, patience . . . love of enemies, and so on [*Experiencia*, 45–46; emphasis added].

God is not a category to be manipulated for the maintenance of the privileged status of dominators—a typical stance of "establishment religion" ("In God We Trust"). This is a betrayal, in the name of God, of the longing for life and liberation of a believing and oppressed people. A faith without the prophetic power to unmask the injustice of the mighty and proclaim "hope against hope," a faith that has been caught and tamed and assimilated to the ideology of the mighty, becomes a legitimating factor for domination, and an illegitimating one for the struggles and hopes of the oppressed for their liberation. These struggles and hopes become "contrary to the faith."[40]

The battle with the ideological nature of the theo-logies of antilife and antihope, the theologies held captive at the heart of a system that oppresses the poor, is part of the struggle to snatch the gospel from the hands of the dominators of this world, so as to prevent it from being transformed into a justification of a situation of oppression that is contrary to God's will (Gutiérrez, *Power*, 21).

A liberative theology seeks to be the liberation of theo-logy. It seeks to be the liberation of theo-logy from its prison of philosophical and cultural categories that veil, rather than reveal, the face of the God of liberation.[41]

Historical

Liberative theo-logy, because it is responsible, is necessarily a historical theology. That is, it is a theo-logy based on fundamental questions arising out of the present, not on universal questions handed down from generation to generation by tradition (Segundo, *Liberation*, 40). Hence the sense of history lying at the foundation of this theo-logy. Hence also the attention it bestows on God's self-manifestation in the *signs of the times*—those temporal, historical signs through which God becomes present in history.

The God question has been historicized, fossilized (Sobrino, *True Church*, 29; L. Boff, *Experiencia*, 42ff.). But in Latin America it arises and is concretized out of the reality of a people historically crucified by poverty, in the face of the radical alternatives of their oppression and their liberation. The God question occurs where ultimate reality occurs: in the life and death of human beings:

> The reality of a crucified people presents—and to my way of thinking, presents in the most radical way—the question of the ultimacy of reality and the reality of the divine. . . . *The historical reality of a crucified people cries out for God*, even before its groans are made the object of thought. Where this reality occurs, there the "problem" of God occurs. *In the face of the alternatives of life and death, liberation and oppression, salvation and condemnation, grace and sin, the transcendent question of God is posed in historical form* [Sobrino, "Fe en el Hijo," 339; emphasis added. See also idem, *Jesús*, 190].

The criterion for the discernment of true faith in God from a false "faith" is therefore to be found on this historical plane, where the real alternatives of human life and death are to be found (Sobrino, "Dios," 112). It is not natural catastrophes that raise the God question. There is indeed a "terrible challenge to the experience of God" (L. Boff, *Experiencia*, 45). But it does not arise from historical catastrophes. It is not the result of insufficiencies on the part of nature. It is the fruit of a structural schema of oppression, determined by the will of a privileged minority of persons who have made it possible to build and maintain an unjust society based on exploitation, profit, and repression.

Here it will be appropriate to cite an observation by Jürgen Moltmann, pioneer in the theology of hope:

> For the eighteenth-century Enlightenment, the world of nature, of principles and ideas, was but a reflection of the power and glory of God. Would human beings only manage to respond morally to this wonderful world of God's, the kingdom of God would be reality. In 1755 the famous earthquake of Lisbon occurred, and optimism crumbled and changed to pessimism and nihilism.
>
> Analogous earthquakes of our times derive not from nature or physical evil, but from history and the sin of dehumanization. For us, Auschwitz is an example. . . . For us rich white dominators, another example is the cry of the starving, oppressed, and racially despised masses [*Experimento*, 70].

Dialectical

Latin American theo-logy is dialectical rather than analogical. For it, the locus of the encounter with God appears not so much in God's analogy with the world, God's reflection in nature, but in discontinuity with a reality that must be renounced: "lived wretchedness." "Things can't go on this way," we say.

Our historical reality of oppression and struggle for liberation takes shape in what is de facto the most apt locus for a comprehension of God's manifestation in our time. The "historically negative"—the calvary of the antilife of the world—is the privileged path of access to Mystery:

> Wretched conditions and a situation of sin and oppression prove paradoxically to be the locus of encounter with God. But God must then be thought of, not as analogous with the God of thought, but as the contradiction of the wretched conditions of real life [Sobrino, *True Church*, 27].

This is why liberation theology has concentrated on such themes as the exodus, structural sin, captivity, conflictuality, and the cross. The very term "liberation"—instead of the "liberty" of the modern European tradition—points in this direction (Gutiérrez, *Power*, 171–78, 188). Liberation is seized only dialectically, as the opposite of oppression (Sobrino, *True Church*, 29).

In liberation theology, these principles of the theory of knowledge—analogical knowledge, dialectical knowledge—acquire importance in virtue of the epistemological rupture or breach presupposed by that theology within the process of its cognition. Jon Sobrino, especially, has called attention to these principles in his reflections on the epistemological status of the theology of liberation and its incorporation of the epistemological breach (Sobrino, *True Church*, 24-38: "Integration of the Epistemological Break into Theological Understanding").

For a better grasp of what is meant by the opposition of these two epistemological principles, and by the epistemological breach, let us consider three factors: analogical cognition; admiration and grief; and dialectical cognition.

Analogy and Its Breach

The fundamental presupposition of analogical cognition is that *like is known by like*. Thus all cognition is basically re-cognition. In the Aristotelian praxic version, like and like go very well together. Analogical thinking presupposes the existence of a correlation between the object to be known and the knowing subject. The new, unknown element is known from a point of departure in what is already known. In theology, analogical cognition functions especially in the knowledge of God. When classic theology—in the main, Catholic theology—speaks of God, it has recourse to a likeness and analogy between creator and creature. These are not the same reality in a monistic sense, but neither are they utterly different realities. Thomas Aquinas reworked the Aristotelian notion of the analogy of being—*analogia entis*—as a way of making it possible to speak of God. God, as creator, has left a mark on creation, in such wise that from creation—an effect—we can mount analogically to God the cause, and attribute certain creaturely concepts to God. We take a concept from the nature or being of creatures, posit its perfection and negate its limitations, and then attribute it to God. From our strength we deduce omnipotence; from our freedom, transcendent freedom; from our compassion, God's mercy.

The conception of analogy posits a moment of breach in the theological cognition elaborated by classic theology. One always had to negate the limited and finite in our knowledge of creatures in order to arrive at knowledge of God. But this breach meant only a *going (infinitely) beyond*. It has not meant a *going contrary to* the creaturely concept. The creaturely concept functions as point of departure in conceptual *continuity* (however distant) with the apex of reality, God.

Wonder as Grief

In Latin America, it is not *wonder* at the positive structure of reality that motivates theological cognition, as it was for the ancient Greeks. The process is precisely the contrary. It is wonder—astonishment, awe, bewilderment—concretized as *grief*—the grief of the oppressed (the negative structure of reality)—that moves one to think theologically. It is in this grief that is found the true *analogy* that makes theo-logical cognition possible. This analogy consists in "the recognition that the present history of the world is the ongoing history of the suffering of God" (Sobrino, *True Church*, 29).[42] Hence the theology of liberation includes a theoretical moment (perhaps not reflexive), viewing the reality of God in God's relationship with suffering: "Because God has willed to join humankind in history, God's sufferings will continue, with humankind and history, until the end of the world" (Alves, *Cristianismo*, 189).

Dialectics and Its Breach

In Latin America, with its long colonial past and neocolonial present, where justice, communion, and universal participation are conspicuous by their absence, where the situation of the masses is catastrophic, theological discourse is necessarily *more dialectical than analogical* (Sobrino, *True Church*, 27–28), and seeks to assimilate the epistemological breach dialectically.

Dialectical cognition knows things in their dissimilarity. The theo-logical, then, will be known *not* in its likeness to created reality and as culmination of reality, in progressive conceptual continuity, but will be known from what is distinct from it—from its contrary, from the negative structures of reality, the structures of oppression as lived experience. Consequently, the concrete mediations of theo-logical cognition—the locus of the encounter with God, the privileged locus of access to Mystery—consists in these realities of oppression, pain, and injustice inasmuch as they indicate, point to (*sub specie contrarii*) their contrary, the utterly other than themselves: liberation, life, and justice, not as realities beyond feasibility in history, but as the negation of present reality, and therefore as comporting a demand for the transformation of that reality (ibid., 28).

The epistemological breach demanded by present suffering calls for a praxic orientation. The experience of actual misery motivates thought, yes, but above all it motivates action. Theo-logy arises in the face of and from the fact of pain. It does not reject an analysis of the historical causes of this pain, but it renounces any attempt to explain the calvary of the world in a cohesive integration of the data of revelation with the data of antihistory. The misery of reality is not, in the final analysis, something to be understood, but something to be combated and eliminated.[43] And this brings me to the next point.

Praxic

Theo-logy is praxic in the sense that it does not arise capriciously. It does not arise in virtue of an academic fad. Its interest is not pure reflection, not even with respect to an ortho-logy of God, an elucidation of the true essence of God. What is important to theo-logy is to respond to God—to correspond, co-respond, to the reality of God in an attempt to inaugurate the reign of God in the crude historical reality structured as antikingdom.

The manner of response to or correspondence with God's ongoing manifestation will consist in the praxis of the justice of the reign of God, and in the effectuation of this praxis from a point of departure in the concrete reality of the poor (Sobrino, *True Church*, 2, 30–31, 281).

In Latin America, the classic question of theodicy, in Leibnitz's original sense of "justification of God," makes its appearance, however implicitly, from a particular viewpoint and with particular nuances. Theology has its external dependencies. Inasmuch as it is the humanly contrived disasters of history, not earthquakes or other natural disasters, that pose the God question, the question of theodicy comes to be mediated by an *anthropodicy*. How is the human being to be justified in our history of oppression and injustice? (Sobrino, *True Church*, 29).

The basic scandal is not that there is suffering in the world despite the existence of God. The basic scandal is simply that there is suffering and injustice in the world. The real question, then, is not how to "square" the existence of God with the fact of human misery. The real question is how to justify the human being in a world of injustice. The God question becomes essentially praxic. The solution to the epistemological breach (for a cognition that is more dialectical than analogical) is not to "think God" from another approach, in such wise that it will be theoretically, ideally possible to reconcile the injustice and misery of the world with the reality of God. To the extent that faith in God enables human beings to battle injustice and misery, and thus strive for a world in conformity with God's design for life and justice, God is "justified," whether or not God and misery are also reconciled theoretically (Sobrino, *True Church*, 30–31).

God's reality is demonstrated in the attempt to reconcile reality—in a history of oppression and struggle for liberation, in the midst of which struggle God maintains an ongoing manifestation, from the depths of the misery of reality, that God may justify, in the sense of re-create, the human being. Consequently anyone who seriously strives for justice is a person "according to God."[44] When all is said and done, the notion of God in a determinate theo-logical view is not discernible on the theoretical level. It can be discerned only in the praxis to which it leads (González Faus, *Acceso*, 28).

The theo-logical reflection maintained by liberation theology seeks to situate itself as a moment in the process of the transformation of the world. It springs from a commitment to a breach with the historical reality of suffering and injustice:

> Without a keen sensitivity and a determination to turn theology into a serviceable tool for orthopraxis, for a social praxis that is liberative, a false and quasi-magical concept of orthodoxy will dissolve theology into universal, ahistorical concepts [Segundo, *Liberation*, 39].

Evangelical

Liberation theology is evangelical in the basic sense of the term: it proclaims the good news of "God-*with*-us" and "*for*-us," in God's radical self-bestowal.

Transcendent Mystery, the creator, has been able to "witness the affliction of his people in Egypt, and hear their cry . . . I know well what they are suffering. Therefore I have come down to rescue them" (Exod. 3:7–8). God continues a self-manifestation in history—in the "chronological today." God's love is greater than the sin of human beings who oppress and murder their fellow human being but fail to destroy the design of God in the "kairological today," and God re-creates life and vanquishes death. Liberative theo-logy proclaims the good news of the reign of God, which is still coming, with its justice and truth, its judgment on the world, and its confrontation with the mighty. As believers, we must rip off our blindfolds and see how God's good news is being proclaimed today through the poor of the earth (IECT, "Letter," 249).

LIBERATIVE THEO-LOGY AND THE MYSTERY OF GOD

A Basic "Thesis Text" ("Primordial Intuition")

The mystery of God as the key to liberation (as approached from the underside of history) is, to my mind, forcefully synopsized in the following lines from the IECT "Letter to Christians in Popular Christian Communities of the Poor Countries and Regions of the World":

> The living power that comes from God is manifesting itself precisely in those places where life is oppressed, enslaved, and crucified on the Calvary of the World. . . . Today, as in the time of captivity, the God who raised Jesus from the dead is hidden in the midst of history, on the side of the poor, working and liberating his people with the victorious power that overcomes death and creates life anew [IECT, "Letter," 247, 248–49].

I propose this "thesis text," as it may be called, with its logic—its way of "seeing" God—as both point of departure and unifying thesis for the dogmatic treatment of my theme.

In this basic vision, I distinguish three force vectors, or thematic points of concentration. (I distinguish them for purposes of exposition and explanation. In practice they constitute a cohesive, closely interconnected whole.)

First, the Mystery of God continues to be *manifested* in history. This is God's historico-salvific self-revelation. Spontaneously, the primordial, original Mystery continues to manifest itself in a self-bestowal in the midst of history, in order to save that history.

Secondly, the Mystery of God is *hidden/identified*. This is *Dios Menor*, "God diminished." God does not remain indifferent to the suffering endured by the victims of history. God's love is expressed in taking up the pain of the world, the calvary of antilife, where life is oppressed, enslaved, and crucified. This is the manifestation of God as *Mystery in hiding*—as God dwells with the lifeless, the humiliated, the vanquished, and the wronged of our history and our society with its oppression, injustice, and structural sin—and as *Mystery identified* with these same victims of history in loving solidarity, not "from without," but "from within": in a historical, ontological solidarity, as God becomes "less," small, poor, a "man of sorrows" (the suffering servant of Yahweh), and the sharer of their abandonment and death. God suffers *with* them and *in* them.

Thirdly, the Mystery of God is *salvific praxis*. This is *Dios Mayor*, the "greater God." Here God is manifested as the liberator God, the giver of Life, who establishes justice and the rights of the oppressed. It is not enough to assert that God is identified/hidden in the midst of history, that God suffers with us in loving solidarity. God starts out from the historical negative, but then bestows on us a self-manifestation as power of salvation, life of the lifeless, liberating the oppressed with a victorious power that vanquishes death and re-creates life in its fullness—the reign of God.

Reading Keys: Hermeneutic Keys

Bipolarity in Language About God[45]

In liberative theo-logical reflection, language concerning Mystery is characterized by a bipolarity, in virtue of which, simultaneously and dialectically, is asserted the mystery of a God *siempre Mayor*, "ever greater," and the mystery of a God *siempre Menor*, "ever lesser."[46] In virtue of this basic affirmation, God's *radical mysteric transcendence* comes to the fore: the ever greater God is the utterly other—God in absolute otherness—the Holy, the Inconceivable, absolute Mystery; in a word, the Transcendent. Conjointly, there is God's *radical historico-salvific immanence*: the ever lesser God, who assumes human otherness without destroying it, God in the incarnation, who assumes lowliness (becomes poor) in solidarity with the lowly and the poor in a suffering love that endures to the death. This is the *mysterium tremendum*, from which we recoil, and at the same time the *mysterium fascinans*, which draws us like a magnet (Pikaza, *Experiencia*, 223–29):

> The Christian God has been explained as a *Dios Mayor*, an ever Greater God. "God is greater than our hearts," the New Testament says (1 John 3:20), and Saint Augustine spoke of God as the *Deus semper major*. This could look like a play on words, just one more beautiful expression for God. And yet, what it basically means is that we cannot exhaust God, we cannot com-prehend God, cannot penetrate God through and through, cannot comprehend the totality of the truth of God, or foresee all God's irruptions in history. In God there is a mystery that overflows our capacities. The consequence is that God unsettles us [Hernández Pico, "Hombre," 41].

It is the prerogative of God's otherness to be radically distinct, to be the Holy One and unmanipulable. This is the point of the biblical conception of God as the Holy One—that is, as distinct, the utterly different one, for this is the meaning of "holy":

For the scriptures, "Holy" is not just one attribute of God among many. Rather it is another way of saying "God." An etymological consideration can show us why. *Sanctus* is the past participle of the verb *sancire*, "to separate," "to distinguish." "God the Holy One" means: the Other, the one who transcends the human being and the world (Hos. 11:9). Everything comes from God, but creation is not a prolongation of God. God dwells in inaccessible light (1 Tim. 6:16f). God alone is Holy—in Latin, *fanum*. Everything else—the *profanum*—is but the antechamber of the Holy. Understood in this way, the holy is inaccessible to the human being, for it defines God's essence (Isa. 6:3). Obviously, then, holiness is something more than a moral quality. . . . *It is the very definition of God as Mystery*, as Otherness, as the other side of what we see and experience empirically. Vis-à-vis the other, and especially the Other, the genuinely worthy and human attitude is an attitude of respect and reverence. . . . Before God, before the divine reality, we have an experience of the *tremendum*—we experience fear shot through with veneration. . . . Then we experience God as the truly Other, distinct from everything we can possibly say, think, or even imagine [L. Boff, *Ave María*, 84–86; emphasis added; see also Gutiérrez, *Dios*, 24–25].

But the greater God is also the lesser God: greater precisely because of having become truly, incredibly, smaller (Sobrino, "Significado," 36).

Boff continues:

This Other, however, is not sinister, but loving and attractive—*fascinans*—a Father and Mother of infinite goodness and tenderness. Therefore the fact that the Holy God is not the world or the human being but something separate from them does not mean that God is found at a distance from, or outside, them. . . . God is especially sensitive to the cry of the oppressed and the lowly (Exod. 3:7–9), through love, which draws near, enters into solidarity, and sanctifies, closing the "essential gap" [*Ave María*, 86].

It is this radically other God alone whom we profess to be free, grace-bestowing self-donation, who assumes our history, refusing to "keep a distance," and approaches us in loving-kindness. Creator of all creatures, God becomes a creature. The one whom "no one has ever seen" (John 1:18) takes visible form. "God, without ceasing to be God, took human form, which was something new" (L. Boff, *Encarnación*, 10–11).[47] Indeed, in virtue of the incarnation we may speak of "God's own humanity."[48] There is no image of the liberator God more unreal than that of an impassible, triumphalistic, neutral, self-satisfied God whose imperturbability the cry of the "damned of the earth" cannot unsettle. Such a God is more like the gods of Olympus, or the mighty of this earth, who live in places where the cry of the starving, oppressed masses cannot be heard (Codina, *Renacer*, 105). The liberator God is present in history, the history taken on by God out of love. God, the wellspring of life, justice, and love, assumes a "radically distinct" reality: poverty, injustice, suffering, and death. Hence God is not to be sought among the mighty, but among the subjected, the "losers," the ones without a future (Ruíz, "Magnificat"; Alves, *Cristianismo,* 184).

This view is very different from that of classic theology, in which "nothing happens" to God in the incarnation because God is immutable: whatever occurs in the incarnation "affects the human nature alone," not the divine impassibility (Gonzáles Faus, *Acceso*, 21; idem, *Humanidad*, I, 232–34). But the divine transcendence, God's "being greater," is not an abstract metaphysical category, placing God ever "beyond." On the contrary, it is a way of positing God's manifestation in incarnation, in what is deepest in history, a history of sin and conflict.

History as Privileged Theo-phanic Locus

For a Christian, history is a mediation of God. Radical historical changes followed by a routine reflection on God would be an absurdity. For a Christian, the radical novelty of history should suppose, in the first place, *the hearing of the new word of God through history.* And then, through this new word, one should ask oneself that never adequately answered or answerable question, the God question. If a historical revolution fails to move us to rethink, to redo, our faith in God, the routing repetition of our belief in God as lord of history will be in vain [Sobrino, "Dios," 107; emphasis added].

History is a mediation of revelation, a "privileged theophanic locus."[49] This means that the locus of concretization of the experience of God is *not* in *nature* or the cosmos, as a nature or cosmic religion would have it, and *not* in *interiority*, or the interior life, as in mystical religion. The locus of concretization of the experience of God is given in *history*, as salvation history. Our religion is historical or prophetical:

The infinite God becomes comprehensible by the revelation bestowed on us. We know very well that this revelation is historical. It is *only* historical. *The sole locus of revelation is history.* The only *locus theologicus* is history, the concrete history of the everyday. If we fail to discover the meaning of history, then neither shall we understand what God reveals to us. God, the infinite Other, is revealed to us in history. One says this all rather quickly, and yet it is the essence of all theology, and the essence of a whole historical process known as the history of salvation, that "Passover" of justice and liberation [Dussel, *Desintegración*, 15, emphasis added; see also Gutiérrez, *Power*, 3–12].

The biblical faith is not some manner of mythic religion based on prehistorical, or, more precisely, ahistorical, mythical event. Nor is it a cosmogonic theory. It does not proceed a priori from an abstract consideration of the essence and existence of God as the Absolute, or as the foundation of being. Biblical language about God has a reference to historical events, and endeavors to read the signs of the times in which God expresses salvific action.[50] The Hebrews did not say that Yahweh *is* or *exists*. They said that Yahweh *acts*.[51] God is made known through works. Biblical faith, then, is to know history and to believe in the God self-revealed in it, to hear that efficacious word. The Bible makes fun of gods who neither hear nor speak. Yahweh's word is *dabar*—simultaneously word and event (Gutiérrez, *Power*, 5). (See Excursus I, p. 40, below.)

Access to God from the World of the Poor

Access to God is not principally effectuated through worship, religious observance, or prayer. These are genuine mediations, but in themselves they are ambiguous. The privileged, unambiguous access to God is through service to the poor, in whom God dwells, secretly and anonymously. Liberative praxis constitutes the surest path to the God of Jesus Christ [L. Boff, *Periferia*, 36; cf. Sobrino, *Christology*, 206–7].

It is not enough to assert that God is revealed in history. The theology of liberation goes a step beyond this cardinal truth of the Christian faith and states that, in approaching human beings gratuitously and freely, God has become accessible to them. Hence the importance of identifying the *locus* from which we have access to mystery. As José Porfirio Miranda has pointed out, the question is not whether one may or may not search for God, but rather whether one searches for God where revelation tells us that God is—in the world of the poor (*Marx y la Biblia*, 82).

The underside of history, which poses the God question so radically, simultaneously reveals the answer, inasmuch as it offers, as Sobrino puts it, "the place of access to God in a privileged world of the oppressed, and insofar as it prescribes the manner of access to God: through the effort to liberate these oppressed persons" ("Significado," 35). This fundamental conviction of liberation theology can be better understood if it is divided into three elements or steps. In its concretization of the locus of access to God, liberation theo-logy, in a liberative key from the underside of history, distinguishes these three elements:

Access to God from History

Access to God does not begin with nature (in a cosmic religion) or interiority (in a mystical religon), but with history, as the space that creates the human being (and not as the modified universal repetition of an idea): it begins with history as real, concrete, and conflictual, with its necessary, inescapable socio-political and economic mediations.

Access to God from the Privileged World of the Oppressed

This is access to God from the "other" history, from the history "of the others"—from the world of the oppressed. This is history in its moment of negativity, history as the "antihistory" of the humiliated and abased (Leonardo Boff), and hence a history of conflict and suffering, an "antilife" history of the world as a calvary—a history whose deepest entrails hold a hidden God in solidarity with the poor—a God of the poor, then, and a suffering Love. The consequence is clear: the locus of encounter and contemplation of Mystery is not in nature, or in the depths of the soul, but in what is deepest in human misery: it is in the poor. Neither illuminist nor quietist may enter here (Fernández, "Lugares," 73).

In his systematic reflection on faith and the praxis of justice, Jon Sobrino identifies and broadens the concretization of the locus of access to God in historical activity itself (*True Church*, 47-63). The practice of justice—as a historical form of love—is suitable, and in some measure necessary, for a concretization of the locus of access to the Mystery of God precisely as Mystery (ibid., 47-53). The practice of justice, unlike philosophical considerations on creation, or esthetic, intellectual, or sapiential experiences, radically reveals the transcendent nature of Mystery, for this mystery bears within itself the demand for an ever "more" in humanization—in the promotion of the life of human beings.

The process of doing human beings *more* justice, and the experience that there are no a priori limits on this "more" (not even to be set by the one practicing the justice), is constituted through the mediation of the experience of the "ever greater God" who has pronounced an unconditional yes upon life, justice, and human beings. The practice of justice, which concretizes the locus of access to Mystery and reveals God's transcendence (Greater God, *Dios Mayor*), conjointly maintains God's radical immanence, from which access is had to God, who is also the Lesser God, *Dios Menor*, identified-and-hidden in the lowly, the impoverished, those deprived of life:

> Access to the *ever greater and transcendent God* comes through contact with the *God who is "lesser,"* hidden in the little ones, crucified on the cross of Jesus and on the countless crosses of the oppressed of our day [Sobrino, *True Church*, 56; emphasis added].

Access to God from a Praxis Liberative of the Oppressed

This is access to God from human history (nature and society) taken in its positive aspect: as a history of struggle against oppression and injustice through the creation of genuine historical conditions of life and interhuman justice. This struggle for justice is a quest for the reign of God, and ultimately the route to the God of that reign and its justice.

Mystery Remains Mystery

The liberator God is revealed to us as Mystery. Christian faith, which begins with the grace that consists in "something having given itself to us," some self-bestowal, recognizes that there is ineffable mystery in God, mystery incapable of being manipulated. To speak of God is to place oneself before original and originating Mystery that remains Mystery eternally.[52] There is a mystery in God that always escapes us, exceeds us. It is impossible to possess it, or make of it a known object. At first sight it appears to be a contradiction to speak of God as mystery in the framework of God's liberative manifestation in history. But the contradiction is indeed only apparent. To speak of God as mystery is *not* to overlook God's liberative call and challenge, nor is it a subtle denial of the concrete historical in a quest for a cyclical history (Sobrino, "Epiphany," 93–97; *Jesús*, 115–49). Nor again is it to open the door to possible temptations of intimistic escapism—to processes of immersive inhabitation that would introduce the human being to mystery only to deny that mystery in its greatness.[53]

Recognition and acknowledgment of mystery demands that we place ourselves before God in an attitude of silence.[54] It demands we listen for God's novel, efficacious word, which is constantly judging and dislodging us all. By the same token, with constancy and humility, we must rethink our practice and thinking, all of it, however much this practice and thinking may have seemed positive and correct—however orthopraxic and orthological it may have seemed to be.

Any theo-logical word—any reasoned word upon Mystery—is always precarious. It is never adequately articulated or articulable. Being mystery, God is never totally embraceable, totally comprehensible. All genuine knowledge concerning God has its quota of nonknowledge (Sobrino, "Conllevamos," 174). Indeed, God is more the object of our hope than of our knowledge. As Gutiérrez puts it, God is "much less what we know than the great hope that we feel" ("Dios," 5–6).

Finally, although history is a mediation of God, God, being mystery, transcends this mediation, cannot be reduced to it. We shall never be able fully and adequately to historicize God. There is nothing in history capable of closing in or exhausting God's presence and activity. In history, limited, imperfect history, God will always be "without a place," without a *topos*, for God is the utopic, transcendent Principle of history. And yet, it is in history that mystery has drawn radically near, as Mystery that is "gratuitous, but not superfluous."[55] God's purpose is to give life in the Son and generate history by the Spirit (*Mysterium Liberationis*), conferring on life and on history a radical sense of ultimacy and transcendence. To "think Mystery" in Christian fashion, in the classic sense of the Augustinian-Anselmian tradition of *fides quaerens intellectum*, is not an abstract, theoretical thinking. It is a thinking that has a historico-salvific character: Mystery has ceased being mystery at one point, that of God's liberative love. It is a thinking that necessarily comports a demanding christologico-pneumatological concretion, as expression of the Mystery of the Father's love, lived in the historical discipleship of Jesus, through the strength of the Spirit (Sobrino, "Fe en el misterio," 145ff.).

EXCURSUS I: HISTORICO-PROPHETIC RELIGION —THEISTIC HERMENEUTICS OF HISTORY

In view of the importance of history as privileged theo-phanic locus, it will be useful to expatiate somewhat on the historico-prophetical nature of the Judeo-Christian religious tradition—that is, on its theistic hermeneutics of history.

Liberation theology in general, and its theo-logy in particular, is an effort to *recover* what is proper and specific to this Judeo-Christian tradition as recorded in the Bible. The kernel of this heritage is in God's salvific activity in history—never on the margin of history, or without passing by way of history. God is the God of history; history is the road to God. The experience of history is space and time qualified for the experience of God:

> Despite the differences from our own world, the most original feature of the socio-cultural world of the Old and New Testaments (in contrast to the Greek world and others) is its *setting of the experience of God in the context of man's historical progress* [Assmann, *Theology*, 35; emphasis added].

In the development of this excursus, I direct the reader's attention to the contributions of Xabier Pikaza.[56] In particular, I shall be following his "Tipificación de la experiencia religiosa" (page numbers cited in parentheses throughout this excursus). His study is a descriptive-phenomenological examination of the cosmic religious experience, the religious experience of interiority, and the historical religious experience.[57] The triple theme is a broad one, and extends beyond the scope of my own work. Hence I limit myself to the descriptive study of *historico-prophetic religion*.

Historico-Prophetic Religions

The historico-prophetic religions are those that, unlike the cosmic or mystical religions, are based on the conviction that *history is the mediation of God's revelation*. Judeo-Christian religion is such a religion.

In the historico-prophetic religions, history is the locus of the dialogue encounter with God that initiates, bases, and directs the path of history, which is a gift of God and the expression of human becoming (p. 256). God's epiphany and the creation of the human being—the anthropophany—converge.[58]

Cosmic religions, or nature religions, interpret the world as the locus of the divine. They discover the presence of mystery through the cosmic order enveloping the existence of human beings (p. 262). History dissolves in the rhythm of the eternal return of things. Reality has no historical beginning—only a great, mythic principle, a kind of root of divinity, seat of the course of the cycles of history, in which all things are finally ever the same (p. 256).[59]

Mystic religions, religions of interiority, interpret the interior life as locus of the divine. They seek Mystery in a process of purification, depth, and interior equilibrium (p. 262). They postulate a kind of primordial fall, in which human souls have descended from a superior, divine level, conceived as stability. Only through a process of profound trial and purification can souls recover themselves, transcend the eternal return of nature that holds them captive, and return to their original divine state (p. 256).[60]

Elements of a Religion of History

The distinguishing elements of *historical religion* are four: (a) transcendence of any intimistic quest for God within human beings alone; (b) God's positive revelation, in personal self-communication; (c) the urgency of an encounter with others, in a triadic model; (d) preclusion of any dualistic dichotomy:

a) Having overcome the sacrality of the cosmos in a struggle with idolatrous polytheism, the religious thrust does not proceed in the direction of interiority, but now *transcends all intimism*, all quest for the divine exclusively within human beings. The deed of religion therefore begins where a word is heard coming from without, from a God conceptualized as endowed with personality.

b) Instead of a religious a priori, we now have a *positive revelation of God*. Mysteric depth is not the locus of the definitive hierophany. Life is not recollection, penetration of one's interior, and consequent transcendence of the evil of the world. Because God transcends what we are and what we are able to do, God's presence can be actualized only through a free deed of personal self-communication, accepted by the believer through the response of a dialoguing faith.

c) *The model of union with God will be triadic.* There is no question of a process of immersive inhabitation that would introduce the human being into the mystery of God in such wise as to deny the transcendent grandeur of God. There is a difference between the human being and God, and this is no obstacle to their union. What is important, then, is not for believers to lose themselves in God, but to real-ize themselves as human beings, in a field of enabling and creative encounter. In other words, between human beings and God there ever prevails the demand of law, the urgency of an encounter with others.

d) This outlook makes it possible to *preclude any radical dualism between soul and body*, between the material world and the spiritual being of the divine. God is not reflected in cosmic immateriality, but in the supracosmic becoming of history. For their part, human beings are neither nature (as cosmic religion would have it) nor pure interiority (as in mystic religion). A human being is a historical becoming, which can be and is based on encounter and communion with the divine. Hence in opposition to the mysteric schema of above-and-below, without-and-within, there is a division marked out between the "now" of a partial realization and the "later" total manifestation of human beings through their encounter with the divine. And so, in opposition to immortality understood as human supracosmic being, the eschatological resurrection is posited, as theologico-humanizing fulfillment of history [pp. 289–90].

The Religion of Israel

The religion of Israel is supported by two pillars. First, there is a *transcending break with the cosmic sacrality and piety* proper to the "epiphany religion" of the fertility cults of Canaan, which interpret God as the numinous backdrop of the cosmos, sacralizing the vital order and divinizing the whole of nature (p. 290).

God is not something "here." God is independent of the rhythm of nature. The cosmos is de-divinized, and appears as the creation of a transcendent God. The earth is to be dominated and transformed, not adored.[61]

Secondly, there is a *theistic hermeneutics of history*—that is, the conviction that history is *theo-phanic* (p. 293). This entails four elements: (1) a distinct locus of God's epiphany (the time of a history); (2) faith as experience of a dialogue encounter; (3) the level of the experience of meaning; and (4) the great novelty that this experience entails.

1) The religion of Israel continues to be epiphanic. What has changed is the locus of God's epiphany. There is no cosmic hierophany as in Canaan, no manifestation of the sacred in the depth of an interior experience as in India. There is only the history of a people, beginning to be conceived as the locus of a new and active presence of God.[62] The sacral epiphany is identified with the time of a history: the call of Abraham, the exodus and the covenant, the wilderness, the conquest of the land, the exile, the return, and eschatological hope (p. 291).

2) Faith is the expression of a dialogue encounter. History as locus of God means that, transcending cosmic fixation and sacral interiority, the course of history is the *locus communis* of the dialogue encounter between God and the human being.[63] The human being's encounter with God, which is the basis of any religious experience, is detached from cosmic space and begins to take shape along the road of a revelatory history (p. 291). In this history, God and the human being coincide, out beyond their differences—God as the one who bursts in with a new word-and-action, the human being as the one who hears the word of the divine call and responds to it (taking the "path of response"). The fullest form of the encounter with God is not cosmic negation of or fusion

with the divine ("losing oneself in God"), but full, creative, and communitarian (because human) self-realization along the path of history.

In the Israelite religious experience, this interhuman relationship is expressed in the covenant.[64] Over against the temptation to find direct routes to God, routes that do not pass by way of the real route of encounter with one's neighbor, the relationship with God is understood and lived on the basis of an encounter-in-solidarity with human beings (p. 297). This interhuman encounter entails a responsibility for the historical lot of others, a social responsibility to construct a nation of equals.[65]

3) Understanding history as locus of God, Israel moves on a level of experience of meaning. The events of history are not neutral. They are open to mystery. They are God's peculiar, proper word:

> For the religious Israelite, the exodus was now not a chance occurrence, but the locus of God's activity in choosing a people. The covenant is interpreted as the field of God's election and human response. . . . The events that have determined Israel's birth as a people (the exodus, the conquest of the land), the vicissitudes of Israel's social configuration (establishment of the monarchy, internal divisions), failures and collapses (the exile), along with signs of hope (the messianic promises), are more than "neutral" events to be explained by the wheel of life. They are God's peculiar word—a word of call, a word of demand or rejection. They are always the word of a transcendent encounter [p. 292].

4) Through this religious reading of history, Israel offered universal culture something new and precious: the *discovery* of history. History is no longer the eternal return of the one and the same. History is seen as a process that is open to the future: the new humanity. Every event, every person, acquires definitive value. Every human being has a responsibility in the fulfillment of each of these events (p. 292).[66]

Israel's Theo-logical Vision

Finally, let us focus on the most significant theo-logical elements of Israel's journey, the elements of its way of looking at God. These elements are transcendence, personal freedom, openness to the future, the radicality of a God at the service of human beings, and a demand for obedience.

Transcendency

From a point of departure in a transcendent God, it is now possible to understand the order and meaning of history. Because God is transcendent, God can freely act and freely reveal the divine will, which gives both thrust and fulfillment to the journey of history (p. 294).

Personal Freedom

Transcendence translates into personhood. God has characteristics that are strictly those of a person: God is autonomous, gives a self-revelation as "mysteric transcendence," speaks a word, which challenges in a tone of urgency, vocation, and justice. God loves, suffers, acts, and answers. Being personal, God can be encountered in dialogue. Faith as an expression of encounter is dialogue with a personal God. Faith is realized in the deed of dialogue. Thus the presence of God "overflows the space of contemplative interiority and is offered in the journey of history, in a dialogue that is a self-expression and self-donation of God, and in which the human being achieves reality" (p. 267).

Openness to the Future—A Religion of Promise[67]

God is mystery open to the future. God is bound by the promise of a new, plenary history that overflows the religious plane of a land granted in eternal stability, a land sacred from the beginning. To believe in God is an eschatological attitude.[68] It supposes a wager on the future. To know God is to hope in God. Thus God is revealed where human beings, joining together as a people—Israel—strive for a future of human fulfillment: strive for a new, transparent humanity, realized and reconciled (p. 263).

A Partisan God

Faith is a trust in God founded on the constancy and fidelity of a God who is at the unconditional service of the human being. Thus the first Israelite creed or profession of faith proclaims God's historical, salvific activity in behalf of the human being, and confers upon God a name in history: "I, the Lord [Yahweh], am your God, who brought you out of Egypt" (Exod. 20:2; Deut. 5:6; cf. Num. 24:8; 1 Kings 12:28; Jer. 2:6; Deut. 8:14, etc.). This "proto-confession" (p. 298) is the foundation stone of the great professions of faith of the Old Testament, and becomes the constant element running through the whole backbone of the two Testaments, by which the radicality of a God at the service of the human being acquires a scandalous concretion: God's "preferential option" for the lowly, the downtrodden.

This constant has been distilled by Karl Barth in the following terms, referring to God's activity in the midst of the happenings of the history of Israel:

> God always takes His stand unconditionally and passionately on this side and on this side alone: against the lofty and on behalf of the lowly; against those who already enjoy right and privilege and on behalf of those who are denied it and deprived of it [*Church Dogmatics* (Edinburgh, Clark, 1957) II/1, p. 386].

Yahweh, the God of Israel, who has been revealed in history, who has delivered Israel from Egypt, is identified as the liberator who seeks to establish justice and right. God is more than provident. God takes sides with the poor.[69]

God: Gift and Demand

God is discovered in a context of obedience and covenant at the heart of the history of a people. The response that God demands is a life of ongoing fidelity to the covenant. This is what is expressed, paradigmatically, in the words "I (Yahweh) will be your God and you will be my people" (cf. Deut. 26:16–19). This is the context that bestows meaning on the "pactual confession" recalled in Joshua 24:17–18 and 1 Kings 18:39.[70]

Israelite theology must have grasped the implication of history and covenant very early (p. 299). We see this from its most complex creed, which is to be found in Deuteronomy 6:20–24. In the background of historico-salvific revelation, we also find the word of the ethico-pactual creed that is determinative of all Israelitic spirituality: the Shema (Deut. 6:4–9, 11:13–21; Num. 15:37–41).[71]

By way of conclusion of this excursus, let me point out that it is this characterization of historical or prophetic religions, especially of the religion and theo-logy of ancient Israel, that provides me with the background for a grasp of the sense of my contention that Latin American liberation theology is an effort to recover what is proper and specific in the Judeo-Christian religious tradition: that history is the mediation of God's revelation, that God has willed to be involved in history. From this beginning, liberation theology—as Christian reflection—will take a further step, and situate this historical hierophany in the light of the incarnation of the Word. In Jesus of Nazareth as personal hierophany, God enters into history once and for all.[72]

CHAPTER 2

Liberative Theo-logy: Dogmatic Articulation

Having treated of the meaning paradigm (hermeneutic key) of Latin American liberation theology in general and of its theo-logical vision in particular, I am now in a position to take a further step and articulate the theo-logical "theory"—the view of God—maintained by liberation theology in its dogmatic aspect properly so-called. This will be a treatment of my theme in its "monographic specificity"—my study of the most frequent theo-logical routes of elucidation pursued by liberation theology, its most significant vectors and thematic nuclei.

This chapter has three distinct parts. First, as my point of departure, I treat of the prime element of the Christian faith: Mystery in its ongoing manifestation. Now I can resume the dialectical bipolarity of language about God as *Dios Mayor* and *Dios Menor,* as greater God and lesser God. Secondly, I treat of the Mystery of God hidden in the lowly, in the poor of the earth, and of this God's love for them, in partiality and solidarity with them, even to suffering and death, the suffering and death of *Dios Menor* on the calvary of this world. Thirdly, I treat of God's manifestation as salvific praxis—as power that saves, fully and abundantly. In this soteriologico-theo-logical axis, I distinguish three moments central to the theology of liberation: liberation, justice, and life—three moments that, although not covering every aspect of the axis, do historicize it.

In concluding this chapter, I attempt to capsulize its meaning in terms of the reign of God—the ultimate and fullest expression of God's design of liberation, justice, and life for the whole human being and for all human beings.

THE MYSTERY OF GOD: ONGOING MANIFESTATION

Self-Manifestation (Autophany)

From the Christian standpoint, the deepest aspect of the mystery of God is the divine self-revelation to history and its salvation (Sobrino, *Resurrección,* 59). The God who liberates, the original and originating Mystery, the Holy and Unmanipulable, whose *esse* is being-Other—otherness, holiness, transcend-

46

ence—is not an everlastingly distant *In Se,* hidden, abiding outside history. God is not self-closed, self-closured, inaccessible mystery; not an entity living impassibly in an eternal, reflex circularity of self-thinking. God is not shrouded in the "abysmal silence" of an "unutterable transcendency," as it seemed to the Enlightenment (Pikaza, *Experiencia,* 14).

By divine initiative, an act of free grace, God has definitively broken the symmetry of the alternatives of being "near" and "remote." God is self-manifested in an unsurpassable and radical proximity of salvation: "The Biblical God is close to [the human being]; . . . a God of communion with and commitment to [the human being]" (Gutiérrez, *A Theology,* 190–94; Sobrino, *True Church,* 141). God is salvation; God's approach is good news. The reality of God, however differently described in various places in the Bible, points ever to the essential nucleus of an ever new manifestation in history, to an "eccentricity" whereby God has undertaken to exercise the act of being conjointly with humans and with history:

> The various descriptions of the reality of God in the Scriptures have something in common: God is described as creator, giver of life; as liberator of the oppressed in Egypt; as *mishpat,* or justice actually operative; as merciful father or loving mother; and finally as love. These descriptions, each with its own nuance, point to what is fundamental about the God of Christian revelation: . . . not a self-centered being but one [that] goes [outside itself] to love, re-create, save, and humanize human beings [Sobrino, *True Church,* 46; see also *Jesús,* 99].

The IECT "Final Document" opens with an acknowledgment of this basic truth. The God of life continues self-manifestation (the *kairological* today) in the course of history (the *chronological* today). God continues to be manifest in the midst of history. Technically, God's revelation in the past and the ongoing manifestation in the "today" of our situation of oppression and sin are to be distinguished. But the genuine signs of the manifestation or negation of God's ever new and efficacious presence in history are there, to be recognized in an act of discernment. If God acts in history, it should not surprise us that we continue to discover an ever new, unforeseen, and liberative manifestation of God in that history. To believe in God involves being open to the new, open to what God can "reveal" to us along unexpected paths.[1] Anything else would be an *in actu* denial of God's being-greater, a denial of trinitarian reality (Sobrino, *True Church,* 2–3).

The IECT document forcefully identifies the locus from which the nucleus of this ongoing manifestation is to be discerned in all its significance. God is revealed in history in a particular, concrete manner: "God gives self-manifestation precisely in those localities where life is enslaved and crucified on the calvary of the world" (Asociación Ecuménica, *Teología*). History as theophanic locus par excellence acquires a scandalous concretion: it is concretized in the antilife calvary of the world.

Paradoxically, it is in wretchedness and oppression that the locus of access to God is to be sought. It is this faith conviction that lends liberative theo-logical reflection its character and nature as dialectical rather than analogical. God is known less by analogy with created reality, less in continuity with and as culmination of that reality, than from suffering, from the negative reality of experienced misery. It is grief, not wonder, that functions as the motive cause, the mover, of theo-logical cognition. Thereby the present history of the world is recognizable as the continuing history of God's passion, and one acknowledges the need to demonstrate God's loving reality in connection with suffering. One acknowledges the need to demonstrate God's suffering love.

God's Manifestation in Jesus of Nazareth

> Being a Christian does not mean, first and foremost, believing in a message. It means believing in a person. Having faith means believing that a certain human being of our own history, a Jew named Jesus, who was born of Mary, who proclaimed the Father's love, the gospel, to the poor, and liberation to those in captivity, who boldly confronted the great ones of his people and the representatives of the occupying power, who was executed as a subversive, is the Christ, the Messiah, the Anointed One, the Son. "These [signs] are recorded so that you may believe that Jesus is the Christ, the Son of God, and that believing this you may have life through his name" (John 20:31; cf. Rom. 10:9). The gospel is the good news because it comes from Jesus the Christ—"Here begins the gospel of Jesus Christ, the Son of God" (Mark 1:1) [Gutiérrez, *Power,* 13].[2]

Jesus, the Truth of the Father

In Jesus of Nazareth, the self-manifestation of the Mystery of God in history acquires its greatest concretion. Jesus, the one sent from the Father, renders testimony that God is true.[3] He is the full manifestation of the Father's truth, and the definitive path to that truth.[4] He is the great hermeneutic principle of faith, and hence of all theo-logical discourse (Gutiérrez, *Power,* 60–61):

> In Jesus we meet God. In the human word we read the word of God. In historical events we recognize the fulfillment of the promise.
>
> This is the basic circle of all hermeneutics: from the human being to God and from God to the human being, from history to faith and from faith to history, from love of our brothers and sisters to the love of the Father and from the love of the Father to the love of our brothers and sisters, from human justice to God's holiness and from God's holiness to human justice, from the poor person to God and from God to the poor person [Gutiérrez, *Power,* 15].

From a point of departure in faith in Jesus, the "problem" of God comes to specific focus and resolution (Sobrino, "Resurrección," 146). To know God—which is to love God—is to know God from a point of departure in Jesus, *locus theologicus* par excellence.[5]

Jesus, the Liberating God Incarnate

Christian discourse on the liberative God maintains, from its point of departure in Jesus, a basic affirmation of Christian faith in all its radicality: that in Jesus of Nazareth the God who liberates has become incarnate in human nature (Gonzáles, *Encarnación,* 16–17). In the eternal design, God has not willed to remain ever "the selfsame," closed up within the mystery of intratrinitarian life. God has willed to be-with human history, from a point of departure in a creation and a covenant, to be sure, but especially through the incarnation (Sobrino, "Dios," 108). For it is in the incarnation that God takes on history irreversibly and for all time. The Word will never shed the humanity that has been assumed.[6] In Jesus, who is the one sent from the Father, the Son (John 3:16), God not only gives a self-revelation in history, God irrupts, bursts into history, and becomes history. The God through whom all creation came into being (John 1:2) has pitched a tent *(eskenosen)* in its midst (John 1:14).

From the first moment of the incarnation, the Word assumed not a generic, abstract humanity—not "human nature" as a universal—but the figuration of a concrete human being of this history of ours. In the Jew named Jesus of Nazareth, the one born of Mary, God takes on a human face (L. Boff, *Encarnación,* 13). Whom no one had ever seen (John 1:18), who indeed could not be seen, was seen (John 14:9), touched, and handled by human beings.[7] The Utterly Other, the Holy One, the ineffable, unmanipulable Mystery, has bestowed itself upon human beings, renouncing distance and assuming human otherness without in any way destroying or modifying it. In measureless love, God has drawn near the objects of divine love, identifying with them in an abiding solidarity. The incarnation is the historical expression of a total surrender to human beings on the part of Mystery. The godhead has nothing to give but itself. As Leonardo Boff says, when we profess that "the Word became flesh," we make a statement fraught with meaning:

> We are professing our belief that *God is here,* is present absolutely, has come to stay, and is named Jesus of Nazareth. By means of this Child, God tells the world and its human beings, once and for all: "I love you." This Word of divine love, now become flesh, does not remain indifferent to the world. No, everything in that world takes on a new meaning. Nothing is totally absurd, for God says: "I love you" [*Encarnación,* 45–46].

The Johannine realism of the incarnation of the Word shows us how to resist any docetist or gnostic temptation. It shows us a God who has no fear of matter—although of course the incarnation is not exhausted in the "physical," the somatic aspect of "taking flesh." It portrays a communication of the mystery of God as *kenosis,* as double diminution: God became a concrete, particular human being, and in fragile flesh (Sobrino, *True Church,* 150).[8] God became poor, a brother in solidarity with sisters and brothers, experiencing pain and learning obedience (Sobrino, "Reflexiones," 244; IECT, "Final Document," no. 30).

The New Testament message of the incarnation as God's nearness and "sympathy" with the human being is a tenet of the theology of liberation from a starting point in God's advance toward the world of the poor:

> Jesus has not become incarnate in just *any* world, but in the world of the poor. He has taken on not just *any* flesh, but weak and errant flesh. He has defended not just *any* cause, but the cause of the poor. Not just *any* lot has fallen to him, but the lot of the poor [Sobrino, "Esperanza," 121].

The incarnation of the God who liberates has taken place in time, in Jesus of Nazareth: "When the designated time had come, God sent forth his Son" (Gal. 4:4). But this incarnation is not a "dated" historical event, occurring only in the remote past. Its historical character is open and dynamic. Jesus' incarnation, his presence hidden away in the history of human beings (especially in that of the poor) takes on newness and continuation in God's assumption of history through the Spirit. This is precisely what constitutes the privileged place of pneumatology, the theology of the Spirit, in a liberative key: a belief in the Spirit not as something outside history, but as something continuously present in history, generating history, re-creating and dispensing life, especially the life of those most deprived of life. All down the journey through history, and without any "self-dilution" in new becomings, God, through the Spirit, continues to assume the socio-historical conditions and conjunctures that render life possible and concrete.[9] History becomes the history of God. Faith in the Spirit, Sobrino says, is the believer's assertion that "human history is God's history, and God's history is human history" ("Fe en el Espíritu," 153).[10]

THE MYSTERY OF GOD: IN HIDDEN SOLIDARITY

> Today, as in the time of the captivity, the God who raised Jesus from the dead is hidden in the midst of history, on the side of the poor [IECT, "Letter," 248].

Latin American liberation theology affirms the mystery of a hidden God, a *Deus absconditus.* The mystery of this God abides in loving solidarity "on the side of the poor," at the very heart of history, and is most accessible from the most negative element in that history: its conflictuality, its sin, its injustice.

A God Hidden . . .

. . . In History

The bipolarity of God's presence in hidden form ("Today . . . God . . . is hidden in the midst of history") points up the fact that God at once conceals and reveals a presence in history in the living, the suffering, the struggles, the hopes, and the deaths of human beings.

Gustavo Gutiérrez broadens the sense of this perspective in a liberative key. As theo-phanic locus, history gives specification to biblical faith: God is present in history and acts in history. This assertion, however, stands in need of two corrective delimitations, which we may borrow from the prophetic tradition (Gutiérrez, *Dios,* 53–55). The first is that, although God indeed assumes history, there is no historical place or occurrence capable of containing, or fixing limits to, God's presence and activity.[11] God will always be u-topic in history.[12] This conviction flows from the biblical notion that God is not manipulable—that one may not invent a God to the measure of human interest. As *Dios Mayor,* God is Lord of truth and freedom. God is above and beyond any attempt to limit the scope of the divine presence and activity. The encounter with God acting in history requires a faith that is open to novelty, and to the repeated, demanding challenge of God issued through that faith.

The second delimitation is that, although God is self-disclosed at the heart of history, the divine presence there is hidden (Isa. 45:15):

God often performs a deed of justice, of liberation, of salvation, *in a hidden manner.* The indwelling of God in history is not effectuated in a simple and obvious fashion, so that anyone going in search of God will find God quickly, directly, or unequivocally. God is within human history, yes, in its tensions, advances, and conflicts. But to find God you have to look, you have to search. This search is a deep spiritual theme in any treatment of the journey to God, any reflection on unprecedented modes of access to this hidden God whose salvific work more often than not travels ways that are not our ways, as we read in Isaiah (55:8) [Gutiérrez, *Dios,* 55–56].

. . . In the Lowly

God's presence in history through the incarnation maintains the mystery of the hidden God: God first becomes present to the lowly, the poor, the humiliated and marginalized of history:

God's smallness and hiddenness is underscored in the fact of revelation through the poor. We are familiar with the straightforwardness of Matthew 25 in speaking of the Last Judgment. The true relationship with the

Lord is a relationship with the hidden Lord. "When did we feed you? When did we give you to drink? When did we visit you when you were ill or in prison?" These are the perplexed questions asked by the just. "When did we see you hungry or thirsty or away from home or naked or ill or in prison and not attend you in your needs?" This is the question asked by those being rejected from the reign of God. "Sticking fast to God"—to borrow an expression from the Book of Deuteronomy—is therefore the establishment of a relationship with a hidden God, which calls for decision, process, search, journey [Guttiérrez, *Dios,* 57; see also *A Theology,* 196–203].

It is in the poor that this hidden God is encountered. God, present in history, acts in that history, identifying with the poor of this world, and concealing in them both the visage and the action of the godhead (ibid).

God's self-manifestation in history follows mysterious paths. The divine presence is revealed and concealed simultaneously.

"You Are the God of the Poor"

The profession of faith of the poor consists less in asserting that God exists than in proclaiming with their lives that God walks the paths of the people, that God struggles in the daily battles of the lowly [CEP, *Credo,* 9].[13]

For liberative theo-logical reflection, the profession that the God who liberates is the God of the poor is its very backbone, as well as its principal point of convergence and unity. This theo-logical reflection is very emphatic on one essential point of the biblical message: the God of the Bible takes sides with the poor and oppressed, at the heart of history, with a view to their deliverance.

One of the richest, most concrete, and best known of popular theological expressions in Latin America, the Nicaraguan Campesino Mass, sings:

> You are the God of the poor,
> a God human and simple,
> a God sweating in the street,
> a God with weather-beaten face.
> And so I speak to you,
> as does this people of mine—
> because you are a worker God,
> a Christ who toils.[14]

The IECT "Final Document," in its section "Evangelization and the Basic Ecclesial Communities," speaks in this same way. Evangelization, it says, is the proclamation—in word and work—of a God who takes the part of the oppressed and delivers them from injustice and humiliation:

To evangelize is to announce the true God, the God revealed in Christ, the God who makes a covenant with the oppressed and defends their cause, the God who delivers his people from injustice, from oppression, and from sin [no. 40, p. 238].[15]

"The God of High Society Is Not the Same"

The Spanish edition of Gustavo Gutiérrez's *A Theology of Liberation* opens with a passage from the novel *Todas las sangres*—"all the bloodshed"—by the Peruvian José María Arguedas, to whom Gutiérrez's book is dedicated. The reproduction of this passage is more than an act of homage. It points to a major truth. Gutiérrez is calling attention to a theo-logical fact of great depth, and one of which oppressed, believing peoples, in their struggles for liberation, in their faith and in their hope, are becoming aware. As the Amerindian sacristan, in the dialogue that Gutiérrez quotes from the novel, puts it, *"El Dios de los Señores no es igual"*: "The God of high society is not the same"—is not the same as the liberating God of the Bible who has taken the part of the poor.[16]

Ultimately, Gutiérrez's theological reflection is an attempt to plumb the sense of God's activity more deeply, from the outlook of the poor (*Power,* 53, 199–200). Here, says Gutiérrez, is where "we shall meet the Lord":

We shall meet him in the poor of Latin America and of other continents. And like the disciples at Emmaus, we shall interpret his words and his deeds in the light of Easter, and our eyes will be opened. Then we shall understand—to cite Arguedas once more—that "God is hope. God is gladness. God is daring" [ibid., 214].

In "God's Revelation and Proclamation in History" (ibid., 3–22), Gutiérrez shows that the relationship between God and the poor constitutes the heart of biblical faith (pp. 8–9).[17] God the liberator, bestowing a self-revelation in history—the basic framework, or skeleton, of biblical faith—"is more than a provident God . . . is a God who takes sides with the poor and liberates them from slavery and oppression" (p. 7).[18] This is why "the real theophany, or revelation of God, is in the liberation of the person who is poor" (ibid.).

God is self-disclosed as Israel's spouse and national protector—but more than this, and above all, as the defender, the *go'el,* of the poor (Ps. 68:6–7). God as defender of the poor is the protector of the people (*Dios,* 29).

Because the relationship between God and the poor is the very heart of biblical faith, one's relationship with God comes to be expressed in one's relationship with the poor. Knowledge of God is not a purely intellectual affair. To know means to love. To know God as liberator is to liberate and do justice (*A Theology,* 194–96). To be just is to behave toward the poor as God has behaved toward the people (Prov. 14:21; see also Exod. 22:20–23).

In the New Testament, Jesus, who is total fulfillment and relaunching God's promise, is the one who bears testimony that God is true. And this is the Jesus who manifests, in depth, the relationship of God to the poor: Jesus reveals to us the mystery of God become poor. As Gutiérrez expresses it:

> Jesus Christ is precisely God become poor. This was the human life he took—a poor life. And this is the life in and by which we recognize him as Son of his Father.
>
> He was poor indeed. He was born into a social milieu characterized by poverty. He chose to live with the poor. He addressed his gospel by preference to the poor. He lashed out with invective against the rich who oppressed the poor and despised them. And before the Father, he was poor in spirit [*Power,* 13].[19]

The Partiality of "God the Ever Greater"

Reflecting on the nucleus of God's current manifestation in history, Jon Sobrino identifies it in God's *partiality* toward the poor:

> In my opinion, God's manifestation, at least in Latin America, is his scandalous and partisan love for the poor, and his intention that these poor should receive life and thus inaugurate his kingdom. . . . This is the great "sign of the times," a sign which is a fact [*True Church,* 2; see also 77, 112].

Sobrino amplifies his assertion by examining Jesus' theo-logical experience. What was God for Jesus?[20] Jesus had inherited a number of traditions concerning God, all of them the products of Israel's particular journey, and diversified in the traditions of Exodus, the prophets, and the wisdom and apocalyptic literature.[21]

Theoretically it is difficult to harmonize all the notions of God that Jesus received from the Old Testament. Of course, Jesus purified them and radicalized them. But his real originality consisted precisely in the synthesis that he made of them, all through his concrete history. "We should not start off assuming that Jesus held some notion of God from the very start. Instead we should assume that in his concrete history he gradually wove together strands from the various traditions about God in order to form his own fabric" (Sobrino, *Christology,* 162).

This synthesis is the product of two vectors: *transcendence* (God is ever greater) and *love* (God's deepest reality is love).[22]

A view of God as transcendence and love comes to novel and paradoxical expression. (1) In the moment of transcendence, the ever greater God is seen to be precisely the *Dios Menor.* (2) God is seen to be lesser in the revelation of the divine *partiality* to the poor, because God is hidden in littleness and poverty. This is the mystery of God's love and transcendence: "God is always greater, because the reality of God is—precisely—love. And God is at the same time lesser, because . . . hidden in smallness and poverty. God's yes to the poor and . . . no to poverty, the result of sin, is what makes it intrinsically possible for Jesus' understanding of God to carry transcendence within itself" (Sobrino, "Epiphany," 92):

> The fact of God's being greater is shown to Jesus in God's loving intentions for the world, but the historical and credible reality of that love appears to him in God's partiality toward the lowly. To Jesus, God is love because God loves those whom no one else loves, because God is concerned about those for whom no one else has any concern [ibid.].

Jesus does not transmit his theo-logical experience in verbal declarations of God's transcendence and love. Jesus has no systematic conceptual articulation. The reality of God's greater being and the reality of God's love shine through in Jesus' own personal experience, in the trusting, obedient conduct of his life. They constitute the presupposition of his preaching, of his reverent behavior, and of his polemics with those who think that they can manipulate the Unmanipulable. At bottom it is the presupposition of his very life, a life so open to the will of the Father.

Transcendence

God is greater than nature and greater than history. Jesus does not express the concept in these terms, but speaks of God as creator (Mark 10:6, 13:19) and sovereign, as incomprehensible (Matt. 11:25–26), as having sovereign power over life and death (Matt. 18:23–25, 10:28), as bearer of a name to be reverenced and not sworn by (Matt. 5:33–37, 23:16–22). Jesus speaks of human beings as God's servants (Luke 17:7–10), and observes that they can serve no other lord (Matt. 6:24).

Still, let us observe, this expression of God's transcendence through the notion of sovereignty and its correlates of respect and reverence for God is not what is *typical* in Jesus' theo-logical experience (Sobrino, *Christology*, 163).[23] For Jesus, God's transcendence typically appears in the accomplishment of the impossible. When Jesus is asked if the rich can be saved, he replies: "For man it is impossible but not for God. With God all things are possible" (Mark 10:27):

> Realization of the impossible, then, is an expression of the transcendence of God. But here the realization is not presented in the classical religious context of miracles or prodigies. Here it is presented in a new and unexpected context: i.e., as a grace that renews and revitalizes human beings, even lost human beings. "Here the impossible is not depicted as supernatural events coming from a world beyond and producing weird consequences in this world. Instead it appears in the fact that the poor, the impious, and the wicked can unexpectedly go back to calling themselves human beings once again" [citing H. Braun, *Jesus* (Stuttgart, Kreuz, 1969), 167]. This realization of the impossible by grace is the way

that God's transcendence is mediated in the eyes of Jesus [Sobrino, *Christology,* 164].

Jesus proclaims God's transcendence in his discussions with the Pharisees—for example, in accusing them of seeking to manipulate God through human traditions (Mark 7:1–17). His defense of that transcendence is all the more remarkable in that these traditions, through which Jesus' interlocutors "nullify God's word," are religious traditions (Mark 7:13).

Finally, God's transcendence is the explanation for Jesus' very life, developing as it does in an ongoing relationship with God—in the constant, obedient effort to identify God's sovereign will, in a life that lets God be God.[24]

A Partisan Love

For Jesus, what is most characteristic of God's reality is God's being greater by being love, and the inseparable relationship between being greater and being the God who is partial to the poor.

How is it revealed that "God is love," along the path of Jesus' life? For Jesus, God is, more than anything else, *Abba.* Jesus has his ultimate experience of meaning not in God's being king, or lord, but in God's being Father. Even if it had not been typical of Jesus to refer to God as Father, the fact that he would do so at all reveals not only his special relationship with God, but also the element of love in Jesus' notion of God (Sobrino, "Epiphany," 92–93):

> It seems almost self-evident to us that Jesus should address God as "Father." But that is not so self-evident at all if we consider the matter historically or logically. Jesus could have used some other expression to signify what he considered to be the ultimate in meaningfulness, though that too would be anthropomorphic. He might have chosen to refer to God as "King" or "Lord," thus picturing the ultimate reality in terms of power rather than in terms of love.
>
> Hence the term "Father" addressed to God by Jesus tells us right away how he pictured the *ultimate ground of reality.* It was not to be viewed in terms of beauty or power but in terms of *love.* That is why he chose to address God as "Father" [Sobrino, *Christology,* 165–66; emphasis added].

In invoking God as Father, Jesus fastens upon the element of love in God. It is a love that, in human language, can be described as infinite tenderness.[25] It is a love whose majesty causes no fright, but is offered in gratuity, liberation, and partiality toward the little and lost of this world. It is a love manifested through concrete historical actions, as we see from the parable of the prodigal son. Hence Jesus' abiding sanction of the use of the word "Abba" in addressing God (Sobrino, "Abordar," 6).

The partiality of God's love is expressed in the proclamation of the kingdom to the poor (Matt. 11:6; Luke 7:22–23). The reign of God is "at hand" (Mark

1:15; Matt. 4:17), and the poor are the ones to whom it is offered (Matt. 5:3; Luke 6:20) (see Santa Ana, *Desafío,* 28–38). For Jesus, God's great deed is bringing the kingdom to the poor. God is the one who comes forward, in the kingdom, as good news for the poor.

Jesus' inaugural discourse in the synagogue (Luke 4:18–19) spells out his program and mission: to bring God's partisan love to expression (Escudero Freire, *Devolver,* 259–77).

God's partisan love is also manifest in Jesus' declarations on the subject of happiness or good fortune and its contrary:

> The poor and the powerless are blest (Matt. 5:1–11; Luke 6:20–22); but there are maledictions for all those who have set their heart on something less than love (Luke 6:23–26), and for all those who use their power to dominate and oppress other human beings (Matt. 23:13–32; Luke 11:37–53). These denunciations do not well up solely from Jesus' ethical awareness. They also stem from his theo-logical awareness, from his conception of God. Because God is love, he cannot tolerate the oppression of the lowly [Sobrino, *Christology,* 166].

Finally, we must note the importance attached by Jesus to love as the way to respond to God (Mark 12:28–34; Matt. 22:34–40; Luke 10:24–27). Because God is love, interhuman love will constitute the approach to God par excellence. No approach to God is possible if it does not correspond to the reality of God's love. The praxis of love of neighbor "is a prerequisite not only for understanding the doxological formula 'God is love,' but also for the experience of God as transcendent, as *Dios Mayor"* (Sobrino, *Cristología,* 148).[26]

Summation

1) The partisan love of the liberating God for the poor is not an elective act of God's will. Rather it is essential to the very reality of God as love (Sobrino, "Dios," 111).

2) The partiality of God's love, far from depriving it of universality, is the very expression of its universality and transcendence. The universality of God's love passes by way of its partiality toward the poor, and it is this partiality that causes scandal (Matt. 11:6; Luke 7:23), by pointing to the concrete locus of its universalization. Only this partiality guarantees that God is God-for-everyone, the only God in existence. The God of the poor is the Father of all (Jiménez Limón, "Meditation," 151–52). God is with everyone, but not with everyone in the same way. God is with everyone in the justice of the kingdom. The good news to the poor constituted by the end of oppression is bad news, too—for those who draw profit from abuse and injustice (IECT, "Final Document," no. 48). God saves the rich and mighty by stripping them of their wealth and power, by felling their idols, by denouncing their alienation and the inhumanity of their sin of exploitation (Santa Ana, *Desafío,* 39–50). God saves the poor and

downtrodden by defending them, by lifting them out of their degradation and misery, by guaranteeing them life, and full human dignity (Míguez Bonino, "Nuestra fe," 8; Sobrino, *Christology,* 214). Every Christian, then—regardless of socio-economic origin—is called to make an option of solidarity with the poor, for whom God has opted, and with whom God identifies.

3) The partiality of God's love for the poor shows us the *gratuity* of that love—the gratuity of a love *addressed to the poor because they are poor,* because they suffer injustice and death, and not because they may be "spiritually poor" or morally good. That is, God loves the poor regardless of their moral and personal dispositions:

> The God who is self-revealed in this preferential love for the poor is a God who loves gratuitously. . . . A God who would love the poor because they deserved it would be perfectly understandable. But a God who loves the poor simply and solely because of their situation of desolation and despoilment, oppression and exploitation, shocks us—and thereby shows us that the love of God who is our Father, the God of the kingdom, is absolutely gratuitous [Gutiérrez, "Itinerario," 59].

4) God comes to us identified with and hidden in the poor, and judges us through our concrete acts of service to the poor. Such acts therefore constitute the sacrament—the efficacious sign—of God's presence in history.[27] This is the indispensable human mediation for the approach to God (Gutiérrez, *A Theology,* 200). A direct relationship with God is always intercepted by the lowly, the poor. The encounter with God passes by way of this mediation. We cannot circumvent it. God renders definitive judgment in our regard—in the sense of a basic judgment of our future—by examining our concrete, historical acts of service to the poor. "Thus, in order to know and to love God, one must come to grips with the concrete life situation of the poor today, and undertake the radical transformation of a society that makes them poor" (Gutiérrez, *Power,* 96).

God: Suffering Love

> God is love and salvation. This is why we hear so much of a liberating God, and with good reason. But God comes to be a liberating God only through suffering [Sobrino, "Significado," 36].

> God is not indifferent to the sufferings of the victims of history. Out of love and solidarity (John 3:16), God became poor, was sentenced, crucified, and executed. God assumed a reality objectively contrary to the divine, because God did not wish human beings to impoverish and crucify other human beings. God's privileged mediation, then, is not glory, or transparency of historical meaning, but the *real suffering of the oppressed.* To say that God took up the cross is not to glorify or

"eternalize" the cross. It is only to show how much God has loved the suffering. God suffers and dies with them [L. Boff, *Jesucristo,* 440–41, emphasis added; see also 420–21].

After its basic affirmation of the mystery of a God hidden in and identified with the crucified ones of history, out of loving solidarity with them, Latin American liberation theology takes a further step, and makes a *theo*-logical statement about human suffering. Here, it seems to me, there are three axial notions. (1) The Liberator God of the poor has not been indifferent in the face of their suffering: indeed, God has internalized the negativity of suffering (the passion of the world and of history is God's passion). (2) God is able to suffer because the most profound reality of the divine being is love: God's suffering solidarity concretizes, realizes the Johannine "God is love." (3) Jesus' historical cross is the culmination of God's loving, suffering solidarity.

We are not dealing here with some doloristic a priori, an attitude incapable of experiencing or speaking of God as hope, joy, and life. Nor is this an apologetic theology, in the sense of a system of answers attempting to provide a theoretical explanation to the why of oppression and the why of suffering in history, so that, as with any "theodicy," or "justification of God," God would be justified. Before the scandal of the suffering of millions of innocent women and men on the antilife calvary of the world, all concepts and theoretical solutions collapse and crumble. Suffering, here, is not to be comprehended, it is to be combated, and with a will (L. Boff, *Jesucristo,* 423). The believer asserts only this, out of a faith in God the liberator: God has taken up this scandal in loving, suffering solidarity. This is the only response to questions about human suffering. The crucified of history, like the cross of Jesus, continue to be a scandal that nothing can soften or attenuate (Sobrino, "Abordar," 19). Sobrino gives special attention to this difficult but fertile theme.[28]

Historical Suffering and God's Suffering Love

What the "third world"—the historical world of the impoverished—privileged locus of God's manifestation, discovers and lays bare is that, however the Mystery of the *Dios Mayor* be formulated, its formulation must inevitably pass by way of the *category of suffering* (Sobrino, "Significado," 36; *Christology,* 179–82).

By the same token, Latin American liberation theology has assigned a privileged place in its reflection to those passages from the Bible in which God appears in relationship with human suffering:

At the crowning moments of divine revelation there has always been suffering: the cry of the oppressed in Egypt; the cry of Jesus on the cross (according to Mark); the birth-pangs experienced by the whole of creation as it awaits liberation [Sobrino, *True Church, 28*].[29]

How utterly distinct God is from what human beings think is discovered only in the God who suffers. This is the unthought-of-element, and the unthinkable element, in the Mystery. God is ever greater in virtue of having become incredibly small. God is greater because of having accepted suffering (Sobrino, "Significado," 36). From the furthest depths of our history of oppression and struggle for liberation, as an expression of absolute proximity to (of sym-pathy with) human beings, God accepts suffering. God's transcendence, utter other-ness, is not an abstract category for asserting that God is outside or beyond history. Paradoxically, to assert God's transcendence is to assert that God is in the deepest recesses of a history of sin and conflict, in its chasms of iniquity and hence of suffering (ibid).

We are confronted here with the thesis, in all its historico-salvific force, that God is not indifferent to the suffering of the victims of history, but maintains a loving solidarity with them, to the point that God is led to accept suffering—to a "co-suffering," as Leonardo Boff puts it:

> When we ask, "Why suffering," God does not answer, but co-suffers. When we ask, "Why pain?," God does not answer, but becomes the Man of Sorrows. When we ask, "Why humiliation?," God does not answer, but accepts humiliation. We are no longer alone. . . . God is with us. We are no longer in solitiude, but in solidarity [*Encarnación,* 64].

God is love and salvation, and this is why liberation theology explains its faith in God as liberation, hope, life, and justice. But God becomes all this only through a solidarity that suffers for love (Sobrino, "Significado," 36).

Latin America has seen the realization of Bonhoeffer's intuition: "Only a God who suffers can save us" *(Resistencia,* 210; see also Sobrino, *Christology,* 197). That is, God saves us not through domination, but through co-suffering.

This liberative theological discourse on God's suffering is expressed in terms of the ever greater being of a God whose *deepest reality is love.*[30] Suffering, as Sobrino tells us, as a mode of God's being, concretizes and realizes the deepest intuition of the New Testament concerning God: that God is love (*Christology,* 217–35).

To say that *agape* is inseparable from God's reality—inseparable to the point that it becomes "Christianly impossible" to discourse upon God without including profession of this reality (Nygren, *Eros,* 139–43)—raises the question of *how* God loves us. Can God love us in such a way as not to be affected by human suffering? This question has nothing speculative about it. The essence of the Christian understanding of God is at stake. Commenting on the cov-enantal explanation of the salvific efficacy of Jesus' death on the cross, an explanation stressing Jesus' function as sacrificial victim, Sobrino observes:

> [This approach] tells us *that* God loved us, but it does not say *how* God . . . loved us and liberated us.
> That is not a superficial distinction, for what is at stake here is the kind

of solidarity that God has with human beings. Does . . . solidarity with us mean that God . . . must go by way of the cross in the midst of countless historical crosses, or in the last analysis does God . . . remain untouched by the historical cross because [God] is essentially untouchable? [*Christology,* 190].

God's love of the world is such that suffering for it is a possibility. God's entering into solidarity in suffering is the "proof," anthropomorphically speaking, that the very being of God is love. Love and suffering are present and inseparably united in the ever abiding mystery of God. There is not much more that the human being can say. Along the same line, Jürgen Moltmann has written:

If love is the acceptance of the other without taking account of one's own well-being, it carries with it the compassion and freedom to experience—even if painfully—the otherness of the other. An incapacity to suffer would stand in contradiction with the fundamental Christian affirmation that God is love. . . . Those who can love are also passible, and can open themselves to the sufferings that love occasions, being superior to them by the force of their love ["Dios," 325; cf. Sobrino, *Christology,* 197].

A view of God from the vantage of the suffering and hope of the poor makes a clean break with the picture of the perfect, immutable, and impassible God *(theos apathes)* of ancient Greek tradition. The philosophical notions that seemed most applicable to the supreme being were those of prime mover, efficient cause, almighty doer. An active love did not seem applicable. Love did not figure among the Greek categories of perfection. If God is perfect, how can God love? To the Greek mind, love is passion, *pathos.* Love means having needs, depending on someone. Consequently, if God is perfect, God cannot love. After all, God is not in need of anything.[31] Total inability to love will entail total incapacity to suffer, or to save in suffering (not in virtue of the suffering, but in virtue of love). The image of the liberating God of the Bible is a very different one.

God's Suffering Love and the Historical Cross of Jesus

God's suffering love receives historical concretion in Jesus' cross. God's solidarity and identification with all the oppressed of history is to the death, even the death of the cross. From out of the deepest abyss of history, God, entering into suffering and death, communicates life, and opens up a horizon of justice, a future of hope.

In his reflections on Jesus' suffering love, Jon Sobrino lays special emphasis on the originality of the Christian faith in preaching a "crucified God."[32] "On the cross of Jesus, God . . . is crucified. The Father suffers the death of the

Son and takes upon himself all the pain and suffering of history" (*Christology,* 224). Let us examine Sobrino's "Thesis" concerning the cross as a *locus theologicus* in reference to God's suffering love, which he propounds in the course of his consideration, "The Death of Jesus and Liberation in History" (ibid., 179–235).[33]

The Cross as Historical Concretion of Suffering Love

Jesus' historical cross, with its dialectic of the presence and absence of God (present for other human beings, but absent for God's son), reveals to us, in a privileged manner, the locus in which God's suffering love, in virtue of God's solidarity with humankind, receives historical concretion:

> God's relationship to unredeemed history is not idealistic and external but truly incarnate; *it is through the cross that the definition of God as love receives its ultimate concretion.* . . .
>
> On the cross God's love for humanity is expressed in truly historical terms rather than in idealistic ones. Historical love presupposes activity, but it also presupposes passivity because it is love situated in a contradictory structure that makes its force and power felt. The passivity involved here is that of letting oneself be affected by all that is negative, by injustice and death. On the cross of Jesus God was present (2 Cor. 5:19f.) and at the same time absent (Mark 15:34). Absent to the Son, [God] was present for human beings. *And this dialectics of presence and absence is the way to express in human language the fact that God is love.* The cross is the contradiction of humanity, but it is grounded on an ultimate solidarity with it [Sobrino, *Christology,* 225, emphasis added; see also Sobrino, *Jesús,* 178–79].

This historicized love does not remain untouchable, invulnerable. It is affected by the negative, by injustice, sorrow, pain, and death. It assumes this negativity *from within,* in the presence of the crosses of history (ibid., 190).

On the cross of Jesus, God is crucified. In the passion of the Son, the Father suffers the pain of abandonment, and *internalizes all the pain, sorrow, and horrors of history:*

> In the Son's death, death affects God . . . —not because God dies but because [God] suffers the death of the Son. Yet *God suffers so that we might live, and that is the most complete expression of love.* It is in Jesus' resurrection that God will reveal himself as a promise fulfilled, but it is on the cross that love is made credible [ibid., 225–26; emphasis added].[34]

The Cross as Breach with Certain Philosophical Principles

Jesus' cross as concretion of God's suffering love calls our attention to the breach that it implies with certain (Greek) philosophical presuppositions, which, in the ontological order (presuppositions concerning God's perfection), as well as in the epistemological order (presuppositions concerning a cognition based on analogy and wonder), block a radical, Christian comprehension of a theo-logy of the cross (see Sobrino, *Christology,* 195–201 [theses 4 and 5]).

Ontological Breach. The Greek ideal of perfection presupposes immutability: the perfect is, by definition, eternal and ahistorical. From this perspective, suffering cannot be attributed to God: it would imply a contradiction. For God to suffer would entail mutability and a setting aside of apathy toward the concrete and the negative of history (ibid., 198).

This Greek philosophical conception of the being and perfection of God precludes recognition of God in Jesus on the cross. The elaboration of a theology of the cross in a liberative key demands, therefore, a clean break with this ontological presupposition.

Epistemological Breach. From wonder at the positive to wonder concretized in suffering, the cross of Jesus reformulates the manner of our knowledge of God. A "natural theology" seeks to know God from the positive elements of reality that we find in nature, history, or human subjectivity (Sobrino, *Christology,* 221). Knowledge of God in the suffering and death of Jesus, by contrast, proceeds from the negative in history—from injustice, oppression, suffering, sin, and death (ibid., 221–24). To the analogical principle, the theology of liberation adds the dialectical. To wonder it adds sorrow and pain as font of theo-logical cognition (ibid., 198; see above, pp. 29–31). In the cross is neither beauty nor order nor power. God appears on the cross *sub specie contrarii.* It is scarcely self-evident that in death there can be life, in impotence power, or that precisely in Jesus' abandonment, God is present. This is what gives a theology of the cross its epistemological breach with analogical discourse:

> We must ask ourselves what joyful "wonder" might mean in the face of Jesus' cross, in a situation where there is little place for joy or wonder. . . . The wonder involved in the process of grasping the truth of the cross is a *highly qualified sort of wonder. Specifically, it is sorrow.* The cognitive attitude that allows for some sort of authentic analogy between the believer and Jesus' cross is that of sorrow in the presence of historical crosses. Here we get a sym-pathy and a con-natural knowledge that enables us to grasp some sort of divine presence on the cross of Jesus and in the overall suffering of the oppressed. . . .
>
> Only in the concrete form of sorrow can wonder help us to grasp what happened on the cross; only in that form can it turn our theological discourse on the cross into something real rather than something illusory or demagogic. . . .
>
> Who can comprehend the aspect of divine revelation in the cross of Christ? The person who feels sorrow in the face of another's misery and who tries to overcome it by bridging the distance between self and the other's misery. Here we have the only authentic kind of analogy for recognizing God in the cross. Mere cognitive analogy and wonder will not

suffice. They are not ample enough to allow us to comprehend the cross of Jesus and to lay hold of the God who may very well be present precisely in Jesus' abandonment [ibid., 199–200; emphasis added].

To know God is to abide with God in the passion of the world. The mediation par excellence of knowledge of God is not beauty, power, or wisdom, but the real crosses of the oppressed (ibid., 198). Knowledge of the *Dios Mayor,* the ever greater God, is given in contact with the *Dios Menor,* the God crucified on Jesus' cross: knowledge of the *Dios Mayor* is given in service to the crucified of history (ibid., 222-23; *True Church,* 54–55). Matthew 25, on the Last Judgment, means that the oppressed are God's mediation. It means that "going to God means going to the poor" (*Christology,* 223):

> The surprise felt by human beings on hearing that the Son of Man was incarnated in the poor is the surprise we must feel to comprehend the divinity of God on the cross. Without such "surprise" there is no knowlege of God, there is only our manipulation of God. It is when that surprise is maintained, when service is rendered to the oppressed, that we "stand by God in his hour of grieving." The resultant knowledge of God is not "natural" but "con-natural"; it is knowledge born of shared communion with the sorrow and suffering of the other person [ibid.].

Life-Bestowing Death. In Greek thought, in virtue of the impossibility of conceptualizing the negative pole of reality, death was not reflected upon in itself. It was considered simply as a passage to another type of life (as in Plato), or as the end of life (as in Epicurus), both views ignoring the reality of death in itself. In such a perspective, Jesus' death has no positive impact (*Christology,* 195). For the theology of liberation, faced with so many deaths on the calvary of the world because of oppression, and the essential necrophilia of the structural mechanisms of injustice, the outlook is different. Gustavo Gutiérrez calls our attention to the opening words of one of César Vallejo's "Poemas Humanos": *No poseo para expresar mi vida sino mi muerte*—"To express my life, the only thing I possess is my death" (Gutiérrez, *Dios,* 23). Gutiérrez is attempting to show us just how death—a certain type of death—has, in its negativity, a positive impact, inasmuch as martyrdom, which is death, communicates life. We can observe this in the historical experience of Jesus' cross.[35]

The Scandal of the Cross (2 Cor. 1:23)

The true scandal of the cross is the *abandonment* of Jesus, the Son of God (Mark 15:37). The distinctive nature of Jesus' death is that the Son, who had preached the nearness of the Father in grace and love as no one ever had before, dies abandoned by that Father (Sobrino, *Christology,* 191-92, 218).[36] The Father surrenders his Son, abandons him to the power of the negative—to sin, injustice, and death. What is the meaning of the Son's abandonment? Four elements can be identified:

1) In the abandonment of the Son appears *God's self-questioning,* and it appears radically. It is God's trinitarian being that makes possible a strictly theo-logical consideration of the cross. The cross becomes the court in which God brings suit against God, internally, within the very being of God. The occasion of the suit is that the Father is abandoning the Son to the power of sin, so that the Son dies and the Spirit fails to generate life and love (Sobrino, "Abordar," 19):

> It is not people who first question God in the presence of human misery. *It is God . . . who questions God,* to use language that is anthropomorphic of necessity. As Luther put it: "No one against God except God." This questioning of God takes the form of abandoning the Son to the inertia of a world that really ought to be called into question. God [undergoes "bifurcation"] on the cross, so that transcendence (the Father) is in conflict with history (the Son) [Sobrino, *Christology,* 225; emphasis added].

Thus the cross opens up to us the fullness of the intratrinitarian process:

> God is a trinitarian "process" on the way toward its ultimate fulfillment (1 Cor. 15:28), but it takes all history into itself. In this process God participates in, and lets himself be affected by, history through the Son; and history is taken into God in the Spirit. *What is manifest on the cross is the internal structure of God. . . .* The eternal love between Father and Son is seen to be historically mediated in the presence of evil, and hence it takes the paradoxical form of abandonment; but from this trinitarian love, now historicized, there wells up the force that will ensure that external history can be a history of love rather than a history of domination. In God . . . the Spirit is the fruit of the love between Father and Son, as tradition tells us. In history, however, this love takes a historical form: It becomes the Spirit of love designed to effect liberation in history.
>
> The work of the Spirit can be described as the incorporation of the human individual and of all people into the very process of God. . . . The Spirit makes us children of God, but it does not do so in any idealistic way. It does so through the structure of the Son. It introduces us into God's own attitude toward the world, which is an attitude of love. But since the world is dominated by sin and hence riddled with conflict, it makes us co-actors with God in history [ibid., 226; emphasis added].[37]

2) In the Son's abandonment appears *God's questioning, God's critique, of history.* In Jesus' historical cross, God voices a protest. God protests the negative of an unredeemed history, submitting the godhead to the power of

that negative. The promised salvation is not realized idealistically, from outside history, but from within history itself. God is and remains mystery primarily because God was on Jesus' cross, internalizing the depths of the iniquity of all history (Sobrino, "Abordar," 11).

3) The Son's abandonment expressed *God's solidarity with humankind.* On Jesus' cross, God was at once present (2 Cor. 5:19-21) and absent (Mark 15:34). In God's absence for the Son, God was present for humankind (Sobrino, *Christology,* 225). In the Son's abandonment appears not only God's critique of history, but God's ultimate solidarity with that history, as the concretion of infinite love for human beings.

4) The Son's abandonment makes it possible for us to reflect on a search for the Christian God on a cross that in its historical projection consists of the *crosses of all the crucified of history* (ibid., 201), crushed by the dehumanization of a life unjustly and prematurely snatched away. In virtue of the cross, on which God is crucified, and takes on all of the suffering of history, God enters into solidarity with all the downtrodden of history:

> This cross,
> imposed on people already crucified
> by the dehumanized life they are forced to live,
> is a crime that will not escape the judgment of God.
> Since God . . . was crucified in Jesus Christ,
> no cross imposed unjustly
> is a matter of indifference to [God].
> [God] is in solidarity with all those who hang on crosses.
> Their humiliation is [God's] humiliation.
> They do not carry their cross by themselves.
> Jesus carries it with them and in them [L. Boff, *Way,* 16-17].

The Cross: A Love That Transforms History

Finally, I must emphasize again that, although the "third world" discovers and manifests that the God who delivers, who liberates, must pass by way of the category of suffering, however this may be positively formulated—liberation theology does not close all accounts with this affirmation. That God must suffer is an important "word," and a necessary one. But it is not the last word. To stop there would be to run the risk of sacralizing suffering. As Sobrino notes, "Christianity has come to be seen as a religion espoused by grief-stricken people obsessed with suffering (Nietzsche) and totally devoid of *joie de vivre* and a sense of responsibility to bring about a better, more humane world" *(Christology,* 180).

The cross of Jesus is much more than a symbol of suffering.[38] It posits a new concept of God, and a revolutionary one, both for a view of God—theory—and for Christian praxis (ibid., 180-81).[39] God does not appear here as resignation, or as a legitimation of a life of wretchedness, but as good news. The cross unleashes life and hope, the cross leads to a praxis of a love that transforms and liberates history. The negative reality of the suffering of the cross, a suffering arising from injustice, abandonment, and death, moves one to think. And above all it obliges one to act.

The spirituality of the cross is not a spirituality of suffering (pace the devotees of pessimism and resignation), but of *discipleship*. It is the spirituality of following in the footsteps of Jesus (ibid., 215–17). And its goal is to take the love that God manifested on the cross and make it *real* in history (ibid., 227):

> [The] spirituality of the cross cannot simply concentrate on the doleful aspects of human existence. Spirituality based on the cross does not mean merely the acceptance of sadness, pain, and sorrow; it does not mean simply passivity and resignation. Of course the crucified Jesus can also give us inspiration when we face trials in life, but that is not what characterizes Christian spirituality as such. Incarnation situated in a concrete context comes before the cross. Hence Christian spirituality must entail imitating the attitude Jesus had when he incarnated himself in a concrete situation. That means we must take a stand vis-à-vis the sinfulness that gives configuration to a given situation. Christians must take a stand in the face of power and be willing to de-idolize it when it tries to pass itself off as God. It is only in that way that our positive proclamation of the good news and its insistence on the primacy of love can be concrete and effective rather than merely idealistic.
>
> The cross is the most peculiar and distinctive feature of Christian faith, but Christian spirituality is not formally a spirituality of suffering; rather, it is a spirituality focused on the following of Jesus. Not all suffering is specifically Christian: only that which flows from the following of Jesus [ibid., 215–16].[40]

The Christian is called to live in the gladness of a self-surrender that takes responsibility for making a better and more human world (Sobrino, *True Church,* 60–61). The Christian is called to responsibility for a world according to the liberative design of God's justice, life, and fellowship.

THE MYSTERY OF GOD: SALVIFIC PRAXIS

> God . . . is hidden in the midst of history . . . working and liberating his people with the victorious power that overcomes death and creates life anew [IECT, "Letter," 249].

Having considered God's loving, suffering solidarity in the *Kenosis* of the cross, we must take a further step and examine God's salvific design in behalf of human beings and their history. From the deepest recesses of history, God opens a new future and a new hope.

The last part of the IECT "Final Document" points up this truth. God's reality is salvific praxis.[41] In the midst of history, God delivers the people from oppression and death. God is salvation. God saves, and in abundance (Sobrino, *True Church*, 51). The "good news" from God is liberation, justice, and the gift of life, and this good news continues to be published. If it were to be "bad news" that had the last word—the bad news of pain and sorrow, suffering and death—vain would be the reality of God and of human action in history (ibid., p. 119, n. 63).

It is significant that the theology of liberation, from its first appearance, has understood itself as "a theology of salvation in the concrete, historical, and political conditions of our day" (Gutiérrez, *Power,* 63). In his *A Theology of Liberation,* Gutiérrez engages in a preliminary reflection on God's salvific action in history. He recalls how history began with creation itself, which appears as the first act of God's salvific work. Creation is the work of a God who saves in history, and inasmuch as humankind is the center of creation, creation is definitively integrated in salvation history (Gutiérrez, *A Theology,* 154–55):

> Salvation—totally and freely given by God, the communion of [human beings] with God and among themselves—is the inner force and the fullness of this movement of [the human being's] self-generation which was initiated by the work of creation [ibid., 159].[42]

The *theo*-logico-soteriological thread of a theo-logy that takes its point of departure in oppression, injustice, and antilife will run through three basic foci: faith in the God of the Bible is faith in the God who (1) delivers from oppression, (2) defends the poor, establishing justice and right, and (3) conquers death and re-creates life. In other words, faith in the God of the Bible is faith in a liberator God, a *go'el,* and a God of life. From its inception, liberation theology has maintained a fundamental reference to faith in the liberator God (a faith arising from the experience of the exodus) who defends the poor (a faith arising out of the prophetic tradition). More recent, and continuing this bifocal axis, is the development of a theo-logy of a God of life in the face of the brute reality of death among the impoverished minorities.[43] In its orientation toward life, liberation theology conceptualizes God as the Power and committed Love who vanquishes death and re-creates life.

The Liberator God: The Exodus Experience

The historical experience of liberation from Egyptian oppression and the journey toward a collective appropriation of the land—the exodus, archetypal and structuring event of Israel's religious awareness—is taken up by the theology of liberation as its great key to an understanding of both the meaning of liberation and the manifestation of God in history.[44] In the exodus, the foundation of Israelitic faith, a God is revealed who is attentive to the cry of the oppressed: "I have witnessed the affliction of my people in Egypt and have heard their cry of complaint against their slave drivers, so I know well what they are suffering" (Exod. 3:7). Here is a God who is present and active in historical liberation causes: "Therefore I have come down to rescue them from the hands of the Egyptians and lead them out of that land into a good and spacious land, a land flowing with milk and honey" (Exod. 3:8).

The thematic motif is a well-known one, and needs little explanation. However, it is important to point out that, for liberation theology, the outlook of a historical faith based on God's liberative activity as the foundational datum of that faith is not found only in the exodus. It fairly impregnates the whole Bible, and inspires manifold readings in Old and New Testament alike (Gutiérrez, *Power,* 5–6). Other biblical themes central to liberation theology are the eschatological promises, the messianic practice of Jesus (hence the attention to Luke 4:16–20, where, using Isaiah 61:1–3, Jesus gives a public account of his messianic program), the kingdom of God, the historical cross of Jesus, and the resurrection.[45]

God as *Go'el:* Vindicator

The activity of God the deliverer, whose self-disclosure in history takes the form of opening it out onto the future, orientates that history in a precise direction: toward the establishment of justice and right (Gutiérrez, *Power,* 6–7). God's irruption in history is calculated not so much to demonstrate power as to liberate and make justice reign. God's power is at the service of justice, and is expressed in the defense of the poor (Ps. 146:7, 9). Yahweh is the *go'el* of the poor.

The *go'el* was the official protector of the family or clan.[46] By extension, and in depth, Yahweh came to be called the *go'el* of Israel. God is the "near relative," the rescuer, protector, and avenger of Israel. But there is more. Above all, God is the *go'el* of the poor within the Jewish nation (Ps. 68:6–7). Yahweh is Israel's *go'el* because Yahweh defends the poor among the people. This is the character, the indelible seal, that marked the covenant (Gutiérrez, *Dios,* 29).

The relationship between the poor and the people, between the poor and the nation, expressed in the assertion of nationhood and the defense of the poor, are not two discrete matters merely juxtaposed. In the covenant, the second gives meaning to the first: it is in justice done to the poor that Israel's true national identity and affirmation are to be found:

Indeed, Israel's identity, the meaning of belonging to the Jewish nation, is the rendering of justice to the poor, rescuing their rights trodden under foot. And when the Jewish people fails to do justice to the poor, it is false to itself as a people. That is, it not only does evil, does wrong, but in violating the pact of the covenant it goes directly against what identifies it as a people and always has: the liberative act of the exodus, the historical experience of having come up from Egypt thanks to its alliance, its covenant, with God.

Once again: to fail to practice justice toward the poor is to turn one's back on the true national identity of the Israelite people. The *defense of the poor* is the *meaning of national affirmation* for the Jewish people— that nation called from Genesis onward to establish the reign of justice and right (Gen. 18:18-19).

In this dialectic of the poor and the people, the poor and the nation, we have what is basic. Israel, the chosen people, ceases to be such if justice is not practiced within it. In so many passages, then, which we need not detail here, the prophets, in the name of God, call the great ones of the Jewish people "Foreigners." For they are foreigners to this people. They do not practice justice, and justice is the meaning, the sense, the raison d'être of the Jewish people. Anyone failing to practice justice ceases to be a member of the people with whom Yahweh has struck the pact of the covenant. The dominator, even a national one, turns out to be a foreigner with respect to what is the very wellspring of the nation. Accordingly, any assertion of national identity that would seek to do without the establishment of justice in the land is a lie, and a manipulation [Gutiérrez, *Dios,* 29-30; emphasis added].

To establish justice, then, is to prolong the liberative act of God. It means living in ongoing fidelity to the covenant that has been struck between God and the people. To know God is to do justice (Jer. 22:13-16), to know God is to establish just relationships among human beings, to know God is to acknowledge the rights of the poor (Gutiérrez, *A Theology,* 194-96). To sin—not to know God—is to make an option for oppression and against liberation. To sin is to make an option against the God who delivered Israel from Egypt in order to establish justice and right (Gutiérrez, *Power,* 9). To be just is to be faithful to the covenant. Fidelity is justice and holiness. To be faithful is to establish justice and right. This, according to the prophets, is true holiness, and the indispensable prerequisite for authentic worship. True worship involves the realization of justice (ibid., 22; *A Theology,* 195-96).

The God of Life "Who Vanquishes Death and Re-creates Life"

Latin American liberation theology has insisted from the beginning on the development of its theo-logical vision from a starting point in God the liberator, and in faith in the God who establishes justice and right. In recent years the development of this approach to the Mystery of God has been broadened in an articulation of the theme of life/death.

This step in liberation theology's theo-logical reflection is not a capricious one. It is rooted in biblical tradition. Liberative theo-logy, as a theology corresponding to reality, has seen itself forced along its path by a cruel reality: the historical problem of a structural injustice that deals death in history. Life is threatened, blocked, and destroyed because the deepest fonts of the real life of millions of Latin Americans are threatened, blocked, and destroyed. St. John testifies that in Christ the Word of life has appeared (1 John 1:1–2). What appears in Latin America, then, is the Antichrist and his world of antilife (Sobrino, *True Church,* 165–66).

Primordial Correlation Between God and Life

The approach to faith in God as faith in the God of life springs from respect for the real, respect for the locus in which the ultimacy of reality is played out in its radical form: the life or death of the poor. In Latin America, then, life and death are pregnant concepts for a step forward in an understanding of God the liberator. But above all they are daily realities, and present the question of God in a historical form (Sobrino, *Jesús,* 190). Do we really believe in a living and life-giving God? Out of the interplay of life and death emerges the primordial correlation between God and life. God's liberative work expresses the design and intent to generate life and defend the right to life of the poor, who are condemned to "die before their time."[47] God means to confront whatever is life-threatening or life-destroying (Gutiérrez, *Dios,* 17–18).

Faith in the God of the Bible is faith in a living, life-giving God. Over and over again in the Old Testament we read that God is a "living God" (1 Sam. 17:26, 36; Judges 8:19; 1 Kings 17:1) (Gutiérrez, *Power,* 5; Vidales, *Cristianismo,* 98–101). There is a profound correlation in the God of the biblical tradition between being the true God and giving life, "between being a living being and engendering life in history. We must not forget that the Jews did not swear by the 'true' God, but rather by the 'living' God" (Sobrino, "Epiphany," 67).[48] Yahweh, the ever-living one, stands in contrast to the "dead gods," the gods of death (Deut. 5:23; Josh. 3:10; Jer. 23:36).

Jesus Proclaims the God of Life

Sobrino approaches this proclamation systematically ("Epiphany," 70–82). For Jesus, God's original plan is for human beings to have life. The realization of life, in all its fullness, including the material basis of life, is the primary mediation of the approach to God (Sobrino, "Epiphany," 70):

> For Jesus the first mediation of the reality of God is life. God is the God of life, and is manifested through life. . . . From the foundational horizon of the archetypal will of God, Jesus observes that God is a God of life, and fosters the life of human beings. This is certainly a primary and generic horizon, which was to become historicized and concrete in the life of Jesus himself. Life will appear as a reconquest of life in the presence of oppression and death; giving life would be salvation, redemption, liberation; life would have to be rescued from death, death itself yielding life. But, logically and in principle, one can understand the God of Jesus only from the positive horizon of life [ibid., 73–74].

Sobrino identifies three points in Jesus' basic understanding of God's archetypal plan with regard to life. The first is Jesus' attitude in explaining, criticizing, transcending, and deepening the Jewish law as the manifestation of God's primordial will that the human being live. This will of God is to be respected, for it is the way human beings are to live with one another.[49]

Secondly, when Jesus speaks of "bread" as an element of life, he is using it as a symbol of all life. One may ask for bread, then, of the Father, and one may pluck grain in a neighbor's field in order to eat (Sobrino, "Epiphany," 86–87):

> Bread and food are . . . primary mediations of the reality of God. This is why Jesus favors and defends them. This is why he eats with publicans (Mark 2:15–17 and parallels). This is why he pays little heed to the ritual ablutions before eating (Mark 7:2–5; Matt. 15:2), the former being human institutions and the latter a divine institution. This is why the miracle of the multiplication of the loaves (apart from the christological and liturgical intention of the evangelists) emphasizes that those who are hungry must be fed, and stresses that they ate and had their fill (Mark 6:30–44 and parallels; 8:1–10; Matt. 15:32–39). This is why the one who feeds the hungry has encountered both man and the Son of Man [ibid., 73].

The third element that Sobrino finds in Jesus' understanding of God's archetypal plan with regard to life is that the reign of God that Jesus proclaims is a reign that, in its ultimate content, is simply and solely human life in its fullness, especially for those who lack that life at the most elementary levels:

> The eschatological horizon of Jesus' mission is the kingdom of God, a kingdom of life for everyone. But, in order to make it a reality, there must be participation in it by those who for centuries have been deprived of life in its various forms: the poor and the oppressed. Hence Jesus' proclamation is partial, and the God of life appears only partially to those deprived of life [ibid., 74].[50]

Jesus is seeking an adequate "place" to establish a relationship between God and life. In continuity with the prophetic tradition he consciously selects a "place" where he can show partiality, God's partiality: that of the poor, who are deprived of life. "It is only in God's partiality towards those without life that there is a guarantee that God is a God of life for everyone" (ibid., 76).[51]

Jesus' defense of a just life for the poor leads historically to his conflictual activity vis-à-vis the powerful—the wealthy, the Pharisees, the doctors of the law, and the ruling class—in the form of denunciation, anathemas, and a general unmasking (ibid., 76–80). The conflict is not reducible to a mere conflict between "mediators," to a personal struggle between Jesus and other persons. No, it is a conflict between "mediations"—between a defense of the life of which the poor majorities are deprived, and the active defense of the unjust life of elitist power groups. This conflictual alternative, as we shall see, is clearly typified in Jesus' death.[52] Jesus, who proclaims the God of life, and defends life as the basic mediation of God's reality, is persecuted. Paradoxically the one who defends and proclaims life is put to death.

Gustavo Gutiérrez works more from the perspective of St. John, whose Gospel asserts that the Word has come into the world that there may be life, and in abundance (John 10:10). Indeed, in this gospel Jesus declares himself to be "the way, the truth, and the life" (John 14:6).[53]

The death of the one who had borne witness to the Father's love, the death of the "Author of life" (Acts 3:15), communicates life. The death passage of the cross shows us the resurrection, the conquest of death, and life at its fullest (Gutiérrez, *Dios,* 24).[54]

The IECT "Final Document" points up this basic truth of the Christian faith when it speaks of Jesus' resurrection from the dead (nos. 30–31). God is described in terms of the concrete act of raising Jesus from the dead.[55] God carries forward the work of salvation by Jesus' resurrection. God does justice to the one who was crucified, and in him to all the oppressed and crucified of history. The origin of life is at work once again: God's "last word" through the Spirit is life for human beings. Jesus' resurrection is the guarantee of the definitive triumph of justice, the triumph of the victim over the executioner (Sobrino, *Jesús,* 176–77). From this moment forward, life triumphs over the power of death in the antilife of the world, in the course of history.

Signs of Jesus' resurrection are present wherever life is locked in a struggle, even one to the death, against death—wherever the forces of life overcome the forces of death.[56] The profession of the God of life leads us to the center of the Christian experience of the Spirit as life-giving gift. The life that comes from God continues to be manifest in the Spirit. The engendering of life is the Spirit's essential characteristic. Through the Spirit, God becomes present, in ever novel ways, down the length and breadth of history, making history give more of itself, as it finds itself impelled by the tension of the utopia of the reign of God—that plenitude of life now inaugurated by the resurrection of Jesus Christ.

The Meaning of Belief in the God of Life

To believe in the God of life is to believe that God's primordial design is for human beings to have life. Therefore to believe in the God of life is to believe that the realization of life in all its plenitude, including its materiality—the means of life—is the prime mediation of God. There can be no faith in God without the deep conviction of the absolute supremacy of life over death. If life is the mediation of God, then any assault on life—hunger, destitution, squalor, oppression, injustice—is an attack on God, on God's will for the life of humankind. A denial of life, therefore, is a rejection of the God of life (Gutiérrez, *Dios,* 63).

To believe in the God of life is to believe that, from the protological horizon of the original will of the God of life, the nature of sin emerges in its inmost essence. Sin is whatever is death-dealing. The keenest aspect of sin in Latin America is in the historical sin by which some men and women oppress others, oppress the majority to the point of causing them to die (Sobrino, "Reflex-iones," 224).[57] Essentially, sin is the denial of God by the annihilation of the life of human beings, which is God's mediation:

> Honesty in dealing with the real leads to the discovery of *sin.* Injustice and the oppression of the majorities reveal to us that which is the most radical denial of God's will and of his very person: the destruction of the created order and the death of human beings. Offense against God and its correlative, subjective guilt, find objective expression in the death inflicted on human beings, either slowly through oppressive structures or quickly through the techniques used by the oppressors. The tradition is fully justified, therefore, in speaking of "mortal" sin, provided the "death" in question be understood as the death not only of the sinner but of the victim as well [Sobrino, *True Church,* 50–51].

One may not connive in the death of the poor majorities in the name of God. Nor can death be minimized in the name of the fullness of Christian life in the eschatological dimension of life (Sobrino, "Dios," 111). What must be accomplished in the name of God is the prophetic unmasking of false gods, the gods of death (the absolutization of riches in capitalism, the idolatry of power in national security regimes), which require victims (the life of the poor—that is, their death) in order to subsist (ibid., 111–12).

Gloria Dei, vivens homo: God's glory is a living human being. This is how Latin American liberation theology arrives at the reality of God from a postive datum.[58] Oscar Arnulfo Romero, bishop and martyr, concretized this truth most meaningfully: "Early Christians used to say *Gloria Dei, vivens homo.* We could make this more concrete by saying *Gloria Dei, vivens pauper*—the glory of God is the living poor person" (*Voice,* 187).

Just as there is no *gloria Dei* without a *vivens homo,* so neither can there be a *vivens homo* without *gloria Dei.* The human being is humanized better and more extensively with God than without God. God is the origin and ultimate horizon of life; God is the demand that life be abundant, the demand for the humanization of the whole human being at every moment, to the gradual exclusion of whatever dehumanizes us (Sobrino, "Epiphany," 96).

Vanitas Dei, moriens homo. To the truth of the foregoing point we must add the "tragic reality on the other side of the coin" (Sobrino, "Epiphany," 67, 76, 80). If death were to have the last word, then life as mediation of God would be "vanity of vanities": vain would be the reality of God, and vain the human being's activity in view of that reality. *The denial of God, a dying human being.* This, at bottom, is the basic problem of theodicy: to "justify" God through the mediation of the supremacy of life—to show that death will not emerge triumphant (ibid., p.100, n. 64).

To believe in the God of life means to believe in God as the one who bestows on life its character of ultimacy—that is, as the one who brings it about that life be really something ultimate, and not merely provisional:

> The fact that life is something ultimate is evident to Jesus when it is seen as the mediation of God, something that is holy and dare not be manipulated, something that must be served and not be used for one's own service, something that is the gift most radically given and something that is most authentically one's own, something that is most concrete and real, and, to be properly understood, can be conceived only as open and limitless [ibid., 91].

Faith in the God of life must pass by way of the demand that life be bestowed *now* on the poor majorities, who die in history (Sobrino, "Dios," 115). A person failing to grasp this demand—that life must be given to the dying majorities—will also fail to grasp, all conceptual profession notwithstanding, the demanding reality of the God of life (ibid.).

CONCLUSION: THE GOD OF THE KINGDOM

The theo-logical vision of Latin American liberation theology, which I have attempted to articulate in this chapter, can be summed up as follows. *The liberator God is the God of the kingdom.* The God who continues to be manifest in history on the calvary of the world, on the side of the poor—hidden in them, in loving, suffering solidarity with them—as salvific praxis (liberation, justice, and life), is revealed in a process: the process of the kingdom.[59]

God is revealed in history in the process of realizing the kingdom. This is God's will (Gutiérrez, *Dios,* 45). The kingdom—"taken in the global sense, as present and ultimate in history" (Gutiérrez, "Comunidades," 25)—is the most complete expression of God's will for history, in whose midst God is active. The kingdom is the transformation and fulfillment of history according to the will and reality of the God who liberates (for it is a kingdom or reign of freedom), establishes justice and right (for it is a reign of justice), and gives life (for it is a reign of life in all its fullness).

Liberation, justice, and life are in reality but dimensions of one sole expression of the single salvific will of a God who desires that the kingdom come.

When the kingdom is not received—when its demands are not met (wherever history is a history of sin)—God is denied, and withdraws. God *is not,* whenever and wherever the kingdom is negated (Gutiérrez, *Dios,* 46).[60] The death of the poor is a rejection of the kingdom because it is a negation of the will to life, a will coming from God (ibid., 62).

By contrast, in the history of grace, God is present, and the "kingdom comes," in the life and liberation of the poor:

> The whole of the biblical record reveals that the struggles of the poor for their liberation are signs of God's action in history, and as such are experienced as imperfect and provisional seeds of the definitive King-

dom. Christians are responsible for discerning the action of the Spirit, who moves history forward, and who creates a foretaste of the Kingdom in every part of the world of the poor [IECT, "Final Document," no. 26, p. 235].

It is impossible, therefore, simply to speak of God, separating God from the kingdom. To separate God from the kingdom is to make an idol of God—to make a god different from the God of Jesus Christ:

God's will is precisely that the kingdom be brought to reality. If we separate God from the divine intent and design, we surely must not believe in God. We are rejecting God's reign. . . . Indeed, the God of the Bible is inseparable from God's will, from the kingdom. Hence any attempt to encounter or comprehend God in isolation from the kingdom is the fabrication of an idol—is the adoration of a different god from the God of Jesus Christ. A god without a kingdom is a fetish, the work of our hands, the negation of the Lord, for a god without a kingdom is contrary to the Lord's designs [Gutiérrez, *Dios,* 45–46].[61]

CHAPTER 3

Liberative Theo-logy as Theo-praxis

Faith in God consists not in asserting God's existence, but in acting as God does (cf. James 2:14–26). Commenting on this passage, Gustavo Gutiérrez writes:

> Practice is the locus of verification of our faith in God, who liberates by establishing justice and right in favor of the poor. It is also the locus of verification of our faith in Christ, who laid down his life for the proclamation of the kingdom of God and the struggle for justice. Easter life is the life of practice: "We have passed out of death and into life, and of this we can be sure because we love our brothers" (1 John 3:14). The only faith-life is the one the Scriptures call "witness." And witness is born in works. To believe is to practice [*Power*, 17].

And Jon Sobrino:

> The continuation of the struggle for the reign of God is the practical embodiment of continued faith in the mystery of God [*True Church*, 61].

Having analyzed the meaning paradigm of liberative theo-logy (chap. 1), and the dogmatic articulation, properly so-called, of this theology (chap. 2), I shall now complete the circle of my analysis with an examination of the *theo-praxic* dimension of the theology of liberation—that is, I shall treat of praxis in view of the justice of the kingdom as the correct manner of "corresponding" to God—responding and conforming to God—in a "praxis according to God" (Teólogos Latinoamericanos, *Iglesia*, 20).

If the God of the Bible gives us "something to think about"—hence theo-*logy*, the necessary *Credo ut intelligam*—all the more does God give us "something to do." The God of the Bible is a "God who acts" (G. Ernest Wright). Believing in this God, then, means more than just enunciating a theoretical

77

judgment. It means *acting in a particular, concrete manner* (González Faus, *Acceso,* 175). Faced with the will of God as expressed in the kingdom, there is nothing for us to do but obey, whatever sacrifices this may entail. God is absolutely, unconditionally demanding (Sobrino, "Abordar," 7). The will of God expressed in the kingdom is to be accepted and *put into practice*—on the level of faith, and of the gratuity of praxis from a starting point in faith. God demands that human beings act in such a way that the objective content of their action will correspond to the content and reality of God's reign of life, justice, and fellowship, in the creation of a world in which sisterly and brotherly communion (a world without oppression) and divine filiation converge (Sobrino, *True Church,* 44).

In the de facto circumstances of Latin America today, it would hardly be possible to undergo an experience of God that would not have the honesty to acknowledge the basic situation of sin created by injustice and oppression, along with a readiness for concrete praxis calculated to transform this situation.[1]

As for the limits and scope of the present chapter: first, I examine its point of departure—namely, the meaning of what I call theo-praxis, and the larger backdrop of the dialectic of grace and exigency in the life of faith. As part of this dialectic I explore God's call to *conversion*—acceptance of Gift—and summons to *mission.*

Secondly, I examine three specific, interrelated praxis levels involved in correspondence with God's initiative in self-manifestation in and redemption of history: three levels of a "praxis *secundum Deum.*" Clearly, correspondence with as radical, total, and demanding a reality as God will engage all levels of human existence (ibid., 43). Still, we can distinguish three fundamental levels at which this demand is perceived and met, three altogether concrete forms of "corresponding to God"—in love, justice, and anti-idolatry. The demands perceived and met at these levels are not just three random demands among so many possible others; they are the demands that are in some fashion the best calculated and most necessary for the achievement of that correspondence.

1) *Praxis of love.* God—who is love—seeks correspondence through the praxis of love. The Christian faith asserts the impossibility of loving God privately, by a love not mediated by a real love for human beings (Sobrino, *Christology,* 168–69).

2) *Praxis of justice.* The praxis of justice is the historical form of love calculated to give life, and render the transhistorical reality of the kingdom a historical reality (Sobrino, *True Church,* 50–51).

3) *Praxis of anti-idolatry.* Faith in the liberator God, the giver of life, calls for struggle against the idols of oppression, the gods of death—in intention and in practice (ibid., 55).

Let us now examine the relationship spanning historical praxis, sin, and the kingdom.

GRATUITY/EXIGENCY: CONSTITUTIVE DIALECTIC
OF THE FAITH-LIFE

The theo-praxis dimension and meaning of liberation theology will best be understood if it is situated in a framework of what Gutiérrez calls the *grace/demand* dialectic that is constitutive of the life of faith ("Comunidades," 24)—in a basic *gratuity* initiating everything, and an *exigency,* a demand of fidelity to the practice of the gift of the kingdom (Sobrino, *True Church,* 43, 281–82). The Mystery of God, while abiding in original transcendence, is given to us through love (who "first loved us"—1 John 4:19), and thus is revealed as "Mystery gratuitous and obligating" (Sobrino, "Resurrección," 150). Belief in God consists not only in knowing that we are referred to God, but also in knowing that we have demands placed on us by God (Sobrino, *True Church,* 57).

The Meaning of "Praxis *secundum Deum*" (Theo-praxis)

The title of this chapter uses a word that could seem inflated or "pretentious," a word that might seem to denote too much: "theo-praxis." I shall attempt to show, however, that it is actually a most apt designation for the correct manner of "corresponding to God" in the practice of the gift of the kingdom (in a "praxis according to God").

We could just as easily be taken aback by Gutiérrez's assertion that "God is practiced" (*Dios,* 6). Actually, as he himself explains, it is a matter of putting "the will of the Father" into practice, of practicing God's kingdom, from a solidarity with the poor and the oppressed. Gutiérrez is referring, then, to the ethics of the kingdom (ibid., 61, 80).

Jon Sobrino speaks of *seguimiento,* discipleship. To believe in God is to maintain oneself, in God's regard, in an attitude of discipleship, of fidelity to the following of Christ, in a readiness to hear the word of God and to put it into practice (here is the unity of faith and praxis, once more) by situating oneself in history as servant of the kingdom after the fashion of Jesus. The following of Jesus is the primordial locus of all Christian theo-logical epistemology.[2]

The first citation from Gutiérrez in this chapter expresses the basic meaning of theo-praxis: to believe is to practice. Practice is the locus of verification of faith in God.

To Believe Is to Practice

The only faith-life is what the Bible calls "witness," and witness is borne in deeds (Gutiérrez, *Power,* 16–17). The well-known verse from James is perfectly clear: "The faith that does nothing in practice . . . is thoroughly lifeless" (James 2:17).

Faith is not gnosis. Belief in God does not consist in the mere doctrinal acceptance of a truth, but in the real-ization—in conformity with the "path," the manner of activity, of God in history—of what we have learned of God noetically. To believe in God is to emerge from oneself and to commit one's life to God and to all men and women in concrete practice. Belief in God is the acceptance of approaching Mystery, in a "correspondence" with the very reality of God in a realization, in history, of what is expressed in the essence of the reality of this Mystery, which is to be love, liberator, and lifegiver, to the end that the *good news* of the kingdom may come to be—may transform itself into—*good reality* (Sobrino, *True Church,* 46–47, 120).

The maintenance of this process of "correspondence" is an experience of the *gratuity* of faith, a faith now no longer merely experienced with new ears for hearing the good news, but experienced as *fullness of grace*—grace in new hands for making a new history:

> I am not denying that a first, general grace gives us new ears for hearing that God has loved us first, that [God] has drawn near to us in love, and that [God] will approach us in a definitive way at the end of time. But the practice of justice concretizes this general grace and prevents it from turning into the cheap grace of those who think they have God at their disposal. The culmination of grace is experienced in the gift of new hands with which to build a new creation. The fact that faith in the mystery of God is itself a grace does not become fully or adequately clear in the first act of faith, but only when faith is sustained at the historical level throughout the process of joining God in the shaping of history [ibid., 62; see also 71–72].

Practice: The Locus of Verification of Faith in God[3]

In transcending simple affirmation and verbal confession, faith in God acquires a certain solidity in reality. We might say that it thickens, or solidifies, into deed and fact. It is verified through concrete deeds, then (Gutiérrez, *Power,* 59–60). The theology of liberation adheres to an authentically traditional proposition: that faith is a journey in obedience, in accordance with the Johannine emphasis of "doing the truth" (John 3:21; 1 John 3:18–19). Faith acts by means of love, St. Paul explains (Gal. 5:6). St. John develops the same theme by linking the knowledge of God with love for human beings.[4]

Theo-praxis: Conversion and Mission

Praxis *secundum Deum,* then, is the framework in which the dialectic of grace-and-demand takes altogether concrete forms. Let us examine two of these forms. The dialectic of which I speak involves God's fundamental call to conversion—acceptance of gift—and to a participation in mission. God calls for a radical change of life, a change peculiar to the commitment to God in God's mission.

Conversion

Every man and woman is called by God to accept the kingdom as a gratuitous gift and to be converted—in a radical change of life, by the power of the Spirit—from injustice and idols to the living and true God proclaimed by Jesus (Mark 1:15; John 16:3; 1 Thess. 1:9). Conversion is emergence from oneself and total openness to God and others.[5] It is openness to the word of Jesus—who is the Word of the Father—in such a way that this word is accepted in faith, lived in hope, and concretized in the praxis of love as realization of the kingdom (IECT, "Final Document," nos. 36, 46, 93). *Eo ipso,* conversion, although it occurs in the sphere of the personal, is not an intimistic, private attitude, but a process transpiring in the socio-economic, political, and cultural sphere in which the converted subject lives, and which must be transformed (Gutiérrez, *Power,* 52–53).[6]

Mission

To believe in God is to commit oneself to God's mission. Gutiérrez examines the familiar passage, Exodus 3:13–15, in which Moses receives the commission to liberate the people, and concludes that God is self-revealed *from within* mission and summons. The immediate context of the revelation of God—of the "I am"—is a historical *responsibility* imposed by God, in the sense of both mission (God's calling and sending) and the option of assuming this task (Gutiérrez, *Dios,* 11).

To Moses it is revealed that God's name is "I am who am." God states who God is. (To the Hebrew mind, the name was the person.) And God does so precisely from a point of departure in the decision to act in history. Although it is true that the "I am" is a statement about self-existence, primacy, absolute principiation, none of this is any indication of a lack of interest in history.[7] And so the passage goes on to instruct Moses to say, " 'I am' sent me to you"—as if God were saying, "Exactly what I am assigns you this mission: the liberation of my people, of whose oppression by the Egyptians I am aware."

God is self-revealed in history, and from history summons us to *mission* (ibid., 26): from history shapes a people whose finality is to become the community of those who accept the gift—with its gratuity—and assume the tasks—the mission—of the kingdom.

"I will be your God and you will be my people" (Lev. 26:12; cf. Deut. 4:20; 1 Kings 8:51; Jer. 7:23, 11:4, etc.) is a basic biblical formula, recurring throughout the Bible and expressing the meaning and content of the covenant between God and God's people in a reciprocal belonging and possession (ibid., 19).[8] God is the God of a people—the "People of God"—which accepts God as *its* God, and God in turn recognizes the people or *God's* people (ibid., 20).

Biblical faith is always contextualized in a pact, an alliance between God and a human group, a community of persons—not a person or persons taken individually. The "your" in "I will be your God" may not be honed down from the collective plural to a distributive plural. It does not mean, "I will be *thy* God" (and "thine" and "thine"). A believer may not and cannot manipulate God; the believer is not God's proprietor. To be sure, it is the person, in his or her full, radical individuality, who has faith.[9] But personal faith in God has meaning only if it is lived not by an individual in isolation, but at the heart of a community, a community of disciples, the *ecclesia,* the community of those who make Jesus' messianic practice their own. Faith is of its nature communitarian (Gutiérrez, "Comunidades," 23). This is the fundamental affirmation at the basis of the reality of church itself, and of the various theologizations of church that appear in the New Testament (the church as "body" of Christ, "people" of God, "temple" of the Spirit) (Sobrino, *True Church,* 309).

The people, the church called together by the liberator God, is a sacrament of liberation. That is, it is an efficacious sign revealing the liberative activity of God in history (Gutiérrez, *Dios,* 26).[10]

It is from this standpoint that liberation theology presses the centrality of the church-kingdom relationship. In the dialectic of grace and demand, a dialectic constitutive of the life of the disciple, it is precisely the relationship between kingdom and church that comes into play—in the demand for fidelity to the practice of the kingdom, God's gratuitous gift. (1) The kingdom of God is the horizon and meaning of the mission of the church; the kingdom, then, is judge of the church. (2) The church, in its orientation to the kingdom, must opt for the poor, in view of the connection between the poor and the kingdom.

The community of the followers of Jesus does not exist as an end in itself. It exists to serve the world in view of the kingdom:

> The kingdom is the horizon and meaning of the church. In the Third World context we must recall that the church does exist not for itself, but to serve human beings in the building of the Kingdom of God, revealing to them the power of the Kingdom present in history, witnessing to the presence of Christ the Liberator and to his Spirit in the events, and in the signs of life in the people's march [IECT, "Final Document," no. 37, p. 237].

The Kingdom—the horizon and meaning of the church—is also the judge of the church that proclaims the kingdom in history (Gutiérrez, "Comunidades," 24). The kingdom stirs the church not simply to reform, but to conversion from its sins, personal and structural, and from its conformism with the spirit of "this age," this world (Rom. 12:2). It obliges it to confess its historical errors, its contradictions and betrayals of its mission (IECT, "Final Document," nos. 38, 82).

The church, in virtue of its orientation to the kingdom, ought always to spring up from among the poor and despoiled, those whom the gospel parable (Matt. 22:1–14; Luke 14:15–24) calls the uninvited. When all is said and done, it is the marginalized, the humiliated, the wronged of society who are invited to the banquet of the king (Gutiérrez, "Comunidades," 24). From this starting point, the church can be a credible witness and living sacrament of the God of the kingdom (IECT, "Final Document," no. 37).

In the "irruption of the poor," with their historical power in society as well as in the life of the church, the church experiences a vital transformation.[11] This is a moment of grace, and of a demanding ecclesial conversion (IECT, "Final Document," no. 20).[12]

LEVELS OF "CORRESPONDENCE TO GOD"

If I am lacking in love and wanting in justice I shall inevitably stray from you, and the worship I offer you will be neither more nor less than idolatry. To believe in you I must believe in Love and Justice, and it is a thousand times better to believe in them than simply to call upon your name. . . . Apart from them I can never hope to find you, and those who take them as their guides are on the road that leads to you" [Henri de Lubac].[13]

Love of God and Love of Neighbor: One Love

Because God is "ever greater," and the deepest reality of God is love, God seeks a "correspondence" on our part in a praxis of love. The correct modality of this correspondence is in the mediation of a real, historical love for neighbor (Sobrino, *True Church,* 74).

God seeks to be loved *in se* and to be loved in others (L. Boff, *Experiencia,* 72; Miranda, *El ser,* 132–33). Love of neighbor, then, is what makes it possible to experience the transcendent God *qua* transcendent, as *Dios Mayor* (Sobrino, *Christology,* 173).

Jesus' Teaching

Historical love as the mediation par excellence of love for God comes to the fore, Sobrino indicates, in those passages of the Bible in which it might appear that love for neighbor could be prima facie incompatible with respect for the rights of God. "As Jesus sees it, God does not choose to claim any right for himself outside of real and effective love for human beings" *(Christology,* 166). Sobrino cites passages in which Jesus speaks about worship, the Sabbath, and the twofold commandment.

Worship

Worship is not understood by Jesus as the autonomous sphere of God and God's rights. If God is love, then a legitimate worship of God that would not be at the same time a manifestation of love would be impossible in the most radical sense of the word. We would be confronted with a strict contradiction between an intended mediation of access to God and the reality of the God to whom access is intended (ibid.).[14] Worship without love for one's brothers and sisters is literally senseless, meaningless, because it neither is nor can be constitutive of a "correspondence" with the God of love.

Sabbath

In the familiar passage on the Sabbath (Mark 2:23–28; Matt. 12:1–8; Luke 6:1–5), Jesus demonstrates the correct relationship between the human being and the Sabbath observance, with a clear displacement of the latter to the former: "The Sabbath was made for man, not man for the Sabbath" (Mark 2:27). In Mark and Matthew the Sabbath has a theo-logical background: the context is one of an apparent or potential opposition between the rights of God and those of the human being. The solution is clear: nothing can legitimately stand in the way of a just relationship among human beings (Sobrino, *Christology*, 168). Because God is love, God is for others (Sobrino, "Epiphany," 92–93). God is not an egocentric being whose reality is to be for itself. It is impossible, therefore, to correspond to God without corresponding to God's loving reality.

If God is for human beings, we cannot have worship of God or a Sabbath without [its] being for human beings. This is the theological revolution for which the ground was prepared in the Old Testament and which Jesus proclaimed openly. As Braun puts it: "God is no longer someone who is served through cultic worship and observance of the Sabbath. Service is no longer addressed to God as if [God] were some reality *in se*. Proper service to God is service to humankind, to human beings in their need. That is the correct observance of the Sabbath. This is authentic worship of God. According to Jesus, correct service to God is not something that simply *can* be service to humankind; it *must* be service to humankind" [Sobrino, *Christology*, 168–69, citing H. Braun, *Jesus* (Stuttgart, Kreuz, 1969) 162].

The Twofold Commandment

The oneness of love for God and love for neighbor appears in what biblical language calls the "greatest commandment" (Mark 12:28–34; Matt. 22:34–40; Luke 10:25–27). All three synoptics have this passage. Although it had a precedent in Hellenistic Judaism, and therefore is not utterly new, this teaching decisively equivalates love of God with love of neighbor.[15]

The "Logic" of St. John. This equivalency receives a fuller development in the thought of St. John. In the Johannine version its logic runs as follows (Sobrino, *Christology*, 171–72; *True Church*, 71–72, 283–84). God has loved us first—the fundamental affirmation of the prevenience of God's gratuity with respect to any activity on the part of the human being (1 John 4:10). God takes the initiative with respect to the world, and God has demonstrated the divine love through the gift of Jesus (John 3:16; 1 John 4:8–10).

Then St. John comes to a radical and surprising conclusion. The correct manner of correspondence to the love of God—who has loved us first—is our love for human beings (John 15:12–17). "God is love. . . . If God has loved us so, we must have the same love for one another" (1 John 4:8, 11).

This "worldly" love, then, is the logical consequence of the priority of God's love for humankind, and the correct manner of response to God's love is to love others. Correlatively, love for one's sister or brother is constitutive of the response of faith. St. John arrives at a paradoxical conclusion: faith is not a mere "responding" to God's love, it is a "corresponding," in a praxis of love, to God's very reality, which is love. "The correct way to make contact with God is to act like God, to share in God's very own reality. If we know that we are loved by God and want to correspond to that love, then we must do what God does: love human beings" (Sobrino, *Christology,* 172).

It is the praxis of love that maintains and supports faith. "That we have passed from death to life we know because we love the brothers" (1 John 3:14), and it is the negation of this praxis that prevents faith from forming.

Of course, St. John also speaks of Christian love for God—the expression of faith. "But what is unique to John is his statement that the right relation to God and the right relation to others are identical" (Sobrino, *True Church,* 283). The demand of love as a grateful turning to God ("loving God") reveals the radical, novel oneness of love for God and love of neighbor. There are not two distinct objects of love here, God and the neighbor. There is only the single experience of the praxis of love, whose materiality is love for neighbor, and in whose formality—when it is practiced without reservation—occurs the experience of God as well, so that this same love can be formulated as "love of God":

When Christians talk about love of God, then, they are talking *materially* about real, historical love for human beings. It is the *formal* nature of this love of neighbor that determines whether it can also be called love of God. If that love is displayed unreservedly and unconditionally, if it is done in the conviction that those who love to the utmost have lived life in all its fullness no matter what happens, then the historical experience of love for neighbor is formally meaningful as love for God.

It is not that there are two distinct objects of love on which one may choose to focus: God or our neighbor. The praxis of love constitutes one unique experience. Materially it is love of neighbor. Formally, when that love is given without reservations, it is also an experience of God and hence can be formulated as love for God [Sobrino, *Christology,* 172].

Which of These Was a Neighbor? Finally, let us glance at the "neighbor." ("Which of these three . . . was neighbor to the man who fell in with robbers?"—Luke 10:36.) There is an intimate relationship between God and neighbor in the Bible (Gutiérrez, *A Theology,* 194–203). In the Old Testament, the neighbor is first of all a member of the community. But the appearance of the classic trilogy—the stranger, the widow, and the orphan—

in lists of "neighbors" is evidence of an effort to transcend these limits. In the New Testament the bond between God and neighbor undergoes a reversal. It is deepened and universalized with the incarnation of the Word (Gutiérrez, ibid., 192–93) and the concealed presence of the Word in the neighbor, especially in the poor person, who, for the gospel, is the neighbor par excellence (Gutiérrez, *Power,* 44). Matthew 25:31–45 is the best evidence of this double process.

Thus, from the urgency of the praxis of love as an option for the poor, the theology of liberation assimilates the biblical notion of being-neighbor as an *active becoming-neighbor* (Sobrino, *True Church,* 52; Gutiérrez, *Power,* 44–45). My neighbor is not only the one who is "close" to my world, the one I meet on my path, the one who asks for my help. My neighbor is also the one in whose path I place myself, the "far-away" one, the "different" one, whom I approach, whom I go out to seek.

Recent years in Latin America have witnessed a very real, insistent discovery of the world of the "other," of the poor, the oppressed—the "other" with respect to an unjust society. It is from a point of departure in one's relationship with this oppressed "other"—the majority—that the biblical notion of being-neighbor as actively becoming-neighbor arises.

The praxis of love as liberative praxis—as praxis of justice—is nothing but the urgent, unconditional impulse, and the correspondence with this impulse, to move toward the poor to become their neighbors:

> The situation of the majorities, which is like that of the wounded man by the wayside in the gospel parable, shows clearly what it means to be a neighbor. It also shows the fundamental wickedness of passing by, of not actively being a neighbor [Sobrino, *True Church,* 52].

"To Know God Is to Do Justice"

> The proper way of being conformed to God is to be concerned actively with the justice of the kingdom of God and with making the poor the basis of this concern [Sobrino, *True Church,* 2].

From its first theo-logical formulations onward, liberation theology has explained faith in the God of the Bible as a demand for interhuman justice. The God of biblical revelation is known through interhuman justice (Gutiérrez, *A Theology,* 194–96; Miranda, *Marx,* passim). To know God is to establish just relationships among human beings. To know God is to acknowledge the rights of the poor. When this demand is not met, God is unknown and absent, and worship of God is impossible.

Jon Sobrino takes up this "central notion of the biblical tradition" (Ellacuría, "Fe y justicia") and subjects it to a more systematic treatment, from a starting point in the profound unity of faith and justice (*True Church,* 39–63: "The Promotion of Justice as an Essential Requirement of the Gospel Message").[16] Sobrino treats faith and justice as distinct, but dialectically related, moments standing in essential need of each other, with neither faith alone nor justice alone enjoying a primacy over the other.

The moment of faith is that of unconditional hope in the *God* of the kingdom. The praxis of justice is the manner of bringing it about that the *kingdom* of God become a reality in history (ibid., 53, 282).

Two main threads run through Sobrino's reflection. First, the practice of justice is essential for a "correspondence" with the God of the kingdom (*True Church*, 40–53). Secondly, the practice of justice is an essential component of faith within the historical process of its realization in such a correspondence (ibid., 53–63).

Just as faith calls for the implementation of a praxis of justice, so this praxis, in turn, exerts a real influence of faith within the process of its actualization. The structure of faith is that of something *in* process (ibid., 54). Faith in God is not a possession but a *quest*. The experience of God cannot be fixed in time. It cannot be undergone once and for all in history. It is essentially a process of growth, and this is why the praxis of justice is necessary for the constitution of the moment of faith.[17] As a consequence, both faith and justice are necessary for corresponding to God's initiative:

> There is no question, therefore, of assigning an absolute priority either to faith or to justice. From the Christian viewpoint priority belongs logically to the decision and action whereby God [is self-manifested] to history and saves it. The response to this initiative is neither faith alone nor justice alone, but Christian existence in its entirety [ibid., 53–54].

The present chapter is concerned with the first of Sobrino's two threads: the praxis of justice as essential for corresponding to God. The requirement of justice is not simply one demand among many that God could make of us. Injustice renders God's own reality vain, for it renders vain God's will for the world and for history (ibid., 57; see also Miranda, *El ser,* 92).

Praxis of Justice as Realization of the Kingdom

The praxis of justice is indispensable for the actualization of the (provisional, but) concrete, real, transhistorical utopia of the kingdom (Sobrino, *True Church,* 66–67):

> Conformity with the reign of God involves not only hope that the kingdom is *coming* but also a practice whereby it actually *becomes a reality.* . . .
>
> God's will is *that* the kingdom should come, *that* human beings should act in a particular way, and *that* their action should have an objective content in conformity with the reign of God. . . .
>
> The kingdom of God is a reality in which the human world is in harmony with the will and being of God. . . . It becomes a world in

which human unity and the divine inheritance of all God's children are coextensive.

This short description highlights the indispensable place of the historical and interhuman dimension of the reign of God, and the objective and nonarbitrary coextension of the reign of God with the ethical requirements of love for human beings. Objective conformity with the reign of God would be impossible without a practice that makes the utopian content of the kingdom a reality. Conformity to the coming reign of God consists in a practice that promotes its content, and is the practice of love [ibid., 44].

Praxis of Justice as Solidarity with the Poor

The praxis of justice promotes an active solidarity with the oppressed majorities in behalf of their life and basic rights (Sobrino, "Oración," 110). From a starting point among the poor, the practice of justice becomes a concrete universal, transcending any generic, idealistic universalization of justice (Sobrino, *True Church,* 47, 51). It is a matter of taking the fact of the oppressed majorities seriously, for it is in the oppression of the majorities that the greatest negation of the will of God is to be found: the destruction of creation, the death of human beings.

Praxis of Justice as Love in Quest of Humanization and the Bestowal of Life

Justice: Love at Work. Love may be described as the correct relationship of human beings with one another arising from the establishment of certain other relationships: whatever is needed to bring it about that the "others," the persons affected by one's own activity, be more—possess more life, and have that life more and more in its fullness, to the point where a common union is attained (Sobrino, *True Church,* 47, 51).

Justice is "the kind of love that seeks effectively to humanize, to give life in abundance to the poor and oppressed majorities of the human race" (ibid., 47).

Justice is a primordial, irreducible form of love, for it takes account of the historical reality of humankind and the social dimension of the human person. Love cannot be reduced to justice, but to neglect justice is to make love something tenuous and idealistic (ibid., 48).

Justice is the form adopted by love in a situation such as the current "third world" situation of oppression, injustice, and antilife (Ellacuría, "Fe y justicia," 21).

Justice: A Way of Bestowing Life. The practice of justice takes its point of departure in the threat to, or denial of, the right to life, and proceeds in the direction of the achievement of life in its fullness. That is, its goal is a life that is truly worthy of the human being. Its goal is the ongoing humanization of human existence, always capable of enrichment and deepening, on all levels and in all historical situations (Sobrino, *True Church,* 186). Sobrino distinguishes three levels at which the humanness may develop: the historical, the transcendent, and the liturgical (ibid.).

The *historical level* includes that of basic human necessities—material, economic, and social—the product, in part, of history, and the positive shaping element of history. The historical level calls for a humanization of structures in the direction of the reign of God:

> This means [the humanization of] the structures in which human beings live and by which the human beings who create them are shaped in the process.
>
> In Christian language this means that structures must be humanized along the lines of the reign of God so that they may promote the satisfaction of elementary needs, basic equality among human beings, solidarity among them, and sharing of power [ibid., 187–88].[18]

It is clear that this level, being historical, is limited, and therefore is fullness of life not in an absolute sense, but only in the sense in which limited reality, deep within itself, is the vessel of the demand for a "more"—for an approach to the ideal of the kingdom. The practice of justice from a starting point in faith should continually encourage and foster this "more," should continually deepen the historical, to the end that it move ever more in the direction of the kingdom.

The *transcendent* level highlights the fact that the human being is a spiritual being as well (but not by opposition to materiality) (Gutiérrez, *Power,* 207). Human beings are signed by a reference to something antecedent to and greater than themselves—God, the primordial origin and ultimate horizon, in whom they find their fulfillment (Sobrino, *True Church,* 186). On the transcendent level, the faith community "offers an explicit cultivation of faith in the eschatological life ["resurrection," "new earth"] wherein God will be all in all. It also offers faith in Jesus who is the first fruit of the new creation; the following of Jesus puts us on the road to this new creation" (ibid., 191).

The *liturgical* level includes the celebration of historical life, expressed from a point of departure in, and with a view to, the transcendent, with the depth afforded by the faith of a community that "believes that the word of God is constantly revealing the depths of the human and pointing out the direction in which the human can become even more fully so" (ibid.).

These levels, though interrelated, enjoy a certain independence, inasmuch as they respond to distinct areas of human life. Accordingly, the humanization of one level does not flow mechanically from the actualization of the others. Life in its fullness is not realized by purely quantitative addition—for example, by the addition of a transcendent "plus" to the limited historical.[19] The practical consequence of this fact is that the praxis of faith in behalf of the fullness of life demands, in any situation, the explicit cultivation of each of the three levels at which human development takes place (ibid., 186). The temptation for the Christian, then, will be the proclivity to praxis for fullness of life in its "more noble" expressions, a praxis concentrated on the transcendent and liturgical levels, independent of the "less full" historical level. This entails a subtle abandonment of faith in the God of life, for whom life, in all its plenitude, including its material basis, is the first mediation (ibid., 187).

As a result, the practice of justice, with its orientation toward the bestowal of life, becomes demanding, severe, and radical, to the extent of entailing—as in Jesus' case—one's readiness for the surrender of one's own talents, and achievements, even life itself (ibid., 58).[20]

Praxis of Justice as Locus of Keeping Faith in God

The praxis of justice, in virtue of its orientation to love and life as the founding reality that is greater than any other, is the locus of maintenance of faith in God (locus of the positive affirmation of the Mystery of God) as "against" and "in spite of" the questioning of this Mystery in history and the temptation to deny Mystery (unbelief arising from the experience of negativity). It is the locus, in St. Paul's celebrated expression, of "hoping against hope" (Rom. 4:18).

The praxis of justice (as praxis of love orientated to the bestowal of life) reveals to us the "more," the surcharge of reality and meaning, but history also contains failure, unrealized hopes, and negative outcomes:

> Justice looks for effectiveness on the historical scene; it seeks to re-create God's damaged creation. Yet [outcomes] are often negative. The just suffer; those who do justice are persecuted; those who try to give life are deprived of life; the poor are told that the reign of God is at hand, but it seems forever distant. These are common experiences; they are also experiences that terrify, not primarily because they leave human beings so insecure, but because they show God powerless in the face of injustice. The fact that "the executioner can triumph over the victim" (Horkheimer) is an expression of the impotence of God and the scandal of faith in God [Sobrino, *True Church,* 59–60].

The historical practice of justice does *not* soften or eliminate this experience of the negativity of faith. The experience of God must include the experience of *obscurity,* must be had in conjunction with the experience of *negativity* (ibid., 59–60).

The practice of justice furnishes an adequate locus for penetrating the scandalous aspect of faith. One must not lose sight of the fact that God's revelation, despite its fullnes, is also scandalous for the human being. The believer must keep in mind God's utterly-otherness, the scandal of God (Sobrino, "Abordar," 3, 19ff.). The praxis of justice also furnishes the locus for abiding in God without attempting to manipulate God. God's manifestation— which has subsumed scandal—is an invitation to (1) abide with the suffering God, and (2) "abide on the underside of history as the place for the obscure experience of God" (Sobrino, *True Church,* 60).

Paradoxically, the praxis of justice offers a structure for a deepening of faith and for the maintenance of faith through its temptation to its own denial, as indeed it must be maintained through that temptation.

Faith can be maintained if, in the practice of justice, there are signs sufficient to maintain hope through the concrete signs of humanization and life that are already present:

> If the poor have the gospel preached to them, if they become aware of who they really are, if they struggle in their own behalf and attain to a greater humanization, if the miracle of . . . solidarity takes place, if fear and resignation are conquered—then life is beng given to those most deprived of it. These are the signs that are a basis for hope [ibid.].

(See Excursus II, below, p. 104.)

Anti-Idolatry Praxis: Faith in God against the Idols of Oppression

> Faith in God means rejection of murderous idols, and this not simply in intention but in practice [Sobrino, *True Church,* 57].

> The church encounters the God of the poor by confronting the idols of oppression [IECT, "Final Document," no. 23, p. 235].

In describing the theo-logical facet of the meaning paradigm of the Latin American theology of liberation, I called attention to its nature as response, to the attention it must pay to the "terrible and devious pact" established between an unjust society and falsified forms of the notion of God, which are ideologically linked to the dominant system.[21]

With this as its starting point and as one step in its process of maturation, liberation theologians have worked on a theology of anti-idolatry (Assmann, "Tecnología," 40–41). For my own theme, this means paying attention to the idolatrous roots of falsified forms of God. Faith in the God of the exodus, in the God of justice, in the God of life, demands a discernment of and a struggle against the idols of a system of oppression that is structurally unjust and "antilife." This system, in order to maintain itself as a system, produces idols that arrogate to themselves the exclusive attributes of God—ultimacy, definitiveness, "untouchableness" (in that they may not be questioned or compromised)—and that have their own *cultus,* one demanding the daily sacrifice of the masses, the violent sacrifice of those who struggle against them. These are the gods of death (Sobrino, *True Church,* 57, 166).

Idolatry: A Basic Problem

The theme of idolatry may seem to refer only to an ancient, primitive problematic, one of uncivilized tribes, or of peoples considered uncultivated. Idolatry can be taken as synonymous with superstition, hence as something no longer presenting a problem. Who, at this juncture in history, would worship idols? (Gutiérrez, *Dios,* 36). And yet the Bible never tires of repeating that to invent false gods is human, and that placing our trust in them and even worshiping them is an ongoing danger to the religious person, to the believer (ibid.; Richard, "Confrontation").

In the Bible, the continual struggle with the problem of idolatry, against false gods, is not reducible to "a sort of intellectual and religious purification, in the direction of monotheism, being wrought in the Jewish mentality" (ibid., 37). God jealously rejects idolatry because the fact that the people places its confidence in something that is not God means that this people will now follow other norms of behavior than those flowing from the covenant established by God with this people—a covenant based on the love of a God who delivered the people from slavery in Egypt in order to establish justice, right, and life. Now this people's behavior will contradict the norms of such a covenant (ibid.).

The underside of history thus furnishes the locus for a grasp of the real alternative to faith in the God of the Bible. The opposite of faith in God is not atheism (the denial of God's existence), but idolatry (Sobrino, "Dios," 111; Gutiérrez, *Dios,* 36; ASET, *Teología,* no. 63, p. 95).

Idolatry is the worship of the gods of oppression, in whose name human beings are dehumanized, impoverished, and put to death. It is not mere rhetoric, then, to say that there are gods of death, gods that, like Moloch, require human lives for their subsistence (Sobrino, "Dios," 111–12; *True Church,* 146). When the powers of death are free to murder, when life is ignored or cruelly cut down, the false gods of death are in power (ASET, *Teología,* 95; Fabella and Torres, *Irruption,* 203).

Idolatry, then, is not a simple lack of faith in the true God, or merely a lamentable noetic error with respect to the invocation of God, or an incorrect categorization of the transcendental experience of God. Idolatry consists in the adoration of a false god demanding victims (Sobrino, *True Church,* 57, 146). These false divinities of death can be religious, or they can be secular—private property, wealth, consumerism, national security, and so on (ibid., 146).[22]

Worshiping the Money Idol

Let us examine, from a biblical outlook, the idolatry of money. "You cannot give yourself to [*douleuein,* 'serve, be a slave to'] God and money" (Matt. 6:24).[23] The vehement biblical condemnation of idolatry is not limited to the liturgical area—the use of images, or prostration before pagan gods (Míguez Bonino, *Espacio,* 17). The prophetic criticism of idolatry has a much broader sense than this, sweeping out beyond the rigid cultic framework and pointing to the substitution of numberless personal or collective idols for Yahweh—the state, power, comfort, money.[24] In continuity with this same line of Old Testament prophetic tradition, we find Jesus' teaching on "belonging to God and money" (Matt. 6:24), as well as St. Paul's on covetousness as idolatry (Eph. 5:5) (Gutiérrez, *Dios,* 37–43).

Gustavo Gutiérrez singles out Jesus' condemnation of the service of money as idolatry. The radical identification of idolatry as the service of wealth (Matt. 6:24; Luke 16:9, 15) is Jesus' own, novel concept (Sicre, *Dioses,* 164ff.).

It is true that the Old Testament contains many passages condemning a preference for gain, money, and interest rather than the works of justice (Jer. 22:13, 15b–17; Exod. 33:31). But the forceful contrapositioning of God and mammon, along with the demand that his disciples make an exclusive option for one or the other, is Jesus' own contribution (Gutiérrez, *Dios,* 38). With precision and emphasis, the Gospels speak of "serving two masters," a figure of speech comprehensible only in a context of the exclusive legitimacy of the service of God. To serve mammon, money, is to acknowledge it as a superior being, to surrender oneself to it, to make wealth equal to God (hence an anti-God). This is precisely the essence of idolatry: the acceptance and service of another god, constituting a rejection of the God of Jesus:

> Inasmuch as, in the biblical perspective, believing in God is inseparable from doing God's will in history, in the matter of the idolatry of money (which constitutes a rejection of God) what is most decisive will not be verbal—whether circumlocutions or conscious, explicit formulations. With precision and emphasis, the Gospels speak of "serving two masters," and not of "believing in two masters." To serve is to behave in conformity with what is recognized as superior, whether we accept its lordship verbally or not [Gutiérrez, *Dios,* 39].

That money falls into the category of anti-God can be seen from the three central notes of idolatry in the Bible. Idolatry involves (1) the placing of one's trust in something other than God, (2) a human production—something that human beings have themselves invented, and (3) sacrificial victims—murderous gods demand victims.

First, idolatry consists in placing one's *confidence* in something other than God. The idolatry or fetishism of the money idol involves placing one's whole confidence in money:

> Let us keep in mind that Matthew 6:24 comes just before the passage that calls on believers to abandon themselves to Providence, with the metaphors of the birds of the sky and the lilies of the field. . . . Yahweh is concerned, with supreme care and attention, for each and every human being and demands that they place their lives in the hands of divine providence.[25] Obviously, then, to place one's trust in wealth, to allow one's hopes and expectations to ride on money, is a prime expression of idolatry. Hence Luke's imprecation: "Woe to you rich, for your consolation is now" (Luke 6:24), and his declaration that the wealthy are excluded from beatitude because their source of security and joy is money, not God, because they seek refreshment, consolation, and the

reward of their efforts in wealth, not God, because the basis of their security is mammon, not providence—because, in a word, they are idolaters [Gutiérrez, *Dios,* 39].

Secondly, the idol is a *human fabrication,* something that human beings themselves fashion and produce, thereupon to deliver themselves, to alienate themselves, to the fetish thus produced, adoring it and sacrificing everything to it:

> Money is the result of human activity. It is idolatry when human beings place money on a higher level than themselves. Here human beings alienate themselves to money, dispose of themselves, deliver themselves, to the very work of their hands to serve it, to allow themselves to be seduced by the result of their own productivity. . . . Now we understand how money, when transformed into God, enslaves the human being. This fetishism of money is idolatry, adoration of the anti-God. Obviously the confidence the idolater (the covetous person) places in a human work (money) will be betrayed. Not to trust in God but in money is the wellspring of death, alienation, and destruction [Gutiérrez, *Dios,* 42].

The third and last of the central notes of idolatry in the theology of liberation is that the god of idolatry is a murderous god, a god of death, for it calls for human victims:

> Rivers of blood flow for the sake of money. . . .[26] Indeed it is in the victims of a fetish or idol that we most clearly appreciate the meaning of idolatry and its radical rejection of God. Idolatry means the death of the poor. Money victimizes the dispossessed. Why, then, is money an anti-God? Why is it possible and necessary for Jesus to raise his voice to set money in opposition to God and say that someone may follow either the one or the other, but not both? Because the worship of mammon means the shedding of the blood of the poor, in the manifold concrete forms that oppression takes in human history. And if you shed the blood of the poor, if you oppress them and trample their rights underfoot and kill them, you are inescapably against the Lord of life. The idolatry of money, of this fetish, this human artifact, is inseparable from, and causally linked to, the death of the poor. It is for this reason that, if we go to the root of the matter, idolatry runs counter to the God of the Bible who is the God of life. Idolatry is death. God is life [Gutiérrez, *Dios,* 43].

Consequently, to have faith in God is at the same time to struggle against the false gods in whose name human beings are put to death. There can be no connivance in the death of the poor in the name of the God of life.

The struggle is not a matter of theory. It is a practice that joins the struggle for justice (Sobrino, *True Church,* 57). Idolatry is not merely "a theological problem and that's all." It becomes a political problem. The antilife system—the system of crucifixion and death—in which the great masses of the poor find themselves, becomes more and more idolatrous in proportion as it keeps on generating death. And to the extent that it produces new idols, this system becomes more and more powerful in its *mysterium iniquitatis.*

There can be no faith in God that does not set itself in opposition to this profoundly idolatrizing system, so as to confront and denounce the gods of death (Richard, "Razón," 7). At the opposite pole from the false deities and their death mediations are found the true God and God's mediation:

> If sin reveals itself in the death of human beings, then grace reveals itself in the human life that is God's first and basic gift to us. If the doing of injustice shows itself to be the worship of false gods, then the practice of justice shows itself to be worship of the true God. If capitalism and national security reveal themselves to be idols, the true God [is revealed] as the one who gives life and desires liberation [Sobrino, *True Church,* 166–67].

Jesus of Nazareth: Paradigm of the Christian Struggle against False Gods, the Gods of Death

In "The Epiphany of the God of Life in Jesus of Nazareth," Jon Sobrino develops a contrast between the God of life and the gods of death. From a starting point in the historical traits of the life of Jesus as set forth in the Synoptics, he undertakes a systematic analysis of the relationship of opposition between the life-giving God and the false gods (the gods created by human beings) in whose name death is generated (in an "idolatry of death").[27] Jesus proclaims life as God's original plan for human beings. It is God's will that the human being live. Life in all its breadth, including its material basis, is God's prime mediation ("Epiphany," thesis 1 and 2, pp. 70–76). Hence the relationship of opposition between the God of life, whom Jesus proclaims and historicizes, and the gods of oppression, including oppression in its most flagrant form, death. These are the "gods of the law," as law is understood by its zealous guardians, and the "political gods" of the Roman state, guarantor of the Pax Romana.

Sobrino distinguishes these three interrelated moments in the struggle of the gods: (1) Jesus' frequent denunciations and controversies (ibid., theses 3 and 4, pp. 76–82); (2) Jesus' exposé of the use of the divinity for the purpose of oppressing the human being (ibid., thesis 5, pp. 82–84); (3) the attacks and persecution suffered by Jesus, even unto death in the name of the false divinities (ibid., theses 6 and 7, pp. 84–91).[28] Let us examine each of these three moments.

Jesus' Denunciations and Controversies

Jesus observes that the causes of deprivation and annihilation of life are not to be found only in the intrinsic limitations of creation. Such deprivation and annihilation are also the fruit of human sin—the product of the free will of minoritarian groups that use their power for their own interests at the sacrifice of the interests of others. Hence Jesus' reproaches, denunciations, and controversies. Jesus reproaches and anathematizes the wealthy,[29] the Pharisees and scribes,[30] and priests,[31] and those who wield political power,[32] exposing the objective oppressive consequences produced by their direct relationship with wealth, knowledge, and power where others are concerned: the masses are deprived of life, in all its various modalities:

> When we scan Jesus' anathemas and rebukes, we see that they contain very sharp attacks on the individuals at whom they are directed, either because they have upset the scale of values, in the case of possessions and power, or because, overturning the values of religion and knowledge, they hypocritically boast of it. But there is something more profound underlying these anathemas. Jesus made it clear that the anathematized were dehumanized themselves—something that cannot take place without dehumanizing others. So, in his anathemas, he does not use merely formal logic, analyzing how certain attitudes dehumanize the human being, but a material logic as well, observing how human beings become dehumanized by dehumanizing others.
>
> The understanding that Jesus had of the God of life lies at the root of this logic. What makes the attitudes and actions of the anathematized intolerable is the fact that they deprive others of life, whether of life itself, or of the possessions, freedoms, knowledge, and the like, necessary for life [Sobrino, "Ephiphany," 79–80].

Jesus proclaims the God of life, and himself historicizes God's proclamation. This brings him into confrontation with the *private interests* of minority groups who deprive others of life.

Sobrino concentrates on five of Jesus' controversies.[33] He distinguishes two levels—a human and a religious—on which the controversy is waged, in order to identify both the nature of each controversy and its theo-logical dimension.[34]

On the human level, the kernel and core of the controversy is a *social activity* taken to be a bone of contention. Jesus takes his meals with sinners. He does not fast. He takes the property of others (ears of grain). He breaks with certain accepted social norms of his time—fasting, respect for private property, the shunning of publicans. In so doing, he unleashes a controversy and explains his motivation: God is first and foremost a God of life, and by this very fact will brook no contradiction:

> Jesus defends the human and historical mediations of whatever is according to the will of the God of life. To the society of his time, these mediations could be of two types: the socially accepted type, such as cures, or the socially unaccepted type, such as friendly relations with publicans, not fasting, and taking what is necessary for life even though it

belongs to someone else. The latter type is what caused controversy, even before it was formulated in religious terms. And, in defending his "antisocial" attitude, Jesus not only provoked controversy, but also declared that God is, before all else, the God of life [ibid., 81].

On the religious level, the bone of contention consists in two miracles of Jesus (the cure of the paralytic and of the person with the withered hand), which, although they contain no intrinsic provocation to controversy, are nevertheless provocative by reason of their circumstances; Jesus claims the power not only to cure the paralytic, but to forgive sins; and the healing of the withered hand is performed on the Sabbath, by which Jesus impugns not the social fact of the Sabbath, but its unwarranted intrinsic sacralization.[35] From this starting point, he sets forth his religious vision of the God of life, defending it against its attackers, and condemning their view of God. "Any alleged manifestation of God's will that runs counter to the real life of human beings is an outright denial of the most profound reality of God" (ibid., 82).[36]

"Theo-logical" Exposé

In the course of his struggle, Jesus discovers that the powers of death find their de facto justification in explicitly religious conceptualizations of life. Indeed, when they put a human being to death, they invoke a certain type of divinity. They engage in an idolatry of death.

Therefore Jesus not only struggles to proclaim the true reality of the God of life, he also *unmasks a determinate conception of God,* in whose name actions are justified that run counter to the reality of God and his will that human beings have life (Sobrino, "Epiphany," thesis 5, pp. 82–84).

Jesus explicitly engages in this unmasking in Mark 7:1–23 (with its parallel in Matt. 15:1–20). Less explicitly, he engages in it with respect to the question of the principal commandment of the law (Matt. 22:34–40 and parallels).[37]

Let us examine Sobrino's reading of Mark 7.[38]

In the face of the Pharisees' attack, Jesus offers two types of response. In the first type he refers to the value of human traditions (Mark 7:6–13). In the second he appeals to genuine purity (Mark 7:14–23). Both responses expose the false use that is being made of legislation: these traditions and laws are a way of circumventing the true will of God and thus allowing oppression of one's neighbor:

What the entire passage from Mark shows is that the Pharisees dealt wrongly with the issue of the true will of God, locating it in laws and traditions merely because they had been declared obligatory. And, in particular, they used—misused—that issue in order to conceal evil acts against a neighbor (Mark 7:22) and to positively oppress a neighbor (Mark 7:12). Hence Jesus' exposé of the spurious use made of legislation as a presumed mediation of God's will, in order to act counter to the true will of God [ibid., 83].

Attacks and Persecution Suffered by Jesus

Jesus' struggle—as expressed in his denunciations, controversies, and exposé—brings frequent attacks and persecutions on him, "causes others—generally the leaders of the Jewish people, who, objectively, invoke other divinities—to reproach and persecute him, the mediator" (Sobrino, "Epiphany," 84).[39] The basic problem is that there are divinities in combat. Hence the persecution suffered by Jesus has an explicitly theo-logical background:

> [Jesus] was persecuted for reasons that have been made theologically explicit in the strict sense: for his position regarding the Sabbath, and for the relationship he claimed with the Father (particularly in John). And there is in the persecution itself a deeply theological symbolism. In Luke, the first attack occurs in the synagogue. In John, the heaviest attacks occur in the temple. The fact that they drive Jesus out of the synagogue and out of the temple is a symbolic expression of excommunication, and of Jesus' nonacceptance by the prevailing religion. Persecution leads to exclusion from the places most closely associated with God's presence.
>
> The essential datum is that divinities are battling; their different mediations are battling; and hence their mediators, too, are battling. Whereas Jesus' controversies point out the fact of alternative divinities, the persecution of Jesus seeks the exclusionary alternative. The false divinities and their mediators want to exclude, and eliminate, the mediator of the true divinity [ibid., 87].

Jesus is violently deprived of his life.[40] He is put to death in the name of the false divinities against which he has struggled. The first thing that stands out about God in the fact that Jesus is killed, is that he is killed "in the name of God." He is killed by those who call on God, and in the very act of calling on God (ibid., 88).

The various conceptions of God that are present in the death of Jesus appear *implicitly* in the political trial, before Pilate, and *explicitly* in the religious trial, before the Sanhedrin.

The Political Trial. What moves Pilate to sentence Jesus to death is not the indictment for rebellion, or for refusing to pay taxes to Caesar (Luke 23:2), but the choice presented in John 19:12–15: Caesar or Jesus, not both. This is not a matter of individual persons, but of symbolic totalities. The alternatives are the kingdom of God and the Roman empire. Each of these socio-political totalities invokes its own, distinct god(s), the God of life who is the Father of Jesus, or the Roman political gods:

> In the trial before Pilate, the alternative of two persons, two mediators—Jesus and Pilate—appears directly. In the realm of "persons" there is very little logic in the trial, and Pilate wants to release Jesus. But if one moves from mediators to mediations, then one understands the conclusion of the trial: Jesus' condemnation to death. For the alternative was

between the kingdom of God and the Roman empire, and each of these two socio-political totalities invoked different gods: the Father of Jesus, and the Roman gods. So Jesus died, not because of a mistake by Pilate, but because of the logic of the divinities of death and oppression. The ultimate reason for which he could be sent to his death, without denying his personal innocence, is the invocation of the divinity of Caesar. Death could be imposed in the name of that divinity [ibid., 89].

The Religious Trial. The choice between *mediators*—Jesus or the chief priests, who were seeking to put him to death (Matt. 26:59; Mark 14:55), and who finally concluded that he must die (Matt. 26:66; Mark 14:64)—and between *mediations* of the true divinity—Jesus or the temple—points to the basic choice between the kingdom of God and the Jewish theocracy based on the temple. And the divinity in whose name the temple stands is the divinity that puts Jesus to death (Matt. 26:63).[41]

Thus "Jesus dies at the hands of false divinities, and they are explicitly invoked for his death, even though, ironically, it is the living God who is named" (ibid., 90).

The meaning of the religious trial and of the political trial, then, lies in the real, concrete choice between the mediations of the divinities that are locked in combat, and the choice will determine life or death for humankind:

> The deepest significance of both trials will not be discovered by considering them as a confrontation between persons, between Pilate and Jesus, between the chief priest and Jesus—in other words, between what we have termed *mediators*. The deeper significance lies in the *mediations* of the true divinity—mediations that are in conflict. And these mediations are associated with the life and death of human beings. . . . What appears in the trials is the *total* character of the alternative mediations. It involves the Pax Romana and a theocracy based on the temple, on the one hand, and the kingdom of God on the other. Hence it involves totalities of life and history, ultimately based on and justified by a certain understanding of God. And as a result of the invocation of the divinities, Jesus was killed. This is the underlying fact that reveals Jesus' historical destiny: the divinities are at odds, and from them life or death results [ibid.].

Diagram 1 (see p. 100) may help to clarify the shaping of the opposition(s) at stake.

Jesus' life ends in a paradox: the one who proclaims the God of life dies. The gods of oppression put Jesus to death. What appears in the judicial processes at the close of Jesus' life is the consequence of what his life has been. Jesus' death cannot be understood in isolation from what his whole concrete life has been, and therefore cannot be understood in isolation from the opposition and conflict between the God of life and the gods of death.

DIAGRAM 1

Three Dimensions of Opposition

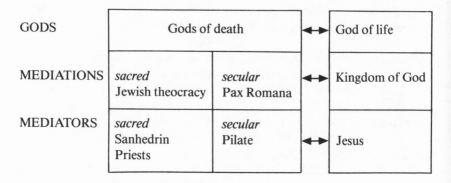

GODS	Gods of death		←→	God of life
MEDIATIONS	*sacred* Jewish theocracy	*secular* Pax Romana	←→	Kingdom of God
MEDIATORS	*sacred* Sanhedrin Priests	*secular* Pilate	←→	Jesus

Faith and Atheism

The experience of the mystery of the liberator God must include the moment of the negative experience of mystery, as temptation to unbelief or as denial of God (Sobrino, *True Church,* 59–60).

In confrontation with the alternatives—oppression (death) and liberation (life)—the God question is historicized. This gives rise to the "problem" of God (Sobrino, *Christology,* 224). Hence the specific outlook and evaluation of the theology of liberation where atheism and its challenge are concerned.

In Latin America, the "problem" of God is not posed in the form of a theoretical debate on the existence or nonexistence of God. Here, "to be or not to be" is not the basic question. It is not to be wondered at, then, that liberation theology has articulated no reflection on the classic "proofs" or "ways" discussed in classic tradition up to the present, from a set of categories that are primarily philosophical, with a view to a possible approach to the existence of God from a point of departure in reason.[42] Nor has the "God problem" been posed from a starting point in the broad, complex, and legitimate (but different from that arising from the praxis of the faith community in Latin America) problematic that begins with "the collapse of the old God of the Western metaphysical ('onto-theo-logical') tradition" (Lotz, "Dios," 404; see also Marion, *L'idole,* 27–48). Nor, finally, does it arise out of the "great crisis, or dissolution, of the divine" as expressed in contemporary European thought (Pikaza, *Dimensiones,* 23–33; "Lugar," 71–76)—for which, in a history (both in nature and in society) presided over by an autonomous rationality (a rationality "come of age," as Immanuel Kant would have it), the very possibility of a positive experience of mystery has been called into question (Gutiérrez, *Power,* 172, 176–86).

The God question, then, is not posed in Latin America as it is posed in strongly secularized regions of the world where God has lost *obviedad ambiental,* a "contextual obviousness" that used to permeate the very atmosphere of a Christian culture (Sobrino, "Abordar," 1). It is not posed from a threatened faith, but from a life threatened by misery and injustice.[43]

In a consideration of atheism in its Latin American concretion, four elements may be distinguished, which, in my judgment, taken together, clarify the outlook of liberation theology on this theme. (1) The oppressed do not primarily question their religious world. They do not first of all ask questions like, "How can God permit such things?" They do not reason, "If God existed, such things would not happen." They render a judgment on the social order that oppresses them and on the distortion to which this order subjects a liberating God. (2) The death of the oppressed gives rise to the "death of God." (3) The obstacle to an approach to the truth of God—to the truth of God's love and justice, the reign of God—is not so much on the rational plane, but on the historical plane: the injustice of reality imprisons the truth of God and impedes its manifestation (see Rom. 1:18; Pikaza, "Conocimiento"). The obstacle to an approach to the truth of God is the atheism inherent in the practice of injustice. The "unjust"—those who oppress their sisters and brothers—appear as the "fool" of whom the Bible speaks, identifying him or her with the atheist with respect to the liberating God (Ps. 14:1, 53:2; Gutiérrez, *Power,* 98). (4) In order to be a believer, one must abandon the gods. The no to atheism pronounced by a believing world paradoxically entails a type of "practical atheism"—an anti-idolatry atheism—proclaimed with respect to the gods of the dominant world. The death and misery that reside in Latin American reality are the fabrication of the false gods of oppression, the false divinities of death, with their prerogatives of "unquestionability," "absoluteness," and "untouchability," with their demand for victims in the form of the lives of the poor, which they need in order to survive.

It will be beneficial to explore these four elements in greater detail.

An Oppressive Social Order

It is not the religious world—faith in God—*that is called into question, but a social order that oppresses and kills.* The specific approach of liberative theological reflection accrues to it from its interlocutor, its historical subject—not the atheist, the unbeliever, but the "nonperson," the "nonhuman" (Gutiérrez, *Power,* 213).

Gutiérrez, in his analysis of the theological route from the underside of history, posits a basic point: that the poor, the exploited classes, the marginalized racial groupings, the despised cultures, do *not* question, at least not at first, the religious world (faith in God, for instance) or its premises. The questioning of the oppressed is primarily directed at the economic, political, and social order that oppresses and marginalizes them, as well as at the ideology that attempts to justify this domination:

The modern spirit, whose subject frequently is the nonbeliever, questions the faith in a context of the meaning of religion. The critique from the standpoint of rationalism and the affirmation of the modern freedoms prefers a debate on the terrain of religion, and the philosophical presuppositions of religion, together with the role of the church in modern, bourgeois society. The questions asked by the 'nonperson,' the 'nonhuman,' by contrast, have to do with the economic, the social, and the political [Gutiérrez, *Power,* 212-13; see also 192-93].

The "Death of God" and the "Death of the Oppressed"

The great challenge for faith in the God of life is the unjust, premature death of the poor person. How is it possible to proclaim the living God when massive antievangelical poverty continues to grow and extend, with its antilife power eating away at all aspects of the life of the masses—economic, political, racial, religious, and spiritual—and accounting for millions of deaths of children, women, and men, all of whom "die before their time"? (Fabella and Torres, *Irruption,* 192-93).

In his work on the epistemological status of liberation theology, Sobrino establishes a bipolarity between the "death of God" and the "death of the oppressed" *(True Church,* 31-33).

European theology, over the course of the last century and a half, and more explicitly since the appearance of the so-called death of God theology, has been influenced by this atmosphere of theological thought:

> In Europe the "death of God" has influenced theological understanding at the level of meaning. In a theistic culture the "death of God" is the most radical expression of the crisis of meaning, whether the "death" be understood as an experience of abandonment (Sartre), as a Good Friday of the speculative mind (Hegel), as a feeling of being orphaned (Nietzsche), or in positive and Christian terms as an ethical exigency accompanying humanity's coming of age (Bonhoeffer).
>
> Among Christians the "death of God" has contributed to a reinterpretation of faith in the specific area of belief. The crucified God is the dividing line between an authentically Christian theology and just any religion, philosophy, or ideology. The crucified God is the most radical expression of God's appropriation of history, not in an idealistic way but in a real way [Sobrino, ibid., 31].

In the context of Latin America as well, the "death of God" is providing theology with its ultimate horizon—but in an unreflected manner, and through a mediation that, in its historical concretion, is different from the European mediation. I refer to the death of the oppressed:

> To begin with, the "death of God" is viewed through the death of the human being (cf. Dussel, "Dominación," 335). That death is real and widespread. If the death of God is the expression of a crisis of meaning, human death is the expression of a crisis in reality. It is not an experience

of being orphaned or of a world that has come of age or of a Good Friday of the speculative mind, but a *real experience of the death of the poor, the oppressed, the Indian, the peasant*. In Latin America, death does not mean simply the disappearance of that which had supposedly given meaning to things (in this case, God), but the triumph of injustice and sin. The theologically correct statement that sin caused the death of the Son is brought home to people in Latin America through the experience of sin continuing to cause the death of sons and daughters. For this reason the epistemological break is formulated not so much on the basis of the death of God as on that of the death of the oppressed [ibid., 32; emphasis added].

Atheism: The Practice of Injustice

The alternative to the practice of justice is the doing of injustice. The alternative to giving human beings life is putting them to death. This is the atheism betrayed by the death of the oppressed. The practice of injustice constitutes a *denial* of God, a rejection of God's will for life, love, and justice (Gutiérrez, *Dios,* 74, 89). This is the "atheism of the practice of injustice."[44] This is the atheism expressed in any perversion of love among human beings, in the exploitation of one's brother or sister that destroys the relationships of solidarity and communion willed by God to obtain among human beings. God is denied inasmuch as the "image of God" in the human being—we have been created to God's image—is distorted by unjust structures, which, by their "defuturizing violence" (Alves, *Cristianismo,* 178), their essential necrophilia, dehumanize human beings and put them to death (Garaudy, *Palabra,* 225).

There may well be among dominators some who profess to be believers. Indeed we find there defenders of what is Christian against "atheistic materialism." And yet, as Gutiérrez has pointed out, "ultimately the dominator is one who does not really believe in the God of the Bible" (ibid., 204).

Anti-Idolatry Atheism

To be a believer, one must abandon the false gods of the system. From a point of departure in the praxis of justice, faith in a liberating God lends paradoxical and positive value to a peculiar form of "atheism" necessary for faith: anti-idolatry atheism (Dussel, *Método,* 244–58). There is no genuine faith without a conscious "apostasy" from idols. In order to believe in God, one must disbelieve in the gods of oppression. You have to begin by being an atheist with respect to the gods of the system.[45] Paradoxically, if faith is to be authentic, it must contain an element of atheism (Segundo, *Nuestra idea,* 226).

Hugo Assmann makes a powerful comparison with the accusation of atheism leveled against the first Christians for rejecting the worship of the official gods of the Roman empire. Today, in like fashion, Christians practice a certain atheism. An abjuration of the gods of oppression and death has now become essential to faith in the God who delivers, to faith in the God of life.[46]

The experience of God in its moment of negativity, as with atheism (all atheism, theoretical, existential, or historico-social), poses the basic question of the *proclamation* of the Christian God. How is one to speak of God? In what words? From what concrete deeds?

In the face of the wretchedness of reality, and in view of the challenge of atheism and the temptation to fatalism or resigned inactivity, the proclamation of the Christian God takes on a new meaning—a meaning that springs from the witness and active ecclesial commitment of a praxis of justice in concrete solidarity with the lowly, the oppressed, whose side has been taken by God, lovingly, unconditionally, and passionately.

Faced with the challenge of the largely nonbelieving modern spirit, Dietrich Bonhoeffer asked his penetrating question: How is one to speak of God in a world come of age?[47] In Latin America, in the face of the unjust situation of the majority—an oppressed, believing people, where the truth of God finds only negative concretion—his question is revised, to read: How is one to speak to nonpersons, the nonhumans, of the liberating love of the Father, and tell them that this love makes us all brothers and sisters? (Gutiérrez, *Power,* 193).

At the same time, evangelization, as the proclamation of the true God revealed in Jesus, supposes a critico-prophetical judgment and discernment of any manipulation of God's name, of "taking God's name in vain" in order to sacralize structures of oppression, repression, and death. Evangelization becomes an ecclesial task of anti-idolatry, and can be effectuated only in confrontation with and denunciation of the idolatrous worship of the powers of this world, the false deities of death, with their demand for human victims.

The salvific, humanizing good news that comes from God will be credible whenever it is lived and proclaimed from the suffering and hope of the crucified of history, the poor. It is from here, as Gutiérrez says, that the community of Jesus' disciples must take up the task that, in Latin America, consists in "making" God present, by the power of the Spirit (*Dios,* 89).

EXCURSUS II: HISTORICAL PRAXIS, SIN, AND THE REIGN OF GOD

In connection with the thesis that the correct manner of corresponding to God, offered in history and approached in the kingdom, consists in the historical praxis of love for the justice of the kingdom (as realization of that kingdom), it will be in order to dwell briefly on two closely interrelated themes of the Latin American theology of liberation: the presence of sin in history, and the relationship between the kingdom as gift and history as human task.

Human History and Sin *(Mysterium Iniquitatis)*

There is but one history.[48] And at the heart of human history is a bipolarity that may be described as a history of grace (*mysterium liberationis*—history in the direction of the kingdom) and a history of sin (*mysterium iniquitatis*—history as negation of the kingdom, history as anti-kingdom) (Sobrino, *Jesús,* 100; C. Boff, *Teología,* 82–85).

In order to be honest with history, not only must we be faithful to history, through an incarnation in the concrete of each moment of its process, and faithful to the course that it is taking, whatever that course may be in a given moment, but we must also keep serious account of the fact that history is shot through with the *mysterium iniquitatis*. History is permeated with the presence of the power of evil. Even in the community that receives gift and mission, there is always the seed of sin and its fruits (Sobrino, "Dios," 123; *True Church,* 108).

If we are honest with history, we shall discover in the experience of history its moment of negativity, and we shall be obliged to take history seriously as a history of sin, with the structural concretions and agents of sin: oppression and death, embodiment of the sin that contradicts God's plan. From a starting point in the antihistory of the humiliated, of the victims of injustice, we find the greatest negation of God and of God's will as expressed in God's concomitance with the kingdom. We find the destruction of creation, the death of human beings (Sobrino, *True Church,* 50–51).

At the same time, historical praxis is the locus of the experience of the "fundamental quandary" (Sobrino, *Christology,* 173). The moment you take the road of love and justice, you feel the sin of the world over you. The practice of justice entails conflict and suffering, even death. This is called persecution. "Sin in its historical reality shows its might and power against those who practice justice" (Sobrino, *True Church,* 52). The practice of the justice of the gift of the kingdom, in solidarity with the masses of the poor in Latin America, has meant, and continues to mean, for a church reborn among the poor by the might of the Spirit, suffering the same repression that the dominant sectors unleash against a poor people fighting for its basic rights:

This repression, unleashed out of hatred for justice, hatred for human dignity, is what today we call persecution of the church. We have the right to celebrate as martyrs the tortured, the disappeared, the exiled, the imprisoned, and the murdered of this people. They are workers, peasants, indigenous peoples, and blacks, men and women and innocent children caught up in their parents' political commitment. They are also catechists, ministers of the Word, leaders of Christian communities, priests and pastors, men and women in religious orders, bishops and martyrs, whom we have the right to celebrate as heroes sacrificed from among the poor [IECT, no. 70, p. 243].[49]

Despite its history of rejection, God continues to inspire the kingdom. God's love is greater than human sin (ibid., no 31). God has pronounced a radical no upon the human history of sin, and a yes upon the history of love and grace (Sobrino, *True Church,* 107, 294–95).[50] Thus the symmetry between the *mysterium iniquitatis* and the *mysterium liberationis* crumbles, and history opens up upon salvation, opens out on its ultimate reality and full sense (Sobrino, "Dios," 127).

The maintenance in history—a history shot through with sin—of the praxis of love and justice "against" and "despite" the sin of the world, is the manner in which human beings may maintain fidelity to a suffering God in the practice of the kingdom.

Personal Commitment and Kingdom *(Mysterium Liberationis)*

The growth of the Kingdom is a process which occurs historically *in* liberation, insofar as liberation means a greater fulfillment of [the human being]. Liberation is a precondition for the new society, but this is not all it is. While liberation is implemented in liberating historical events, it also denounces their limitations and ambiguities, proclaims their fulfillment, and impels them effectively towards total communion. This is not an identification. Without liberating historical events, there would be no growth of the Kingdom. But the process of liberation will not have conquered the very roots of oppression and the exploitation of [human beings by one another] without the coming of the Kingdom, which is above all a gift. Moreover, we can say that the historical, political liberating event *is* the growth of the Kingdom and *is* a salvific event; but it is not *the* coming of the Kingdom, not *all* of salvation. It is the historical realization of the Kingdom and, therefore, it also proclaims its fullness. This is where the difference lies [Gutiérrez, *A Theology,* 177].

God's ultimate design for human history is that the kingdom come to realization. What has already been set forth concerning God's demand—the promulgation of the commandment of love, the formal relationship between faith and justice, and the concretion of the faith moment from a starting point in the practice of justice—demonstrates the impossibility of an objective correspondence with the approaching kingdom in faith alone (as the acceptance of a truth) or in hope alone (Sobrino, *True Church,* 45).

The response to the kingdom that is God's is given in faith and hope that the kingdom come. But this response is also a practice of the kingdom to the end that the kingdom come into being (ibid., 44). Faith and hope must be maintained in practice in the struggle for a kingdom that is never attainable in its utopian aspect, but calls for concrete configurations, anticipating the kingdom, down through the course of history (L. Boff "Salvación," 385–87; *Jesucristo,* 27ff.). Faith in God is basically nothing else but continually giving historical, imperfect form (*topos,* "topia") to the transhistorical utopia of the kingdom (Sobrino, "Dios," 109; *Christology,* 230: L. Boff, *Jesucristo,* 257–58). In the kingdom, transcendence and history are unified.

The kingdom relationship—transcendence and historical commitment—presupposes a tension—that of continuity and discontinuity—which merits a brief examination and nuancing (Míguez Bonino, "Fe en busca," 161–82). The kingdom is not actualized on the margins of history. It is not the negation of history as a mere episode deprived of relationship with the kingdom (which would be religious "reductionism"). But neither is the kingdom the natural dénouement of history (which would be an overoptimistic evolutionism). On the contrary, history issues in the kingdom (eschatological plenitude) through the medium of suffering, conflict, and judgment. The kingdom transforms and fulfills the "corporeality" of history and the dynamic of love and justice that have been operative in history. "There is no love lost in this history" (Juan Luís Segundo).[51] But in its quality of eschatological plenitude, the kingdom is not the work of humankind but of God (Sobrino, *True Church,* 73).

The IECT "Final Document" furnishes us with a clarification of the profound and complex relationship between the kingdom and human history. This clarification, in my judgment, synthesizes the outlook of the Latin American theology of liberation:

The coming of the Kingdom as God's final design for . . . creation is experienced in the historical processes of human liberation.

On the one hand the kingdom has a utopian character, for it can never be completely achieved in history; on the other hand, it is foreshadowed and given concrete expression in historical liberations. The Kingdom pervades human liberations; it manifests itself *in* them, but it is not identical *with* them. Historical liberations, by the very fact that they are historical, are limited, but are open to something greater. The Kingdom transcends them. Therefore it is the object of our hope and thus we can pray to the Father: "Thy Kingdom come." Historical liberations incarnate the kingdom to the degree that they humanize life and generate social relationships of greater fraternity, participation, and justice.

To help us understand the relationship between the Kingdom and historical liberations we might use the analogy of the mystery of the Incarnation. Just as in one and the same Jesus Christ the divine and the human presence each maintain their identities, without being absorbed or confused, so too is the eschatological reality of the Kingdom and historical liberations.

The liberation and life offered by God surpass everything that we can achieve in history. But these are not offered outside history nor by bypassing history. It is all too clear, however, that there are other forces in the world, those of oppression and death. These are the forces of sin, personal and social, that reject the Kingdom and, in practice, deny God. . . .

The Kingdom is grace and must be received as such, but it is also a challenge to new life, to commitment, to liberation and solidarity with the oppressed in the building of a just society. Thus we say that the Kingdom is *of God;* it is grace and God's work. But at the same time it is a demand and a task for human beings [nos. 33–36, pp. 236–37].[52]

CHAPTER 4

Liberative Theo-logy: An Evaluation

The three foregoing chapters of this book have been concerned, respectively, with the hermeneutics, the dogmatics, and, shall we say, the "praxis" of the Latin American theology of liberation in its theo-logical perspective. My intent has been to explain that perspective in a systematized way. With special reference to Gustavo Gutiérrez and Jon Sobrino, I have sought to organize and articulate what in my judgment constitute the fundamental and foundational concepts of this theo-logical vision from the "underside of history."

The purpose of this fourth and final chapter, as its title indicates, is on the level of *judgment*. Here I shall undertake a critical evaluation of my theme, taking up its basic content, and identifying the whys and wherefores of its theses, its values, and limits, and then presenting my own systematic reflection.

I propose to develop this chapter in four steps: (1) *Overview:* Without any attempt to review in detail each of the subthemes already studied, I shall offer a concise definition of the basic theo-logical axes configuring, in their ensemble, the view of God proper to the Latin American theology of liberation. (2) *Value judgment:* Here I am on the level of *judgment* in the strict sense, the object of that judgment being the scope and limit of the subject I have been examining throughout this book. "Between the lines" I may also read what liberation theology does *not* say—material not expressed, but certainly not necessarily denied. (3) *Prospective reflection:* Here I shall draw up an "agenda" for the theology of liberation in coming years, with respect to the theme I have been pursuing. (4) *Final reflection:* Last, I have a personal observation to address to my own ecclesial tradition in light of the completed study.

THEO-LOGICAL OVERVIEW

The theo-logical view, "in a liberative key," from the "underside of history" can, in my opinion, be summed up after the fashion of a *profession of faith*. It seems to me that this will be the best and most forceful way to isolate the profound *praxic-ecclesial-doxological* sense of the *theo*-logical propositions of the theology of liberation—that is, this will help us see what manner of life and ecclesial praxis will lend meaning to these propositions. It will not exhaust the Christian kerygma, any more than any other faith-confession in the life of the church. It will seek to set in relief a concrete faith-life.

Concretely, theo-logy "from the underside of history" is: faith in the Mystery of the Liberator God of the poor—a faith lived (actualized), proclaimed, and thought *ecclesially* (reference to the community nature of the life of faith), at the heart of an active solidarity in the sufferings, struggles, and hopes of the poor of the Latin American nations (reference to the praxis of faith).

The view, the profession, that I here seek to articulate has no pretentions to the theoretico-formal character of a dogmatic definition.[1] It will be articulated instead in an expository-narrative manner. It is intended to be in continuity with the history of faith—hence with salvation history—as lived and reported all through the pages of the Bible. Hence its *doxological* nature: it will seek to express in theological language what has already been expressed in the language of celebration, and in real life in the language of ecclesial praxis.[2]

The structure of this faith-confession will be basically trinitarian. That is, its assertions will be grouped with reference to the reality of the Mystery of God revealed as Father, Son, and Spirit (hence the trinitarian structure of the *Mysterium liberationis,* and therefore of the experience of God).[3]

Profession of Faith

We believe in God, *the Father,*
  our Father, and the Father of all humankind,
  Mystery of Love,
  Original and Ineffable, Holy and Unmanipulable,
  Giver of life,
  Creator of history:
  the Space to be free human beings,
  who continues *self-revelation*
  on the Calvary of the world,
  where life is crucified and destroyed
  by injustice, oppression, and sin.
  The Father is on the side of the poor—
  of the lowly, the lost ones, of this world,
  the exploited classes,
  marginalized cultures,
  and racial groupings victimized by discrimination—
  liberating his people with a victorious might
  that establishes justice and right,
  vanquishes death,
  and re-creates and humanizes life.

We believe in *Jesus of Nazareth,* Son of God,
  True Human Being and True God,

the Truth and definitive Way to the Father,
Witness to the Father's Love
our Elder Brother in solidarity with us,
Liberator of all humankind.
By his historical, messianic practice
he proclaimed the *Kingdom of God*—
free Gift of the Father,
Good News for the poor,
ultimate design for the whole of creation.
Refusing to keep his life to himself,
he made himself the servant of others
to the death, death on the cross.
But the Father raised him from death, with power,
as Firstborn among many sisters and brothers,
New Adam, Firstfruits of the New Creation,
by the *Resurrection,*
the triumph of God's life and justice.

We believe in the Holy Spirit,[4]
Principle and Source of Life,
bond of Love
between the Father and the Son,
between God and human beings,
between one human being and another.
the Spirit is the Generator of history,
Transformer of all things,
novel Presence of God in the midst of our history,
who speaks to us through the "signs of the times,"
who makes us hear the cry of the poor,
who calls us to a radical change of Life,
who leads us to a recognition of our freedom to love
as creative sons and daughters of the Father,
as sisters and brothers to one another,
who calls us to the following of Jesus,
creating the community of his disciples,
who animates us, and enables us
to be a free and efficacious sign of the Kingdom,
who sets in motion a loving praxis
lived in hope,
concretized in our history,
and orientated toward the justice of the *Kingdom,*
God's utopia—
a new heaven and a new earth
for the new humankind.

VALUE JUDGMENT

If the state of domination and dependence in which two-thirds of human-ity live, with an annual toll of thirty million dead from starvation and malnutrition, does not become the *starting-point* for *any* Christian theol-ogy today, even in the affluent and powerful countries, then *theology cannot begin to relate meaningfully to the real situation.* Its questions will lack reality and not relate to real men and women [Assmann, *Theology,* 54; emphasis added].

"Dialogical Openness" to Liberation Theology

Well aware that "any reading is, at bottom, an interpretation," as Xabier Pikaza has put it—that any reading of a subject is always done in light of certain "pre-suppositions," in guise of a theoretical framework—I was alto-gether frank, in the Introduction, as to this part of my methodology. When it came to a minimal global theoretical framework, I began with a decision for belief, a longing for liberation, and an ecumenical spirit. It was from within this theoretical framework, I stated, that I would read and analyze the theo-logical "logic" of the Latin American theology of liberation.

As I now approach the task of rendering a value judgment with respect to the topic under consideration, the theological framework remains the same. With this framework as my starting point, I wish to maintain a *dialogical openness* to the theology of liberation.

My evaluative judgment is not to be one of polemical confrontation.[5] As is well known, liberation theology, in various ecclesial and even nonecclesial contexts, within and without Latin America, has been the object of study, discussion, evaluation, and, in some cases, outright rejection.

My personal judgment is that the Latin American theology of liberation, as a theological "open road" to be traveled by the church in Latin America, is useful and necessary, both ecclesially and theologically.

Any theological schema, of course, as a communitarian "understanding of the faith," is limited and imperfect, while always perfectible. The history of theology bears clear testimony to the scope and limits necessarily attaching to any Christian theological discourse. The consequence for us is equally clear: the theology of liberation must live in a permanent state of self-criticism, lest it succumb to the classic temptation of theological totalization—the temptation to seize upon *a* theology and present it as *theology.* Christian faith, founded on the gratuitous activity of God, obliges the theologian to come forward as a servant of the truth rather than as its owner.

From its starting point in the faith-praxis of an oppressed, believing people, which has found in its faith the courageous spirit and motives to pursue the goal of liberation, the Latin American theology of liberation, born as critical reflection ("second act") on this praxis ("first act"), is performing its *diako-nia*, which is the raison d'être of theology in the life and mission of the church.

From its particular social and ecclesial location in a concrete historical context, liberation theology offers its prophetic word (Geffré, "Conmoción"). It makes its contribution to the renewal of the universal task of theology (Schillebeeckx, "Presentación"). It would be a mistake to think that the theology of liberation is interested only in Latin America. To be sure, it is contextual. Theology is always contextual, hence relative and limited. But the theology of liberation aspires to universality. Juan Luís Segundo, in his reflections on "our idea of God," makes a statement that I want to cite here, and not in a chauvinistic spirit:

> When historical sensitivity and ecclesial flexibility converge in it as never before, Latin America, a *peripheral* Western cultural complex, can be, for itself and for the whole of Christianity, the seedbed . . . of *a new idea of God closer*—at long last—*to Christian revelation* [*Nuestra idea,* 51; emphasis added].

The Outlook of the Poor: Key to the Understanding and Evaluation of Liberation Theology

In chapter 1, I sought to explain, in its basic elements, the "hermeneutic key" of liberation theology—its meaning paradigm. This, we saw, is nothing other than the outlook of the poor: the poor as *privileged theological locus* from which to situate and concretize the material and accents of a theological discourse.

It is an easy matter, then, to see why such a perspective or outlook, so decisive for an understanding of the theology of liberation (the level of *seeing*), must at the same time—in its capacity as the "backbone" that supports and keeps in place the content and emphases of the "word" of this theology— become the point of departure for any critical evaluation (the level of *judging*) of its contributions and limits. Liberation theology must be judged in any given area—here, in the area of its theo-logy—not merely on the basis of its statements taken in themselves (here, its theo-logical ones), by way of a purely textual analysis, but also on the basis of their reference to their larger text, their reference to the historical matrix (the real contradictions of history, the position-taking, the ecclesial praxis) that has made these statements possible, and that lends them meaning. Otherwise, dialogue, evaluation, and theological discussion will themselves all be bereft of meaning.

The breadth of this subject calls for a selection of basic subthemes to be subjected to a value judgment strictly so-called. Starting from the outlook of the poor as the guideline supporting and unifying various commentaries, I propose to single out the following reference points:

1) the poor
2) theological method

3) the Mystery of God: the poor as theo-phanic locus of the "God of the poor" (constituting at once the infrastructure and the point of major convergence and unity of the theology of liberation)

4) theo-praxis and ecclesiology.

The Poor

The poor person does not exist as an inescapable fact of destiny. His or her existence is not politically neutral, and it is not ethically innocent. The poor are a by-product of the system in which we live and for which we are responsible. They are marginalized by our social and cultural world. They are the oppressed, exploited proletariat, robbed of the fruit of their labor and despoiled of their humanity. Hence the poverty of the poor is not a call to generous relief action, but a demand that we go and build a different social order. . . .

The option for the poor, taken in the commitment to liberation, has brought us to an understanding that the oppressed cannot be considered apart from the social class to which they belong. This would only lead us to "pity their situation."

The poor, the oppressed, are members of one social class that is being subtly (or not so subtly) exploited by another social class [Gutiérrez, *Power,* 44–45].

If the poor are a theological locus, it becomes necessary to answer the question, "Who are the poor?"

If we are to be honest about reality, there can be no question about the validity of taking the world of the poor as the point of departure for theology. Still, terminology has lent itself to considerable confusion, ambiguity, and indetermination in Christian circles, and the very term "poor" may stand as an example.

From its earliest formulations, Latin American liberation theology has sought to fix and concretize its language about the poor in such a fashion as to break with a universalizing ecclesiastical language that uses the concept of the poor as an abstract universal. I hope that, in the course of my considerations on the meaning paradigm (chap. 1), I have identified with sufficient clarity the elements that constitute the "perspective of the poor" for liberation theology: the historical irruption of the poor, the new historical hermeneutics, the dependency-liberation polarity, the mediation of socio-analytic discourse, and a new understanding of the political. These elements are important, and must always be present for an understanding of the perspective of the poor in the Latin American theology of liberation. Not to take into account the scandalous situation of the poor, who constitute a majority of the world population, will automatically issue in a misunderstanding of liberation theology. On a deeper level, more seriously and more radically, it will issue in a failure to grasp the liberative power of the poor in history and their evangelical message. For

Jesus, God is the One who draws near, in the kingdom, as good news for the poor. To be sure, I do not imply that the poor are the sole depositaries of the faith. Nor have I any intention of denying that those who are not poor may have faith.[6]

The evangelical option for the poor, practiced in solidarity with them in their own liberative practice, has led to an understanding of the *destructive* and *structural* nature of poverty. Hence the central place assigned by liberation theology to an *analytical mediation* as the route to a discernment of the "objective logic" of the historical causality and structural mechanism at the root of the situation of the poor. The itinerary of many Christians in Latin America as they move toward an understanding of poverty is the following:

1) Poverty is destructive. It is a threat to the life of the poor, hence is genuinely "mortal."

2) Poverty is not a natural "accident" of mere want. It is not politically neutral. Poverty does not obey a kind of blind, inexorable social fatalism.

3) Poverty is structural. It is the historical product of an unjust system of impoverishment determined by the will of a minority of human beings in serving interests and benefits that are not those of the majority. Hence we may speak of a dialectic: there are poor because there are rich, and there are rich because there are poor.

4) Poverty calls for struggle. Poverty is perceived (is felt), is analyzed (is seen), but most of all demands struggle (calls for action).

Protest, ethico-prophetical indignation at the reality of the poor, is a necessary first step. The next is the articulation of a practice in solidarity, lucidity, and efficacity. Good will is not enough. Neither are lyric outcries in behalf of the poor that ignore the underlying causes and structural mechanisms that generate poverty. I shall have something more to say about the levels of this ecclesial praxis of assistance when I come to speak of the value judgment of theo-praxis in its ecclesial sense.

Creaturely Poverty or Material Poverty?

The option for the poor has led to the discovery of the historical catastrophe of a poverty that deals slow, sure death to thousands and millions of human beings. To speak of the poor, then, is to speak of their concrete, real poverty. In my view, this is one of the values of the perspective of the poor that must be maintained in face of the constant temptation to spiritualize that perspective. This material aspect of poverty lends a fuller meaning to the traditional correlation between poverty and God. To the question, "Who are the poor?" theology has responded: "To be poor is synonymous with being human. Poverty is part and parcel of the human constitution as a creature. Every human being, as such, is needy, incomplete, and limited in self-realization, especially with respect to death."

This "creaturely poverty" is a human attribute, undeniably. But, in my judgment it is not a sufficiently radical definition of poverty, either from the viewpoint of the Bible (which contains the concept, but does not present it in terms of poverty), or from that of historical reality. The poor, living in the hard reality of material poverty, function as indicators of a situation of contradiction that goes beyond the basic human condition into the area of the subhuman, in virtue of its radical character of spoliation and antilife. Their real situation, then, is doubly hard: besides creaturely poverty, they must also suffer the unjust burden of real, historical poverty. They are truly "the crucified of history," condemned to a slow death "before their time" by reason of oppressive structures, and a more rapid death by reason of repressive structures.[7]

This being the case, the gospel invitation is transformed into an *urgent call to defend their basic right to life,* along with the material *means* to life, without which no one can live in even a minimum of human dignity. To take seriously the primary material levels of life—the material, corporeal life of human beings—is to revalidate a theology of creation in terms of a re-creation of life.[8] As Sobrino has insisted, the poverty of two-thirds of humanity means that God's creation is imperiled and vitiated. The very fact of being alive, and of coming to be alive, of placing nature and its resources at the service of the full satisfaction of basic human necessities, is an expression of God's primordial will of life.

We are not dealing with a merely anthropological or socio-economic problem here. We are dealing with a theo-logical problem in the strict sense. If poverty is the expression and product of sin, being the absolute negation of the will of the God of life, then the re-creation of the life of the poor is the way to assert "the absolute of life," from a point of departure in the primary realities of life. Life becomes a mediation of the experience of God. From within an active practice in defense of the life of the poor emerges an understanding of what Irenaeus meant with his cry, *"Gloria Dei, vivens homo"*—which Archbishop Romero reformulated concretely and prophetically: *Gloria Dei, vivens pauper* (*Voice,* 187).

Reading the Reality of the Poor (Seeing)

The option for the poor does not automatically guarantee a correct reading of the historical reality of the poor. In fact, a certain training in "traditional Christian principles," with its disregard for historical reality, has made us Christians insensitive, even hostile, to the mediations of socio-analytic discourse.[9] To what type of analysis and to what theory shall we accord the "epistemological privilege" that is in question here? What theoretical explanation of the mechanism and structures of society in general and of the reality of the poor in particular will afford the best understanding of these mechanisms and structures?

Analysis of Reality: A Committed, Partisan Act

When it comes to the reality of the poor, we find ourselves faced with readings that are not only different but contradictory. Choosing a reading presupposes the taking of a position vis-à-vis reality, and this in turn commits and adapts the mediation of scholarly socio-analytic instrumentality.[10]

The "Epistemological Privilege of the Poor"

The theology of liberation is interested in an "illumination" and "empowerment" of the praxis of faith from within solidarity with the poor. Accordingly, the social locus here, the option for a determinate analytical mediation, lies along the concrete axis of the *liberation of the poor.* Hence "epistemological privilege" conferred on a determinate social analysis is the "epistemological privilege of the poor." What is needed is a reading of the human condition that will afford the best possible knowledge of the economic, political, and social causes and mechanisms of the current situation of impoverishment of the majority of human beings, and of the concrete conditions of breach with the prevailing system that will initiate a liberative forward march in history.

Structural-dialectical Analysis

The Latin American theology of liberation has opted—correctly, in my judgment—for a reading of the poor from a structural-dialectical social analysis.

This analytical stance is not content with *phenomenological* social analysis, or mere registering of facts (the fact of injustice, of unemployment, of infant mortality) that does not get down to causes. The spirit of a phenomenological analysis is that of passive awareness, and the action it recommends is *assistentialistic* or *pragmatic:* it pays attention to facts simply as presented.

Nor does Latin American liberation theology settle for a *functionalistic* social analysis, a view of society as an organic whole, a body hosting multiple functions, which , when they function organically—in the correct interrelationship of whole and parts—manage to maintain the harmony of the whole.

Functionalistic analysis is superior to phenomenological, inasmuch as it does not rest content with simply listing facts. It sees facts in their mutual relationships, in their conjuncture, prioritizing the harmony of the social whole. Society is in harmony, it says, when everything functions. It is concerned for the functioning and harmony of the social whole. Reforms may be needed, but without interrupting the overall balance of society.

When dysfunctions occur—for example, in the case of the poor—reforms must be brought about to achieve the recovery of social equilibrium. The spirit of this type of analysis is a critical, in contrast with a passive, awareness, and the action it proposes is "reformist."

Structural-dialectical analysis is an analytical approach that begins from facts (on the level of phenomenology, then) and conjunctures (on the functionalist level), and then proceeds to the structural mechanisms of the Latin American social configuration of dependent capitalism (Gorostiaga, *Entender,* 32–74). Precisely on this accout is it called *structural* analysis—because it looks for the structures underlying conjunctures and facts. Conjunctures and facts, it holds, are understood only if they are grasped in the framework of the manifold structures, mechanisms, and institutions by which dominant sectors exercise their dominance in the economic, political, and cultural spheres of society (IECT, "Final Document," nos. 12–18).

The *dialectical* nature of this structural analysis lies in the fact that it sees the social whole not as something in harmony, but as something in conflict, by reason of the spoliation and exploitation, subtle or overt, by which one social class is despoiled of the fruit of its labor by another social class. It sees the social whole as permeated by a conflict of class interests between capital, concentrated in the hands of a few, and the labor force.

The *radical* nature of the critical awareness that is the spirit of this structural analysis proceeds from its insistence ongoing to the roots of the facts. This awareness is expressed in a concrete practice, which, in view of the prevailing conflictuality (it lives and thinks peace in the midst of conflict), demands not reformation, but *transformation* of the system. It promotes the creation of a liberative forward thrust in history, with a sharing by all in the means and goods of production, to the end that all may be guaranteed the full satisfaction of their basic needs (work, food, housing, health, education) and the creation of the true conditions of life, justice, and freedom.

This, then, in all brevity, is the nature of the socio-analytic mediation that furnishes liberation theology with its point of departure for a reading of social reality. I make my own the words of Leonardo Boff on the theological use of structural-dialectical analysis:

This is why the theology of liberation opts for the dialectical analysis of social reality. Liberation theology holds that this is the analysis that better answers to the objectives of faith and Christian practice. And it is here that use is made of the analytical instrument devised by Marxist tradition (by Marx himself, by the various contributions of socialism, by Gramsci, Althusser, and other theoreticians). The utilization that liberation theology makes of this instrument is not servile. Dialectical analysis is science, divorced from its philosphical presuppositions, divorced from dialectical materialism. *Science* is knowledge submitted to control by experimentation and verification. *Philosophy* is a universalizing interpretation of being and global history. It is Marxist science, and only science, that will serve our purposes.

In the analysis of social reality in the dialectical approach, the data of social anthropology and social psychology, along with considerations of history, also come into play. Everything must conspire toward a *structural and causal comprehension of the situation of poverty* in which millions of Latin Americans live, a situation that, within an ethical framework, must be considered inhumane and unjust [Boff and Boff, *Salvation,* 50; emphasis added].

Source and Reference of Spiritual Poverty:
Material Poverty

I have asserted that one of the values of the Latin American theology of liberation is that it has found the basic meaning of being poor in real, material poverty: the poor are those who are threatened in their basic right to life. Now, does this reading on the part of the theology of liberation entail a material-temporal reductionism at the expense of "religious" or "spiritual" aspects of poverty? A word of explanation is in order. In my opinion, what we have here is not a "materialistic reductionism"—an evaluation of poverty that excludes and thereby detracts from the "specifically Christian" notion of poverty in the gospel notion of "spiritual poverty"—but a case of being profoundly "honest with reality."

A perception of the raw reality of the poverty of the Latin American masses calls for a rejection of any attempt to mask or conceal that reality, either socially or "religiously."[11] The Christian commitment to the poor, entailing as it does the denunciation of all abstract spiritualization of poverty (Ellacuría, "Bienaventuranzas," 118), has led to a dialectical rescue of the profound evangelical notion of "spiritual poverty." Faithful to its roots in the gospel, liberation theology takes spiritual poverty not as the dissimulation or eviscera-tion of a scandalous reality, but as an *acceptance* of gratuitous Mystery, as *openness* to God's will for love and justice, as *spiritual infancy* (Gutiérrez, *A Theology,* 296–99). An authentic attitude of spiritual poverty can emerge only from a commitment to those who suffer real poverty, and it is only from the depths of an attitude of spiritual poverty that it is possible to commit oneself to the world of the poor as a real, material world. From out of the mist of the poor of the earth, in conscious and clear identification with their life, their struggles, and their hopes, the gospel call to be poor is experienced in *solidarity* and *protest:*

> Evangelical poverty began to be lived as an act of love and liberation toward the poor of this world. It began to be lived as *solidarity* with them and *protest* against the poverty they live in, as *identification* with the interests of the oppressed classes, and as *indictment* of the exploitation of which they are the victims.
>
> The ultimate cause of exploitation and alienation is selfishness. The deep reason for voluntary poverty is love of neighbor. Poverty—the fruit of social injustice, whose deepest roots are sin—is taken up not in order to erect it into an ideal of life, but in order to bear testimony to the evil it represents. Our sinful condition, and its consequences, were not assumed by Christ in order to idealize them, surely, but in order to redeem us from sinfulness, to battle human selfishness, to abolish all injustice and divi-sion among human beings, to suppress what divides us into rich and poor, exploiters and exploited.
>
> The witness of poverty, lived as an authentic imitation of Christ,

instead of alientating us from the world, places us at the very heart of a situation of spoliation and oppression. From there it proclaims liberation and full communion with the Lord. From there it proclaims, and lives, spiritual poverty: total availability to God [Gutiérrez, *Power,* 55, emphasis added; see also *A Theology,* 299–302].

Theological Method

The theology of liberation offers us not so much a new theme for reflection as a *new way* to do theology. Theology as critical reflection on historical praxis is a liberating theology, a theology of the liberating transformation of the history of [humankind] and also therefore [of] that part of [humankind]—gathered into *ecclesia*—which openly confesses Christ. This is a theology which does not stop with reflecting on the world, but rather tries to be part of the process through which the world is transformed. It is a theology which is open—in the protest against trampled human dignity, in the struggle against the plunder of the vast majority of people, in liberating love, and in the building of a new, just society [of fellowship]—to the gift of the Kingdom of God [Gutiérrez, *A Theology,* 15].

Methodolgy

Living and thinking the faith from the world of the poor has led Latin American theologians to pose the problem of *methodology*—the problem of the route, the way, by which one proposes to do theology. It was evident from the beginning that it would be impossible to reflect theologically from the poor as point of departure without a reflection on method. When it is asserted, rightly, that the newness of liberation theology is neither in its language nor in its thematic, but in its methodology, we must keep in mind that its method is inseparable from the outlook of the poor. Only thus shall we be able to avoid an abstract theoretical approach that fails to go beyond an examination of "conditions of possibility." We are dealing with something altogether concrete: a new manner of doing theology, from a starting point in faith as lived and thought (in the sense of the "understanding of faith") in an ecclesial practice in solidarity with the poor. The "methodological root" of liberation theology is to be found in an *identification* with the anguish and the hopes of the poor regarding their basic right to life.

The Central Theological Problem

If there is anything *specifically Latin American* in this theology, it is the fact of having taken the situation of oppression and impoverishment of the masses of Latin America as the *central problem* of its theological reflection. The historical situation of the suffering, oppression, and systematic death of the impoverished majorities of the "third world"—two-thirds of the world population—constitutes, without a doubt, the *major challenge* to the life and mission of the church today. The poor— in their particularity—become a genuine universal.

Search as a Basic Attitude

The inhumanity of the reality of the poor is far too harsh for us to be able to sidestep the question of how we have thus far been living and reflecting on our faith, in the church and in society. New, rich, and serious questions arise. Old certitudes and securities fall. Theology suddenly finds itself with the task of following a road under the sign and rubric of *search,* of quest, as its basic attitude. The challenge of the poor rules out recourse to the theological procedures of the past if this will mean reiterating old answers. Theology must emerge from the infertile schema of the "eternal return" of the same questions and answers, always coming and going *from within theology itself* and passed on from generation to generation by tradition. In practice this has been tantamount either to leaving new questions without answers, or offering old, inapplicable, and conservative answers. Thus theology loses contact with reality. Isolated from the challenge of historical processes—such as liberation processes—theology falls into irrelevancy, into a kind of "historical limbo," bereft of the prophetic force needed to confront historical processes, and failing to have any repercussions on pastoral theory and practice. Theology must be intent on interpreting the word of God directed to us here and now. It cannot allow itself to be reduced to a search for "orthology"—orthodox formulations.

Zeal for biblical orthodoxy in the Protestant tradition not infrequently conceals conservative political options, and lends ideological reinforcement to the status quo. In the name of an orthodoxy that manufactures security at the price of presence to the difficult, ambiguous depths of history, we hear warnings of the danger of a theology that would speak so much of the poor as to fall into a "horizontalistic reductionism" of the faith.

In my judgment, what is actually happening is just the opposite. Reduction of the faith, and of the theological task, occurs when, despite the cry of the poor, we fail to open our eyes to the "signs of the time," frightened as we are by the novelty of the manifestation of a God who has been revealed in predilection for the poor. Search, from among the poor, is what specifies the method of liberation theology, in the original sense of "method"—a way, a route, to be followed in thinking, ecclesially, a faith that is *lived,* that is experienced. The route to be traveled is projected on the basis of three mediations—three means utilized by liberation theology for the performance of its task in the service of a liberative ecclesial praxis (C. Boff, *Teología*):

1) socio-analytic mediation *(seeing)*
2) hermeneutic mediation *(judging)*
3) praxico-pastoral mediation *(acting).*

Hermeneutic Mediation

I have already made some remarks bearing on socio-analytic mediation above, in the section on the poor (p. 113). Praxico-pastoral mediation will be treated below. Here I touch on hermeneutic mediation, a very sensitive point in the Protestant tradition (Kirk, *Liberation,* 143–308; Padilla, *Teología).*

The point of departure of my evaluation is the question, How are the Bible and the historical reality of the poor to be articulated, interrelated? This articulation is neither self-evident nor is it anything mechanical. It must be submitted to the mediations of historical analysis (the social sciences) and biblical analysis (the biblical sciences), in order to be able to lend a coherent articulation to a theology that will now be capable of elucidating efficaciously the historical reality of the poor in the light of God's word. What is God saying to us (on the faith level) from the historical situation of the poor (from the level of historical, social reality)? And how may one make an illuminating Bible reading from the historical reality of the poor? Can simply any reading of the Bible be used? Or are there ways of reading that are disqualified by the Bible itself as contrary to its principal, basic intention?

It will be impossible to give these questions an exhaustive response here. In themselves they fully justify treatment in separate monographs. In the pages that follow, I address only the task of explaining what these questions presuppose. To my mind, we are in a "second Reformation" today where a reading of the Bible is concerned, in the sense that one must rescue the sovereign liberty of God's word to say, in our historical situation (the *chronological today*), what is authentically liberative (the *kairological today*), in order to correspond to this ever challenging word in a creative, renewed obedience of faith.

First, a preliminary word on the "hermeneutic circle." The analogy of a circle with reference to the hermeneutics of liberation theology may give the impression that we are dealing with something in which all points have an equal value. But God's word (always normative) and our situation are *not* identical realities, however it may be that the word of God has never been spoken on the margin of a historical situation—however it may be that God's *logos* has become history. We must have neither word without history (religious reductionism) nor history without the word (historicist reductionism). An old principle of biblical hermeneutics has it that "a text without reference to context becomes pretext." Here, then, the biblical text read without reference to the historical situation becomes ideology. My own terminological preference is for "hermeneutic circulation" (Casalis, *Ideas,* 61–66), and I distinguish the following interconnected and mutually fecundating phases in this simultaneous circulation: (a) from the situation of the poor to the word of God, and (b) from the word of God to the situation of the poor. That is, hermeneutic circulation moves simultaneously from history to faith, and from faith to history.

The foregoing brings us to the following explanation, which proceeds (1) from the social location of the Bible reader to (2) the level of a praxis-in-obedience by way of (3) a discernment of ecclesial practice in the reading of the Bible—critical discernment of the questions arising from a given situation, and historico-salvific discernment of this same situation.

Social Placement of the Reader

From what vantage do we read the Bible? What is our basic option? Do we begin with an option for the poor? Our interpretation of the Bible must be examined with respect to the praxis from which it originates, the praxis from which our reflecting is done.

A reading of the Bible that fails to keep account of these conditions, yet laying claim to being an objectively biblical, scientific reading in faith, will sooner or later, in virtue of its methodological and epistemological naivety, be reabsorbed by the more profound mechanisms of oppression. Instead of discovering what the word of God actually says with respect to a given situation, it will be the unconscious mouthpiece of the experiences and ideas of the dominant classes and groups. There is ever wider agreement that all alleged "impartiality" is a sign of conscious or unconscious partiality in the very point of departure.

Critico-liberative Reading of the Bible

To what extent has one failed to read the great biblical theme of poverty? Does the manner in which we have read that theme end, without conscious intent, in a legitimation of the situation of the poor, which calls precisely for transformation?

With reference to my theo-logical theme, what is the authentic image of God presented to us in the Bible? Is it that of a God of resignation, or that of a liberating God who loves justice?

Discernment of the Questions of the Present

A liberative reading of the Bible—that is, a reading more interested in *being liberative* (more interested in method) than in *speaking of liberation* (theme)— is a reading with a decisive *fulcrum* in the form of questions arising from the present, which supposes a church community of great sensitivity to the most significant challenges of history, and always attentive to the signs of the times.

Every age has its own questions and problems, and reads and rereads scripture from a point of departure in these problems. The theo-logical vision of the theology of liberation has invited attention to *certain biblical perspectives* as better corresponding to our specific situation. From its inception, then, liberation theology has centered on certain points that have proved particularly illuminating: the identification of Christ with the poor (Matthew 25), the exodus/liberation theme, the unity of history (creation, salvation, and the eschatological promises), faith acting by love, Jesus' option for the outcasts of his time, the conflictual sense of Jesus' liberating messianic practice, and the proclamation of the reign of God.

Historico-salvific Discernment of the Historical
and Social Situation of the Poor

In light of the history of the foundational and generative facts of faith and its basic paradigms—life, justice, sin, idolatry, fellowship, reconciliation, salvation—we "judge," we "interpret" the situation, the historical reality, of the poor. Does this reality evince the acceptance of God's liberative plan (*mysterium liberationis*), or the negation of God's will (*mysterium iniquitatis*)? We move from faith to history, and from history to faith.

Enlightened by the word received in faith, we experience, in a first moment, "ethico-prophetical indignation" at the harsh reality of the poor. "This situation is a negation, a refusal, of God's will!" we cry. God's creation is threatened and eviscerated. For the Bible, the situation of spoliation and oppression in which the poor find themselves is a situation of sin (Gutiérrez, *A Theology*, 291–96).

Praxis-in-Obedience

Our reading of the Bible and the demanding mediation of the "hermeneutic bridge" is not situated so much on the cognitive level, the level of comprehension and interpretation, as it is on the level of the praxis and obedience of *faith*, which, "informed" by love (which is a practice, not a theory), *becomes* real faith. It is a matter of reading the Bible in such a way that, by the inspiring power of the Spirit, it becomes the wellspring of God's living, effective word. This word moves us, at the heart of a conflictual history, in the direction of a praxis that will further the justice of the kingdom. From a status of solidarity with the poor, we have rediscovered the liberative message of the Bible with respect to the oppressions of our time. The Bible guides us to an in-depth perception of the situation of the poor, and helps us to situate ourselves fully within conflictual reality in a practice of solidarity-in-assistance (on the level of acting).

From the Ecclesial Tradition of the Poor

Is the methodological novelty of Latin American liberation theology in contempt of ecclesial and theological tradition? Certainly not.

1) The theology of liberation is not so naive as to think that it stands at the beginning of church history, and so to deny or ignore the value of so many centuries of history and theological reflection. It is impossible to articulate a liberative theological discourse without confronting the theological awareness of the Christian community past and present.

2) The theology of liberation has no pretensions to an exclusive message, or to its own private revelation, the earmark of sectarianism. In my judgment, liberation theology, on this level, moves in a dialectic involving the tension between the "relevance" and "identity" proper to every risk and commitment in Christian history. Fully aware of belonging to Christian history—conscious of its continuity, its *identity*—it takes up the challenge of the historical situation of the poor today—the challenge of *relevance*. It lives an ecclesial commitment

that sinks its roots deep in the Christian identity, and then goes in quest of a further identity that will give it the power and ability for historical commitment and involvement. Christian identity is not something to be safeguarded. It is a matter of quest. The proper note of the Christian is not on the order of "distinction and separation from" something, but of "identification with" something.

3) The theology of liberation takes up the fertile tradition of the church in order to reread it from the outlook of the *poor.*[12] Its purpose and intent is to concretize that tradition in a novel fashion. The point of continuity with church tradition is given to it precisely in the outlook of the poor. From solidarity with the poor, the great prophetic church tradition of acceptance of and service to the poor, in attentiveness to their cries and hopes, is resituated and reassumed today. For liberation theology, following the path of this history is mandated by its own historical continuity (Gutiérrez, *Power,* 43–44).

Liberation theology embraces tradition in a tension of continuity—and—discontinuity (breach). Hence it is under the necessity of marking ruptures and establishing limits. "Third world" reality, not out of any eagerness for "originality" on the part of liberation theology, but from a necessity imposed by the search for meaning vis-à-vis the challenge of the poor, demands breach and differentiation.

It demands *breach* with a static theological tradition—with a kind of universal, abstract, frequently idealistic, *theologia perennis,* which claims to take its point of departure in "principles" or "values" and always to move along a horizon of theological totalization, without any reference to, openness to, or honesty about the real, without honesty about the queries and question marks of history.

It demands *differentiation* from other currents of contemporary theology, by reason of its distinct historical matrix and distinct theological interlocutor. We have grown clearly aware that the so-called "univocal universality" of "theology" (instead of "a" theology) has been nothing more than the particularity of the European experience of Christian faith (Dussel, *Desintegración,* 191). Today, thanks to the contribution of the social sciences, we know that theology, like all thought, is bound to social processes—that it belongs to a "historical bloc," according to Gustavo Gutiérrez, borrowing the classic expression of Antonio Gramsci (Gutiérrez, *Power,* 213).

Hence the differences established and the limits underscored by liberation theology. The theology "of the center," it has lent great thrust to personal spirituality and missionary expansion, is found wanting in the face of the urgencies of the "third world." Accordingly, in Christian communities committed to the liberation processes, a discourse on the faith is being developed that proceeds from these communities' own historical and ecclesial experience. This is one of their ways of "giving an account of their hope" in the liberator God, from the underside of history. For the first time in many centuries, an effort of reflection on the faith is arising outside the classic centers of theological elaboration. We have discovered our own ecclesial and theological identity, for we have discovered the basic fact of our dependence and domination.

The Latin American theology of liberation is not a priori anti-European or pro-"third-world," thus stated abstractly and generically. It is a theology of liberation, which is closer to those Europeans who are struggling, in solidarity, for liberation, than to those Latin Americans who are struggling to maintain dependence and domination in our great homeland, Latin America (Richard, *Iglesia,* 18–19).

THE MYSTERY OF GOD

The Poor as Theo-phanic Locus

In the irruption of the poor, the church is experiencing a profound challenge. What is at stake is something more radical than a challenge coming from more than one direction, or a more accurate perception of the harsh reality of the poor. The church is experiencing the judgment of God's word bursting in on the liberative history of the poor. Never before had we so clearly heard the word of God as when it came to our ears through the piercing cry of the poor, in a "real epiphany of God's word" (Dussel, "Dominación," 346–47). This is a time of grace and ecclesial conversion, an inexhaustible wellspring of new spiritual experience: a spirituality of solidarity with the poor. For at the basis of the theology of liberation lies a spiritual experience: the encounter with the Lord in the poor and oppressed along the pathways of Latin America. The poor, as "nonpersons," as the humiliated and crucified of history, but in the power of their struggle and unshakable hope, are a *locus of God*—a privileged, a special theo-phanic "place."

What does this imply for the theo-logical vision of liberation theology? What does it mean to have the poor as locus of the revelation of Mystery? It seems to me that the key to the answer is : If, for a Christian, history is a mediation of God's revelation, then God's revelation in history wins a specific and scandalous concretion in the poor of the earth.

Mystery has come to the little ones of this world, and now resides in them. God is on the side of the losers, on the side of the debased of history, those whom history has brought low. God overturns the human ideas of God as power, grandeur, and domination. *Dios siempre Mayor* has taken the initiative in becoming incredibly little in the lowly.

Liberation theology, consequently, insists that theo-logical knowledge of God is more dialectical than analogical, and depends on the theo-phanic value of a liberative and loving praxis starting with the poor, in whom God is hidden. Thus we have an *analogia agentis*[13] rather than an *analogia entis.*

Paradoxically, it is in the situation of the poor as antihistory, as situation of sin and antilife, that we must seek the locus of the revelation of Mystery in history, which Mystery, of course, will not appear in continuity with, but in *contradiction and contrast* with, this situation of misery.

As locus of God, the poor reveal God to us by the *via negativa,* inasmuch as their situation is contrary to God's will. Theo-logically, the poverty of the "third world" means that God's creation is *threatened,* that God's primordial plan for human beings is being *perverted.* The daily poverty of two-thirds of humanity, which puts millions of human beings slowly but surely to death, represents the *vitiation* of God's creation (Sobrino, "Esperanza," 114-15).

The poor, as locus of God, reveal God to us *positively* inasmuch as God assumes this threatened, vitiated history, and is present in its midst on the side of the poor, in order to re-create life and open up a future of hope (hope in the kingdom) from the negativity of history—from the negativity of injustice, sin, and oppression.

Theo-phanic Value of Praxis from a Point of Departure in the Poor

The "third world"—in its formal quality as a world of the poor—reveals God by way of furnishing the special place of access to God that is to be found in the world of the poor, and by way of requiring access to God through the effort to liberate the oppressed, in whom God is present. Again we have the *analogia agentis.*

With this as my starting point, I turn to three pairs of disjunctive alternatives:

Messianism or the Evangelizing Potential of the Poor?

God's option for and identification with the poor is not based on any merit or virtue in the poor. To hold the contrary would be to sacralize the poor. God seeks the sacralization neither of the poor nor of poverty. What is at stake is the manifestation of the radical gratuity of God's transcendent, universal love, historicized efficaciously when God seeks the little and lost of this world, and turns to the poor *because they are poor,* regardless of their moral and personal dispositions. The poor have nothing to offer God in the sense of having any merit, virtue, or other title by which they might solicit God's acceptance of them. The poor of the earth are those whose lives are threatened, who are crucified by history on the cross of poverty, who suffer the violence of an objectively unjust system.

What is at stake is the justice of God's kingdom, God's primordial plan that the poor have life and that the kingdom thus be inaugurated. Accordingly, God identifies with them, and makes their cause God's cause, *polemically.* "The right of the poor is God's right" (Echegaray, *Apurando,* 13-21). This is why we have had to say, in virtue of our faith, that the poor are the locus of God (a theo-phanic locus)—that in them God is present in person.

All believers, then—whatever their socio-economic origin—are given the demand, and receive the gift, of making an option of solidarity for the poor, of living a "passion for God in a passion for the poor" (L. Boff, *Espiritualidad,* 20-24). A twofold relationship is established here. A "passion for God," striving to serve God in a first instance, is transformed into a *diakonia* of the poor, so that now it is they whom one seeks to serve, in a second instance. The poor, in virtue of the harsh reality of being poor, become what Christians call a sacrament, an efficacious sign of the presence of God in history, and thereby evangelize those who at first sought to evangelize the poor. Through their suffering faces, the face of Christ beams anew on the world:

> Commitment to the poor and oppressed and the rise of grassroots communities have helped the Church to discover the evangelizing potential of the poor. For the poor challenge the Church constantly, summoning it to conversion; and many of the poor incarnate in their lives the evangelical values of solidarity, service, simplicity, and openness to accepting the gift of God [Puebla, "Final Document," no. 1147, in Eagleson and Scharper, 265–66].

Analogia Agentis or *Analogia Fidei?*

The absolute primacy accorded in Protestant tradition to faith is well known. The classic example in our own century is the position and attitude of the celebrated Swiss Reformed theologian, Karl Barth.[14] His thesis is that, by reason of the "infinite qualitative difference" between God and the human being, it is radically impossible to discover a way to the knowledge of God from history. There is but one way of knowing God: by revelation. The point of departure here is faith. Hence we may speak of an *analogia fidei*. Human beings can know God not by reason of their own quest, but because God has granted self-revelation.

Barth's position is of undeniable value. The primacy of God's activity in self-revelation to history, freely manifesting God's love, is maintained. The moment of essential gratuity, without which faith simply dissolves, is maintained. God has approached humankind by grace. This is not a human achievement. God's approach to us is not by reason of our merits. However, human merits must be defended against a fideistic reductionism that would limit and impoverish them. The gratuity of God's activity does not mean that the human being is in a state of total passivity. This would entail a contradiction. Were this to be the case, God's self-disclosure to us would be pointless, for we could not offer even a minimal *response* to the proposal of God's word. A classic maxim of theological tradition is apropos here: "God saves us, but not without us." Along the pathways of history, in justice, love, and hope, there is a way open to Mystery. It is not closed beforehand or condemned to failure.

Liberative praxis—as *analogia agentis*—must be recognized and defended as that which makes possible the apparition of the Mystery of God in historical activity. Of course, God, *siempre mayor*, is irreducible to our praxis. Praxis does not automatically lead to God. God is not necessarily at the terminus of human praxis, is not necessarily its culmination, however correct (ortho-praxic) that praxis may be. Still, all ortho-praxis is open to the Mystery of God, tends toward God—for God manifests the divine life, lays it out for us to see, in a commitment of liberation and justice for the poor. "Those who take love and justice for their guide are on the road that leads to you" (de Lubac). A liberative praxis, in the form of efficacious love for the poor, constitutes a sure path to the God of the poor.

Where is the point of departure? In faith, in virtue of an *analogia fidei,* or in liberative praxis, in virtue of an *analogia agentis?* Faith and liberative praxis are not identical. They are distinct moments, with distinct specificities. But they are not thereby contradictory. They do not negate each other. In Jesus, God incarnate, present at the heart of history, the dilemma dissolves. By reason of the fact that God has become a human being and assumed history, the human being and history have assumed sense and meaning, and are open, in their darkness and conflictuality (in a history of oppression and struggle for liberation) to the *Mysterium Liberationis.* Mystery has ceased to be mystery at one point: love. When the threatened lives of the poor are defended, when the truth is told where lies prevail, when love is practiced in the midst of hatred, and those historically deprived of love are loved, when new relationships of fellowship and sharing are created, then "God walks in our own journeying." A liberative praxis, and the moment of faith (grace as contradistinguished from human goodness or merit), both get under way, are set in motion, when they are authentic, when they have the same end: the human being's encounter with the liberator God, and the liberator God's encounter with the human being:

> This is the basic circle of all hermeneutics: from the human being to God and from God to the human being, from history to faith and from faith to history, from love of our brothers and sisters to the love of the Father and from the love of the Father to the love of our brothers and sisters, from human justice to God's holiness and from God's holiness to human justice, from the poor person to God and from God to the poor person [Gutiérrez, *Power,* 15].

Atheistic Knowledge of God or Theistic Ignorance of the Human Being?

The emphasis that liberation theology gives to the indissoluble bonding between the praxis of justice and the knowledge of God—part and parcel of the prophetic tradition—has been criticized for its alleged implication that there could therefore be an "atheistic knowledge of God" (Bandera, *Iglesia,* 263–65). It seems to me that, at the present moment in the church in Latin America, the real problem lies in precisely the opposite direction—namely, in a *theistic ignorance of the human being*—in the tragic situation in which persons professing themselves to be believers ("theoretical theism") deny God in practice ("practical atheism") by ignoring the cry of the condemned of the earth—or, worse, profess themselves to be believers while actually occasioning these cries by creating relationships of injustice and death. As Gustavo Gutiérrez has put it: "Dominators reveal themselves for what they really are—the 'fool' of the Bible, the atheist, who refuses to believe in the God of deliverance" (*Power,* 98; see also 208–9).

The God of the Poor

Liberation theology begins with the reality of God. It is a "theology of God," if we may use that tautology, developed from a starting point in a situation in which the truth of God has been preserved, has not lost, as it has in heavily secularized milieus, its "contextual obviousness." The classic question of theodicy, like that of an aggressive, protesting atheism—both of which, reasonably indeed, appeal to the fact of the poor—is not the decisive problem for the oppressed, believing peoples of Latin America. But neither do these pilgrim peoples believe in a god who is explanation (plugging the dike) or resignation ("sympathetic comforter"). Instead they believe that "God is hope, God is gladness, God is courage." God appears as a saving, humanizing Good News, giving rise to an active hope and a demanding liberative practice.

Hence, in my judgment, the specificity of the Latin American theology of liberation consists in its elucidation and concretization of the revelation of the Mystery of God as *God of the poor.* It is this concretion-and-profession that is the backbone of liberation theology, its point of convergence and unity. The poor are the key to a grasp of the sense of God's revelation. God is the Father of *all* men and women. But precisely because God is Father of all, the divine self-revelation is that of God of the poor. Here it is crucial to make a careful distinction between the *order of being* (the ontological level) and the *order of knowing* (the epistemological level): the God who *is* the loving Father of all is *made known* as God of the poor.[15]

Between God and the poor there obtains a primordial hermeneutic circulation: from the poor to God and from God to the poor. When one reflects, from the outlook and perspective of the poor, on the "logic" of the mystery of God—on God's historico-salvific manifestation—the mystery of God becomes transparent and omnipresent, throughout the length and breadth of our history (and from top to bottom), a history of struggle for liberation on the side of the poor. And thereby the mystery of God also becomes "omni-absent" in structures of injustice, oppression, and sin.

This is the source of the criterion used in liberation theology to discern whether and where there is, or is not, a manifestation of God in history. We are no longer dealing simply with the polarities of nature and grace, sacred and secular, history and transcendence. We are dealing with the biblical categories of *grace* (history of grace) and *sin* (history of sin). Grace is whatever renders God present, and sets history in motion toward the kingdom (in its eschatological fullness). Sin, by contrast, will be whatever denies and clouds the liberative will of God in history—whatever presents an obstacle to the coming of the fullness of the kingdom, that free gift of the Father, to us today.

With this basic thesis of liberation theology as a starting point, I can go on to identify four theo-logical notes that, in my judgment, at once sustain that theology, explain it, and characterize its vision of the God of the poor.

Revealed in Self-Donation

It is possible to speak of the God of the poor only from a fundamental datum of Christian faith: God has been revealed as God of the poor. This theo-logical truth can be approached only from God's own self-revelation. This statement has at least three implications. (a) It is to God that revelation belongs *essentially*. Taking the initiative, by way of free gift, out of fullness and not out of need, God has engaged in self-revelation. This revelation is self-communication, self-gift, and hence "God's revelation is itself salvation," a salvation offered first as good news for the poor. (b) History is the locus in which the Mystery of God is revealed as God of the poor. It is not within the compass of my interior life, my subjectivity, my individual awareness, and it is not within the compass of pure rationality or nature (it is not purely in the cosmos) that God bestows self-revelation. It is in *history* that we find the specific locus of the *presence* (history of grace and acceptance) or *absence* (history of sin and rejection) of God's revelation. (c) In Jesus of Nazareth—in his life, death, and resurrection—God has been manifested *definitively*. The Mystery of the God of the poor has been historicized and brought radically close to us in Jesus. God's revelation in Jesus is in continuity with Old Testament revelation, but Jesus radicalizes, expands, and fulfills it. As definitive witness of the Father's love and truth, Jesus sets us down at a new beginning.

For Jesus, God's great act is the approach of the kingdom to the poor. God is "the one who approaches in the kingdom" as good news for the poor. In this revelation and historicization of God's nearness, of God's approach, in Jesus, the incarnation as *Kenosis in solidarity with the poor* is basic: this was the life that Jesus—"the rich one who made himself poor" (cf. 2 Cor. 8:9)—took on himself, and thereby revealing to us the Father's love.

Here two brief remarks will be in order. First, it is significant that the Latin American theology of liberation has developed a christology as a "first act," and then used it as a springboard for the development, in a "second act," of its theo-logy. Thus liberation theology participates in the larger theological effort to restore Jesus of Nazareth to his "special place in God's determination" (Duquoc, *Dios,* 33), as against the theo-logical danger of creating an image of God that would be more deistic than trinitarian, closer to the metaphysics of an absolute being than to the God of Jesus of Nazareth.

Secondly, the theology of liberation, in thus propounding God's activity of self-revelation in history, does *not* pretend to be making a theoretical advance toward a new concept of revelation. The question is not one of the possibility of revelation, or whether God has actually engaged in revelation, or whether the human being has the capacity to receive the truth of God. Anchored as it is in the Judeo-Christian tradition, liberation theology applies itself to an *explana-*

tion and concretion of the locus, the *place,* that is the mediation of revelation. The question is rather, *How* does one approach and correspond to God from the *place* where God has said that God is present? Whoever wishes to know God must seek out the specific locus of God's revelation. What is at stake is a critical corrective of the grave sin against the Spirit. We sin against the Spirit when we discount the possibility of God's having chosen a specific place of revelation, and when we are scandalized that this locus is, in a privileged way, the world of the poor.

"Utterly Other" (Transcendent)

God, in becoming "God of the poor," reveals to us mysteric transcendency. To God belongs the reality of being the Utterly Other, the radically distinct, the Holy and Unmanipulable. At the same time, God has become little, and thereby credible, by nearness to the crucified of history. If God could have "become other" only by ceasing to be what God had always been and is, then God would not be the Absolute, the Mystery irreducible to our way of understanding, to our theology, indeed to our faith itself. From the otherness of the "other"—the poor person—liberation theology professes and defends God's transcendence.

Transcendence here is not the abstract "transcendence" of a "God-beyond," as in the logic of the old dualistic schema: God is "up there" and the human being is "down here." Transcendence here is the term used in the Latin American theology of liberation to denote God's presence in the depths of human history. God has taken solidarity with human beings so seriously as to willingly risk a share in their historical life, with all its poverty and fragility.

Quite correctly, liberation theology has tended to eschew the mediation of a metaphysical tradition that finally converted God into a "conceptual idol," so that in practice it has hidden rather than revealed this passionate God, incapable of conceptual manipulation, this God who "wagers on humanity," and undertakes to re-create life—the life of humankind and the life of nature, at the heart of our history—to the point of taking up suffering, abandonment, and death, in order thence to open up a future of hope that transcends history.

Given its starting point in the discipleship of the God of the poor, liberation theology comes into conflict with any theo-logical view that, in "defense" of God and God's mysteric transcendency, reduces language of and about God to the "spiritual," to the "religious," thought of as a sacred, autonomous, separate sphere floating above conflictual historical processes with their real economic, political, and social dimensions.

When theo-logy is developed in this manner, it emerges as a "transcendent" way of legitimating oppression (Duquoc, *Dios,* 25). Theo-logy disembowelled of the force of its doctrine of the incarnation, and lifted above the compass of the historical and mundane, blithely coexists with an unjust, inhumane and inhuman system of oppression. It finds it possible, without criticism, to welcome to the categories of filiation and fellowship—as sons and daughters of

God, and sisters and brothers of one another—persons who find themselves in a social dynamic of conflict generated by the contradictory, inhumane "logic" of the antikingdom of discrimination, violence, and death that is the prevailing system of transnational capitalism.

The Latin American theology of liberation does not deny the transcendent, gratuitous nature of faith in God. Faith in the God of the poor is not an ideological superstructure. What this theology denies is the falsified transcendent, religious, sacred legitimation of an inhuman, irrational practice of oppression, which is essentially atheistic, in that it denies and negates life and the utopia of the kingdom.

The fact that God has irreversibly assumed history is no reason for us to sidestep history. We need not resort to false dualisms in order to approach and know God. God's transcendence, far from referring us to abstract, ahistorical realities, refers us to, turns us in the direction of, the ultimate horizon of life, justice, love, and truth. The absolute mystery of the God of the poor, as Mystery, makes it possible for history to give ever more of itself, for human life to become truly worthy of the human being.

Liberator

A liberative theo-logical discourse rests upon and is sustained by the axis of the *Mysterium Liberationis*. God has sundered, once and for all, the symmetry of "possible salvation or possible reprobation." God is salvation. The "understanding" of Mystery can eventually be given conceptual and doctrinal formulation. Faith seeks to understand. But that understanding will have to maintain permanent roots in the mystery of salvation in history, whose "recapitulation" is ever and ineluctably Jesus of Nazareth. Only from him, only from this vantage, will a theologian be able to advance in the understanding of the trinitarian structure of our salvation and the trinitarian reality of the liberator God of the poor.

As the first councils of the early church affirm, God is Father, Son, and Spirit: God engages in liberative self-donation as Father, by the Word of the Son, in the power of the Spirit, down the pathways of history. This is "the way God is," and this is the way that the salvation and life that come from God are manifested in history, so that it becomes possible to engage in a strictly theological consideration of history. God has not willed to remain eternally "the selfsame," eternally shut up in the unfathomable mystery of the immanent relationships of love, relationships *ad intra*. God engages in self-bestowal, in order to be with the history of humankind, from creation and covenant onward, in the definitive nearness of the incarnation of the Son and the assumption of history by the Spirit. History is the history of God. God is in us, and we are in God.

Liberation theology, without pretension to speculative comprehension, holds what Rahner calls the "basic axiom" of the Christian faith: the total unity/identity of the "immanent" Trinity and the "economic" Trinity, the

Trinity of the economy of Salvation. *As God is, so God is self-revealed.*[16]

The God who is revealed in history as the god of the poor is the one and only God. There is no other. There is no God-*in-se* different from, separate from, apart from God's self-manifestation in salvific praxis. To God-*in-se* belongs the mystery of being God-with-us, Emmanuel. The reality of that "with us," in the last analysis, is God revealing for our benefit what is expressed in the essence of God's reality: to-be-love, liberator, lifegiver.

In order to speak of God "liberatively," that God may come to be and continue to be a liberator, we must always take our point of departure in God's self-manifestation in salvific praxis. Only from this starting point does it become reasonable to dare to speak of the reality of a God-*in-se* considered as communion-and-love, now no longer as point of departure but as point of arrival. The trinitarian reality of God, what the reality of Mystery contains "forever and from all eternity, of the 'other' with respect to oneself," is not some incomprehensible, useless mathematical curiosity (Sobrino, "Abordar," 2). God is not mystery-for-speculation. God is mystery-of-salvation, and this is why salvation has a trinitarian dimension.

A Crucified God

Faith in the God of the poor is profoundly dialectical. To believe in the God of the poor is to maintain faith in a God who is at once deliverer and crucified. On the cross of Jesus the radical nearness of God acquires its dimension of greatest credibility and its dimension of unmitigated "scandal." On the cross God delivers up the Son, and God is crucified. Here, it seems to me, there are three elements to be identified:

1) The cross expresses and concretizes the authentic *loving solidarity of the God of the poor with humankind.* Because God was crucified in Jesus, there is no historically crucified people—despised racial minority, marginalized culture, or oppressed people—to whom God is indifferent. God co-suffers with their degradation and antilife.

2) The cross expresses and concretizes *God's rejection of unjust suffering.* On the cross God takes on the pain and sorrow of the history of sin, thereupon, from within that history, to open it out on a totally different future: life for humankind, hope for the crucified. In Latin America the cross has been seen as a symbol of suffering, but God has not called the poor of the earth to suffering, to become the suffering servant of Yahweh. This people of poverty, "a people historically crucified," is crucified *against* its will and the will of God. It is the sin of the world that continues to despoil it of everything and, especially, to snatch away its life. The cross expresses God's no to suffering and oppression. The primordial will of the God of life finds in the cross its ultimate consequences. The reality of salvation passes by way of historical condemnation. As Jon Sobrino has said so powerfully, God has submitted to the power of the negative—of evil, injustice, oppression, sin, and death. The promised salvation is not actualized miraculously from outside history, but from within the

greatest negativity of history, from its deepest "depths of iniquity."

3) The cross invites us to *share with God*, in loving, liberating solidarity with the world and history. In history the cries of Egypt's oppressed continue to echo. We hear Jesus' cry on the cross. The whole of creation is groaning until now, suffering the birth-pangs of the liberation it hopes for. From the cross, with a compelling demand for fidelity to the real, we are invited to "abide with God in passion *with* and *for* the poor," in unconditional solidarity with "the condemned of the earth." Life, ever menaced by the powers and structures of antilife, and hope, frequently against all hope, must be maintained through signs and deeds of struggle. This is the concrete way to believe in the life and hope that spring from the cross.

By way of concluding this section on the Mystery of God, I have two further observations to make.

1) The theological vision of liberation theology is set forth in *"historico-economic" language* rather than in *"ontologico-immanent" language*. The Latin American theology of liberation does not engage in an essentialistic discussion of the nature or being of God *in se*. Its point of departure contains no primary reference to the classic dogmatic formulations concerning the Mystery—although neither does it have the slightest interest in ignoring or denying them.

The theology of liberation is a *narrative* reflection—that is, a recital with a starting point in God's revelation from within concrete activity. God loves, suffers, delivers, gives life, establishes the kingdom. Liberation theology is more nearly akin to the tradition of biblical thought, as a "confessional narration" of the redemptive deeds of God in history, than to the Western tradition of "onto-theo-logy" (Pikaza, "Trinidad").

Its language about God moves ever within the compass of a *dual* affirmation: of God and the poor, God and history, God and liberation, God and life, God and the kingdom. Liberation theology insists upon its right to integrate into its theo-logical discourse the outlook of the poor, the conflictuality of history, the aspirations of a people for liberation, the struggle for life. It is less interested in theoretical novelty than in the obligatory concretion of its language. No theo-logy can prescind from this responsibility and this risk. No theo-logical language may neglect this "conjunctive way" if it is to have any pretension to fidelity to God's manifestation. It is impossible to engage in a reflective discourse upon God's activity in history by alluding simply to God, and not to history.

When it is asserted, in the Spirit, that "the history of humankind is God's history, and God's history is the history of humankind,"—or that "God is in us and we are in God"—or, as the fathers of the ancient church had it, that God is "Father," "Son," and "ourselves"—we are asserting that all the complexity of history, in its *negativity* (as history of sin, a historical condemnation) and its *positivity* (as history of grace, of salvation), is also the complexity of God's experience. This is how we assert that God is the God of history—that God assumes history, although without being "diluted" by history. History is an open road to the experience of God, and historical experience lived from the concretion of love and hope is mediation for the experience of God.

2) *God continues to speak.* In rescuing the specificity of the Judeo-Christian tradition—history as theo-phanic locus—liberation theology is underscoring something of importance: that *God continues to speak a new word in history.*

The theology of liberation has written no grand tractates on God. But it has done something more important. It has let God be God, "has left God at liberty" (Duquoc) to speak a word of judgment upon us, without placing any prior limits, without presupposing that we already possess God's word. The basic activity of the Spirit in history is to generate the living word historically, by referring its hearers again and again to the original Word, Jesus Christ.

These assertions of liberation theology pose a serious problem for the various types of biblical fundamentalism that we observe at work in Latin America (Ramm, *Fundamentalismo,* 60–61; Dillenberger and Welch, *Cristianismo,* 212). Fundamentalism holds that, in the history of the foundational, generative deeds of the faith, the "germinal events" of the faith—the deeds of God in Israel (in the Old Testament), the birth, life, death, and resurrection of Jesus and the history of the apostolic community up to the year 100 (in the New Testament)—the word of God in history has been spoken adequately once and for all. Although history continues open to the future and the Parousia, it mediates nothing important for God's word, which has already been spoken, and has been recorded in the Bible. The poor, the processes of liberation, constitute a great silence. They are not a "theo-logical locus," a challenge, a "sign of the times." The category of "application" —central to fundamentalism—implies that the *only* thing that we can do is to attempt to apply the Old and New Testaments (their situations and their texts) to the historical situation in Latin America (as if the biblical word were a sort of *logos asarkos,* a "word without flesh"). We hear of a reading of the Bible *for* rather than *from* Latin America.

Things are not that simple. I think that it will be apropos at this point to underscore the importance of acknowledging and maintaining the central place of the Bible in continuity-and-discernment with the word that God today continues to speak (the "signs of the times") *from* and *in* our situation, by the Spirit present in history. There is no *word* of God without its historical context.

Here I make my own a statement of Jon Sobrino pointing in this same direction. With a view to its better comprehension, I divide it into three moments:

[1] As Christians we must profess that God is self-revealed in Jesus of Nazareth, that God is revealed after the fashion of Son—that the definitive filiation and fundamental structure of correspondence to the Father has been revealed. This is inalienable, and without it faith, as "Christian," is deprived of its logical and historical sense.

[2] But on the other hand it is equally evident that the three years of

Jesus' public life fail to exhaust the possibilities and modalities of history. Therefore we have asserted that in Jesus has been revealed the basic structure of correspondence to the Father, of how to hear and respond to God's word. But obviously, we cannot find in Jesus *all* the concrete ways to respond to God's word, precisely because God is Lord of all history. God is a God of history.

[3] The first Christians had the same conviction. And therefore, in conjunction with faith in Jesus as Son of God, they believed in the Spirit of God, Lord and Lifegiver, who continues to be present in history ["Dios," 116].

Elsewhere Sobrino underscores the importance of the historical element in the role of pneumatology for the Latin American theology of liberation:

Arguing a priori, if pneumatology has any role to play in the real life of the Church, if we accept that the Spirit of God continually acts in history and in the Church, then we should not be surprised by the idea that we are to search continually for the manifestation of God in our times. Nor should it surprise us that the manifestation will take on new forms during new times. To deny this would be to deny the action of God's Spirit; it would be to deny the "greater" being of God, of which the New Testament and tradition tell us. It would be to deny the first and most orthodox of all truths about God: the trinitarian being. To be frightened of new forms in theology is to be frightened of God [*True Church,* 3; see also Avila, *Teología,* 169–211].

Liberation theology will insist that, because God is the God of history, docility to the Spirit is more necessary today than ever before. One must allow the Spirit to breathe where the Spirit wills, one must recognize the signs of the times, whether they occur within or without the church, one must take history in its devolution, change, and novelty, without any attempt (pneumatologically illegitimate) to set limits of space or time to God's ongoing manifestation. God continues to speak a word in history, in depth and novelty. "Let those who have ears to hear, hear" what the Spirit says from history.

THEO-PRAXIS AND ECCLESIOLOGY

In this matter of the idea of God, one's way of living is more important than one's manner of expression [William of Saint-Thiérry, *Aenigma Fidei,* PL 180:398, cited in Segundo, *Neustra idea, 12*].

The theology of liberation—not out of any depreciation of the noetic aspect of religion, however—respects, the profound meaning of this statement. It is basically not a question of demonstrating an intellectual understanding of *Dios siempre Mayor.* What is basic is not a noetic elucidation of the true essence of

God by way of an "orthology," but an experience of the reality of God in the task of inaugurating the kingdom. It is a matter of being introduced into, and living, the very life of God, in a "praxis according to God." Gustavo Gutiérrez calls it, provocatively, "practicing God" (*Dios,* 6).

Jon Sobrino is altogether on the mark with his "primordial circulation" between God's revelation and "realized faith" ("Abordar," 4). The way to respond to God is to correspond to the reality of God—to live out in history what is expressed in God's essence. The "practice of God" is, on the one hand, a *historical* practice, and on the other, a *communitarian* practice. God's revelation always creates a community, a people. Theo-praxis, as response to God, entails a demanding ecclesial concretion.

Theo-praxis: A Way of Corresponding to God

From its first formulations, the Latin American theology of liberation has insisted in marking a breach with every kind of idealism, any ahistorical, purely theoretical cognition (Gutiérrez, *Power,* 58–60). Hence the central place it accords the biblical perspective, for which knowing does not have a purely intellectual sense, but an active, participatory sense.

Praxis is integral to the very concept of faith—and not merely as the result and expression of faith, but as a *dimension of faith itself.* Believing praxis is faith—faith acting in concrete deeds of love and hope. Now, if faith thus implies praxis as something intrinsic to itself, then theo-logy cannot be limited to the *cognitive* dimension of faith. It will have to keep account of its *theo-praxic* dimension, as well. Faith, as re-sponse to the pro-posal of the God who delivers us, is total surrender (in one's knowing and deciding and acting). To believe in God is to act in a concrete manner in a praxis according to God— theo-praxis. Faith in God acquires texture and consistency in concrete deeds, and thereby transcends simple affirmation and verbal profession.

For the Old Testament prophets, "knowledge of God" and "practice of justice" are indivisible. In the Synoptics and St. John, faith entails the following of Jesus. For St. Paul, the faith by which a human being receives the gift of justification is operative only in love. The Letter of James takes all this up and formulates it as a dynamic interrelationship between faith and the works of faith: "Faith without works is as dead as a body without breath" (Jas. 2:26). The First Letter of John asserts, profoundly, that only they know God-who-is-Love who love their brothers and sisters. Works are acts of love, not good argumentation!

A "praxis in view of the justice of the kingdom as the correct way to correspond to God" is, in my judgment, an adequate translation, with all the appropriate biblical and ecumenical depth, of the relationship between faith and works. It safeguards, historically and dialectically, the two poles of tension—faith and works—constitutive of the only correct response to God's absolutely gratuitous salvific manifestation. A response to the God of the kingdom will be given neither in faith alone (without works) nor in works alone, but in the *totality of Christian existence.* Faith is the free gift of the Father, but the practice of justice, as praxis of love, prevents that gift from degenerating into "cheap grace." The character of faith in the mystery of God as grace does not appear in all its fullness, does not appear adequately, in the first step of faith. It comes to light only "when faith is sustained at the historical level throughout the process of joining God in the shaping of history" (Sobrino, *True Church,* 61). The just will live by a faith that acts by love. Paul and James are inseparable here, and "what God has joined together, let no human being sunder."

Theo-praxis in Solidarity with the Poor

> In recent years it has seemed more and more clear to many Christians that, if the church wishes to be faithful to the God of Jesus Christ, it must become aware of itself *from underneath,* from among the poor of this world, the exploited classes, despised ethnic groups, and marginalized cultures. It must descend into the hell of this world, into communion with the misery, injustice, struggles, and hopes of the wretched of the earth— for "of such is the kingdom of heaven." At bottom it is a matter of living, as church, what the majority of its own members live every day. *To be born, to be reborn, as church,* from below, from among them, today means to die, in a concrete history of oppression and complicity with oppression [Gutiérrez, *Power,* 211; emphasis added].

The community of Jesus' disciples is the locus whence is proclaimed and celebrated faith in the Mystery of a God who bursts into history with the power of a kingdom that judges the world and even the church. From within the activity of hearing, accepting, and serving the poor, the church proclaims the good news of the God of the poor. Without a church that experiences, proclaims, and celebrates the Mystery of God's presence in the lowly, the oppressed, the good news runs the risk of being lost in the oblivion of a world of injustice.

*Deed (*Diakonia*)-and-Word (*Kerygma*)*

From the underside of history, Dietrich Bonhoeffer's pastoral question— How is one to speak of God in a world come of age?—becomes, instead: How is one to tell the nonperson, the pauper, the beggar, that God is liberator, that God has become radically close to the crucified of history?

The response of liberation theology lies along a twin axis: (a) we can proclaim the liberator God of the poor only with concrete deeds and (b) only from deed is the proclamation of the liberator God *by word* understood. The word will emerge from the deed, and the deed from the word. Jesus of Nazareth—heart and soul of the gospel message—is the *Verbum caro factum,* the Word become deed. The conclusion is clear: the proclamation must take flesh in history, must "become history," coming down to those who dwell in the "cellars of history."

Once more, liberation theology is seen to be radically dialectical. It maintains, in terms of deed-and-word, the centrality-and-oneness of the New Testament service-and-proclamation *(diakonia-*and-*kerygma)* bipolarity. Without the deed—of hearing, accepting, and serving the poor—proclamation by the word is empty, it floats in weightlessness. Deed has historical consistency and force in itself, because what basically counts is deed, whereas, of course, word expresses deed and completes it. "To speak out a lived experience, to speak out about a deed, leads one to live it and perform it more consciously and more profoundly" (Gutiérrez, *Power,* 17). By contrast, when the church fails to live the word it proclaims, it will end by proclaiming by word the kind of life it lives. Solidarity with the poor is the touchstone of the authenticity and credibility of the proclamation of the Christian God. In a society marked by injustice, solidarity with the poor constitutes the *terra firma* from which one may speak of a God who has drawn near to the lowly.

Theo-Centric Ecclesiology: Toward a Liberative Ecclesiology

Proclaimed out of deeds in solidarity with the poor, the gospel has a distinct manner of "calling together *in ecclesia."* In the poor of the earth the church has beheld the face of God. Those who have been the witnesses of these apparitions cannot but shape a liberative form of being-church, a form centered on the reign of God. Long has the church succumbed to the temptation of ecclesiocentrism. It has sought to build itself *from within,* with a view to its increase and preservation in the world. This is the mentality of christendom.[17] A more recent outlook, that of the Second Vatican Council, has moved the church to "think itself from without," from the world—a hostile, unbelieving world, a world of technology, liberalism, and Marxism. From the historical situation of the "third world," the church has more clearly understood its call, in fidelity to the God proclaimed by Jesus, and by the power of the Spirit, to be reborn *from below,* from among the poor—the exploited and oppressed classes.

The base church communities, or popular Christian communities, are like a "trial kingdom," where the world should be able to see "the people, the land, and the blessing" that God desires for all humankind. In this "descent," this *ecclesial kenosis,* the church is gradually rediscovering its own identity and mission as sacrament of the reign of God in history (Ellacuría, "Iglesia," 707–22). Now it will proclaim, in deeds of life, love, and hope, the reign of God proclaimed and inaugurated by Jesus. Now its ecclesiological vision will be *theo*-centric.

Levels of Ecclesial Praxis

Church praxis from a point of departure in solidarity with the poor is a loving praxis. At bottom, it is a matter of historically concretizing that original theo-logical "word," "Love one another," in order that God's love—whose measure is measurelessness—may dwell among us and win credibility. "Only by an unconditional solidarity with the condemned of the earth can we venture to speak of the love of God in our regard" (Rahner, *Sacramentum,* I, 125).

The faith community is called to a praxis of hearing, accepting, and serving the poor as the expression of its genuine meaning and purpose. Let us briefly sketch these dimensions or levels:

1) *To hear the poor* is to listen to their challenging word revealing to us the inhumanity of their misery and oppression, and the power of their hope and their yearning for liberation.

2) *To accept the poor* is to accept those "not invited to the banquet," in their value, in their dignity as human persons, and in their word, as locus of the presence of God in history.

3) *To serve the poor* is to "go directly to the people," in concrete deeds of efficacious love. That is, it is to assist efficaciously in the liberation of the poor. The poverty of the poor is not a call to a generous relief action, but a demand for the transformation of their situation. Generous relief actions help the poor, but fail to promote their own liberative capacities as active subjects of the process of transformation of their situation. Who experiences and suffers the consequences of oppression more intensely than the poor themselves? Who, then, is better prepared to grasp the urgency of liberation?

Listening to the poor, and the deed of accepting them, moves to action—to a practice-in-solidarity of help. The Christian faith asserts the impossibility of loving God directly. Love of God *must* be mediated by a historical love of neighbor. And the poor are neighbors par excellence, who move one to draw near to them (by listening to them, accepting them, and helping them).

Up to this point, everyone may be in agreement. Complications arise when we pose the question of the concrete mediations of our loving praxis in history.[18] Christian love of neighbor does *not* contain within itself the criteria of its historical realization. Further: the church, in virtue of its location in history, is shot through with social conflictuality (Gutiérrez, *A Theology,* 272–79; Sobrino, *True Church,* 194–227). It is impossible to ignore the serious differences of opinion and practice prevailing in the church in this matter. And it is here that the Latin American theology of liberation has proposed its interpretation of the church contributions to the life, hope, and liberation of the poor of Latin America. This interpretation is neither exclusive nor isolated, but it seems to me to be rooted in the gospel, and in the best ecclesial tradition of the defense of the poor (Leuridan, *Justicia;* Codina, *Renacer,* 57–87).

If it is true that, in this world and our history, *there is only one way of being with Jesus,* and that way is to opt for those for whom God, unconditionally and passionately, has opted, to place oneself on their side forever—it is nevertheless also true that, in the discipleship of Jesus along this path of incarnation in the world of the poor, in defense of their imperiled lives, it does not fall to the church to guide and direct history. The place of the church is not on the front-lines of the liberation processes. It creates no political parties, no popular organizations, and does not come out in favor of a party line (Míguez

Bonino, "Nuestra fe," 8–9). What, then, can we and should we do? From an incarnation in the world of the poor (from the "underside" of history), the church has a mission of *active defense of the right to life of the poor.*

Negative Moment *(via negativa)* of Denunciation and Exposé

This is the moment of a special kind of "whistle-blowing," the moment of a prophetic denunciation of the oppressive and repressive *structures* that, slowly or violently, deprive the poor masses of life—the moment of an exposé of the historical *causes* of oppression (made possible by a socio-analytic discernment of the mechanisms at the root of the historical and social situation). From an ecclesial viewpoint, the situation of the poor cannot be allowed to remain at the level of uninformed opinion. The presumed impossibility of a scientific under-standing, through a serious historical, structural analysis, of at least the more determinative aspects of the misery of the reality of the poor, represents at the present time one of the more effective ideological mechanisms called into play by the system of domination. It is an abiding paradox that many of our churches, which proclaim "the future" with such insistency, and hold with such certitude to the "last things," refuse to accord even a minimal degree of certitude to any understanding of the historical situation of daily domination to which most Latin Americans are subjected.

This moment of Christian denunciation entails the denunciation of an abstract spiritualization of poverty, and the rehabilitation of the biblical con-cept of the poor as the defenseless victims of the mechanisms of oppression (Tamez, *Bible)*. At the same time it will be important to attend to—to judge, to discern—the distorted images of the God of the poor, images caught up in the dominant ideology, that render theo-logy a "religious superstructure" func-tioning for the preservation and sacralization of unjust economic structures responsible for the antilife of the poor. In Latin America there is a greater danger than unbelief: that of the historical heresy of tailoring the liberating message of the gospel to the measure of the interests of the powerful and their practices of domination. We may cite Atahualpa Yupanqui's lyric poem, "Preguntitas sobre Dios"—"little questions about God." It is harsh, but it will help purify our faith. In its conclusion, we read:

> A God watching over the poor?
> Maybe and maybe not.
> But one thing's for sure:
> God's out to lunch
> with the boss today.

Hence, precisely, our positive evaluation of a peculiar type of atheism—one opposed not to the world of believers, but to the dominant world and its idols of oppression—an anti-idolatry atheism, then. When God is transformed into the guardian of the established order—or better, the established disorder—

"atheism" becomes a necessary condition of faith as practiced in the struggle for justice and the transformation of history. Evangelization, as proclamation of the true God, is an anti-idolatry task. The church encounters the God of life, the God of the poor, by facing up to the false divinities of death, the idols of oppression.

Positive Moment *(via positiva)* of Affirmation, Accompaniment, Proclamation, and Celebration[19]

Here we go directly to the poor, in active defense of their sober hope—"to live!"—and thereby confessing that the church really does believe in the God of life. The defense of the poor means:

1) *Being the voice of the voiceless.* The defense of the poor calls for the assertion of the truth of their reality, the justice of their silenced yearnings and struggles. It is from here that the church proclaims the God of the poor, proclaims a God who strikes a covenant with the poor and defends their cause as their vindicator.

2) *Accompanying the poor in their efforts for liberation.* This is the active continuation of the incarnation of the church in the world of the poor. It is not something to be done just once. A concrete incarnation entails readiness for ever new incarnations, in the specificity of each given moment. This accompaniment includes the defense and encouragement of the decision and capacity of the poor to mobilize and organize in the formulation of their own liberative self-projection forward in history.[20]

3) *Imbuing them, as persons and as a people, with the Christian spirit, in their efforts and struggles,* in the conviction that with this spirit the poor give more of themselves. "It means making them aware of their limitations, and criticizing their mistakes and sins, precisely that they may be enhanced as a people" (Sobrino, "Aporte," 126).

4) Contributing, from a starting point in faith, and through the hope of the church itself, to *keeping the active hope of the poor alive* in their most difficult moments. Liberation processes are arduous. They have their moments of "fundamental aporia" (Sobrino, *True Church,* 33–38; see also 59–60). In the midst of pain and suffering, the radical nearness of the liberator God, who is also the crucified God, keeps one from despair. It is the dialectical maintenance of this nearness that fuels the doggedness of hope.

5) *Celebrating life in the depth given it by faith.* This is the praxis of celebration. From a starting point in the deed of solidarity that defends the imperiled life of the poor, the church joyously celebrates the salvific activity of the God of life, and the fullness of life manifested by the liberation (the death and resurrection) of Jesus. The crowning moment of this celebrational ecclesial praxis is the Eucharistic celebration, the Lord's Supper, with its constitutive dialectic of *memorial* (Paschal memorial) and *freedom* (openness to the future) (Gutiérrez, *Power,* 12, 16)—a memorial that is not a fixation on the past, but

the necessary condition for making the past present in view of the future—not a sad, nostalgic recall of bygone times (*in illo tempore . . .*), but the full openness of hope and gladness, in a freedom calculated to create the future.

In the breaking of the bread, the bread that is wanting on the tables of the poor of the earth, the life of the Risen One is rendered present by the power of the Spirit, and acknowledged so to be present. It is a life that re-creates life, a life that assures us that sin, oppression, and death will be ended forever. Celebration and a committed wager on life, far from being opposed, call for and reinforce each other.[21] Nowhere in the church in Latin America is the praxis of celebration lived with greater fervor, intensity, and joy—in the midst of daily suffering and struggle—than in the Christian communities that have taken up a praxis in solidarity with the poor. It is not a matter of naive, escapist merriment, the fruit of a lack of awareness of the daily reality of antilife and suffering experienced by the poor. It is a Paschal joy, a joy by way of pain and death, but expressing its deep trust in the liberating love of the Father, whose last word is life for human beings, hope for the crucified of history.

Ecumenical Dimension of an Ecclesial Praxis in Solidarity with the Poor

An ecumenism from a starting point in a crucified people has two dimensions. First, just as it is true that the poor evangelize the church, it is no less true that the poor show us, and open to us, the road to Christian unity. In a world of exploitation and misery, the gravest division is that created by injustice. From a praxis of love in solidarity, the profession of "one Lord, one faith . . . one God and Father of all" (Eph. 4:5–6) finds a solid basis for an advance toward unity in the enterprise of the proclamation of the kingdom (evangelization), in liturgical celebration, in the work of theology. Hence the ecumenical character of the Latin American theology of liberation. The poor challenge us to fulfill Jesus' last wish "that all may be one" (John 17:21)—that we all, Catholics and Protestants, and on a deeper level all men and women of all races and cultures—come to constitute the people of the daughters and sons of God, a people among whom the relationship with the Father becomes really possible in virtue of the fact that we all become truly brothers and sisters.

Secondly, a practice-in-solidarity of helping the poor demands and promotes Christian solidarity among the churches. To defend the poor is to study their situation thoroughly, and expend time and resources in defense of their lives. Thus the defense of the poor demands and promotes the solidarity of the universal church and local churches, between mission churches and those that provide missionaries, and among the various Christian confessions, in a process of "mutual support among Christians" on the historical, ecclesial, and "theological" (in faith, and in the practice of love and hope) levels (Sobrino, "Conllevamos," 157–78).

The "particularity" of the church in the "third world," incarnate as it is in the world of the poor, defending them and persecuted for their sake, becomes transformed into a genuine universal. The new Christian *oikoumene,* the new "catholicity" of the churches, emerges from the "particular situation" of the church of the "third world."

PROSPECTIVE REFLECTION

A liberative theo-logical reflection is a theology of pilgrimage—a theology of the open road, not a road that comes to an end somewhere—in growth, diversification, and maturation. Many a task still lies ahead.

Those who look for rigorous, exhaustive systematization in theological material may feel cheated by the failure of liberation theology so far to offer either a systematic tractate on the Mystery of God or a varied, broad quantity of theo-logical articles and essays springing from its vaunted concrete historical context. Indeed, one might say, not entirely groundlessly, that even a general dogmatic structure is still rather wanting. But let us not minimize the accomplishments of liberation theology. Theological systematization cannot proceed in dissociation from the life and mission of the faith community, cannot consist in a mere chain of ideas without praxic content. Theology is always a response—a praxico-pastoral mediation—and ought to constitute a challenge to historical processes.

The theology of liberation, as the condition of its effective *diakonia* in behalf of the church and historical processes, must now proceed with its in-depth elaboration of its theo-logical *theoria,* its way of "seeing" God. Here, I think, are some of its tasks.

1) In virtue of its aspirations to universality, and as a precaution against any possible temptation to chauvinism, the Latin American theology of liberation should continue to broaden the universality that it has thus far attained, and do so from an ecumenical perspective. The dialectical tension between life and death, manifested in so many ways in the "third world," provides an opportunity of plumbing the meaning content of faith in the God of life in dialogue with theologians of Africa and Asia. It is likewise necessary, and urgent, to strike up a dialogue with theological undertakings in a liberative key in the countries of the so-called center, the North Atlantic world. Finally, liberation theology should be in dialogue with theologians of countries conducting socialist experiments, in Europe as well as in the "third world."

2) It seems to me that it will be important and valuable to carry out studies on the experience of God in the complex compass of Latin American *popular piety,* the religiousness of a people simultaneously oppressed and believing, in the implications of this experience as an expression of the genuine liberative power of the people.[22]

3) Another important work will be the collection, systematization, and study of the extensive *theo*-logical output stored in the documentation of popular Christian communities—liturgical celebrations, testimonials, poetry, songs, drama. Taken together, they form a living and most rich vein of authentic liberative spiritual theology.

4) From a starting point in its basic underlying theo-logical theory, I judge it important to have more, and more deeply pondered, monographs on the basic intuitions of liberation theology in the field of biblical studies.

In a biblical framework, Sobrino's reading of the Synoptics with respect to the manifestation of the God of life in Jesus of Nazareth has seemed to me to be most worthwhile, and in some measure a paradigmatic exercise in hermeneutic circulation.

Other theo-logical lines of scripture ought to be taken up as well—for example, the Psalms, the songs of the Suffering Servant, the Book of Job (Gutiérrez, *Dios,* 63–86). Of particular importance would seem to be the image of God in the Book of Revelation, with its themes of conflict and judgment.

5) Another valuable approach is to be found in the emphasis placed by liberation theology on the "abasement of God," on the presence of God's mystery of concealment-and-identification on the crosses of history. Given the weight of a Christian tradition of "dolorism" and "crucicentrism," liberation theologians should take up, and develop from a biblical outlook, with God's manifestation in history as its main axis, the sense and meaning of earth, bodily life, joy, and hope.

6) The *dogmatic* theme presenting the richest opportunities for further work is the *trinitarian vision.* The theology of liberation has been well advised to renounce any speculation on the trinitarian reality of God *ad intra,* limiting its reflections to the trinitarian dimension of God's relationship with history and human beings,—studying the trinitarian structures of salvation. But it will be important to draw the basic *consequences* of God's intrinsic trinitarian reality. Here a triple thematic will appear:

(a) The trinitarian life as model of life in community *(koinonia).*

(b) In the christological approach of the theology of liberation, the original dyad, the "original dual unity" of *Father-and-Son* is crucial (Pikaza, *Orígenes,* 503). The expression is Pikaza's, and denotes the interpersonal encounter in which the Son, in trust, obedience, and unconditional fidelity, gives himself to the Father. This trust is evidenced both in Jesus' prayer, and in his obedience and fidelity to his mission, to death on the cross.[23] The task of developing the "ambital dyads" of Father-and-Spirit and Son-and-Spirit remains to be performed (Pikaza, *Orígenes,* 503ff.).

(c) It has become commonplace to observe that a reflection on the Spirit, and on the presence of God by the Spirit, constitutes the great hiatus in Christian theology (Comblin, "Missão"). American theology of liberation, in virtue of its basis in a spirituality (the spiritual experience of encounter with God in the poor) must contribute to filling this pneumatological vacuum. It must help rehabilitate the importance of the presence of the Spirit—in whom God becomes present as principle and origin of life all down through history, generating that history. The Spirit opens our ears to the groans of the "condemned of the earth," fires our hearts, destroys the structures of oppression, and causes us to be reborn as church, from the lower regions of the earth to the solidarity of the kingdom.

FINAL REFLECTION

An utterly other God seeks an utterly different society [Helmut Gollwit-zer].

By way of conclusion of this final chapter, enunciating an evaluative judgment of the Latin American theology of liberation, I take the liberty of addressing—the Evangelical—a word *ad intra*. To my own ecclesial tradition I think that the theo-logical reflection carried on by liberation theology has several ways of both questioning and enriching our own Latin American evangelical theology. This word will be a "last" word only chronologically, not logically. It is not intended as a "final conclusion." It is not intended to function as a kind of "safe arrival" at a tranquil port of destination. It is meant as a *point of departure* for an ongoing quest of the liberator God of the poor.

We journey toward God; we do not possess God. We know that we shall never render Ineffable Mystery a known object. We know that the last word of faith on God is that "mystery remains mystery." Happily, when we speak of God we have no experts or specialists on the subject. We have only seekers, and the only thing that they can do is share, in community, the results of their search and encounter, inviting us to pursue it with them along the same path, attracted by the Mystery fascinating, gratuitous, and demanding that has won credibility by drawing near to the poor and promising that they are to have abundant life.

Discerning the Signs of the Times

Our evangelical theology, in order really to be evangelical, in the original sense of the term—the good and joyful news that comes from God—must live in a state of permanent attention to God's ongoing manifestation. We must therefore be attentive to the kernel of God's manifestation in contemporary signs of the times—attentive to God's challenges coming to us through the cry of millions of poor throughout the world, especially in Latin America.

The history of Latin America is *not* God's great silence. In it and through it God continues to speak to us, in a novel manner. To deny this possibility is to deny that the Spirit continues to act efficaciously in history. We sin against the Spirit when we fail in openness to historical novelty as the manifestation of God, when we are unwilling to let the scales fall from our eyes to see the kernel of God's manifestation today, unwilling to hear the good news of God proclaimed by the Spirit through the poor all over the world (Isa. 42:18-20). To "let God be God" is to let God speak a new word, a word ever "living and effective" (Heb. 4:12).

Open History

If history is a special theo-phanic locus—if God has definitively and irreversibly assumed our history, and the incarnation and the presence of the Spirit are now central to that history—then the conflictual history of oppression and struggle for liberation must be accorded the value of, and taken up as, a *locus of struggle and creative human self-realization.* In this history—the only history we have—we are called upon to accept the gift of the kingdom in obedience to a creative praxis that envisages a world transformed into a reign of justice and a communion of sisters and brothers.[24] A personal experience of God thus becomes a historical experience rooted in the building up of the kingdom.

The mystery of God acquires a sense of gratuity and totality that transcend—that are irreducible to the framework of my own encounter with God, my personal salvation. God is the one who bestows meaning on the lives of all men and women, the one who is lovingly and salvifically self-manifested to the world and the cosmos in total re-creation.

Faith in God is the sustaining rationale in the face of all fatalism and resigned inaction, all mixture of stoicism and "providentialism" in the midst of suffering, failure, and struggle with evil and injustice. It is our sustaining rationale in the face of any temptation to accommodation with the status quo, enabling us to refuse to see the latter as a "necessity of nature" and thereby to renounce prophetic protest and the transforming activity of history. History is not the eternal recurrence of one and the same thing. It is not something already over and done, the inexorable fulfillment of the will of a God who predestines it.

God, in radical self-bestowal to humankind, opens history to us as the space of human actualization. Faith, acting as it does in hope and love—in the praxis of hope and love—insists on assuming history to transform it from below, in order that life, not yet possible for the majority of human beings on the Calvary of this world, become ever more possible and real, as God's primordial will of life demands. Faith demands the social effectuation of real life (Ellacuría, "Reino").

The task of the believer will be to seek, on the level of human rationality, the instruments of struggle and of transformation of history.[25] Every narrowly "religious" consideration condemning history to irrelevance in the name of an ahistorical vision of salvation, every "religious" consideration reduced to pure interiority, and thus more the religiousness of the gnostic or mystery religions than of the Bible, must be abandoned.

The powers of personal and social sin are present in history. Human history is a history of grace and sin. The structures of oppression and antilife are signs and effects of the evil that takes flesh in concrete alienations. Accordingly, it is God who invites us *not* to acknowledge as God's work a world such as it is structured today, a world so ill constructed—and to struggle for the dismantling of its mechanisms of violence and antilife.

The history of the oppression of the poor poses a *human question* as to its socio-economic meaning, its material, ethical, and political meaning. But this question has a *theo-logical scope:* God's creation is seen to be imperiled and destroyed.

If the world thus configured, with its Calvary of antilife, can and ought to be considered a harsh reality negating God's will in the crucified lives of so many men and women, then it will be in its transformation, in conformity with God's design of life, that the truth of our relationship with God will be verified. In the language of the Bible, knowledge of God is not something purely intellectual or subjective. The kingdom of God as transcendent goal, as eschatological fulfillment, is not the negation of history, but the elimination of the sin of history, the elimination of its unjust social structures.

The utopian character of the kingdom is not verified in some "imaginary image of a filling up" of what must be wanting in history. The kingdom will rescue, transform, and plentify the "corporeity" of history and the dynamics of a love-in-solidarity operating in it. This is why fidelity to the kingdom demands anticipatory concretions—"signs"—in history.

"God is the sole Absolute. All else is relative." This is the "Protestant principle," and is to be maintained (Dillenberger and Welch, *Cristianismo,* 288–90). But it stands in need of one necessary qualification. Although, from a point of departure in the Absolute, the historical, as "penultimate reality," must indeed be relativized—only the kingdom of God in its eschatological fulfillment is the "Ultimate"—it is no less true that this very principle demands we take the relative very seriously, in a dialectic of "distinction" and "nonseparation."[26] History is the place where the Absolute anticipates the "ultimate," anticipates the reality of the kingdom. The reality of historical liberations, however limited and "penultimate" they may be, are signs of the kingdom manifesting itself *in* them, without of course being identical with them.

Wagering on Humankind

The tragic reality of human sin has not set God's liberating design at naught. God has not come into the world in Jesus to destroy humankind, but to re-create it in all fullness (John 3:17). Because God has become a human being and assumed history, humankind has meaning, and is open to the new, in hope. The incarnation is an affirmation of the world and of history.

I am not pleading for a naively optimistic humanism that fails to take sufficient account of the history of sin, whereby some human beings marginalize others and deny them their basic right to life, and thus denying, negating, the primordial will of the God of life. What is at stake is that "the only point in believing in human beings is that God believed in them first" (González Faus, *Identidad,* 68). It is a matter of taking our faith in the liberator God seriously, in openness to liberative undertakings in history—limited undertakings, surely, but open to the greater reality of the kingdom inasmuch as they humanize life, and generate new relationships of communion and participation.

We must break, in practice and in theory, with all pessimism claiming to be based on a religious view of the human being, such as the pessimism so typical of the self-styled anti-Pelagian anthropology of most of our Protestant tradition. The danger of this pessimistic view is all the greater in Latin America today by reason of the influx of Evangelical missioners from the Anglo-Saxon world and the type of hermeneutic key they promote for study of the Bible.

With all the force of an absolute a priori, it is argued that "history is failure," that "today's liberations are tomorrow's oppressions," that one must "be liberated [spiritually] from the idolatry of [material] liberation"—that, finally, it is "God, not the human being, who will have the last word." In a universe of closed horizons, where there is no possibility of anything new in history, where the historical initiative and activity of the "condemned of the earth" for their own liberation is a priori doomed to failure, faith becomes simply impossible. The greatest peril of this pessimistic anthropological vision is in the "ideological function" that lurks within it, in that it promotes a religious practice of separation and historical escapism.[27] Thus this vision, however unconsciously, comes to be an effective contribution to the preservation of the status quo of injustice. The biblical, ethico-prophetical, religion of historical and prophetic hope disappears—and this, paradoxically, in the name of fidelity to the Bible.[28]

Here the kernel of the Marxist critique of religion maintains its validity. The experience of God entails the moment of tension between God's no to the history of sin and condemnation, and God's yes to life, to the struggle for a world of justice and fellowship, and to the creation of a new humankind. God's yes is the source of our hope, which, though often a "hope against hope" (Rom. 4:18), supports us and enables us to continue unflagging in our activity—to say yes, "against" or "in spite of" the negativity of history as locus of the temptation not to struggle. A failure to have hope leads one to live according to the ethic of death. The contrary leads one to live according to the ethic of life, which, taking its thrust from the yes *of* God and a yes *to* God, drives us to discover the sense of our activity, and to make a wager on a dynamics of life. This is the ethic of faith, hope, and love.

Room to Be Persons

Faith in the liberator God of the poor is the profession that God *alone* is liberator in the authentic sense of the word. This is not in doubt. The question is only *how* God is that liberator: whether *without* the human being, as a power imposing itself "from on high," from above—or *with* the human being as active *subject* and not merely passive object of liberative activity in the midst of history. Once more we find ourselves at the intersection of the coordinates of that classic and complex problem of God's *concursus:* of history as human activity and God's activity, as gift of the Father and human creative task. I accept the challenge of saying a word about this problem. Of course, accepting the challenge does not mean resolving it.

In the face of demands that we go and transform history, that we build a social order in which new relationships of freedom and justice are generated among human beings, we meet with a theo-logical "logic" asserting that the "privileged dialectic is the dialectic between God and the human being" (Gonzáles Faus, *Identidad,* 75). This dialectic is expressed in terms of a radical *confrontation*. God and the human being are asserted here in a contradictory manner, such that the human being's historical initiative comes to be seen as a challenge to God, a way of "squeezing God out," and we are tempted to say, "It is God, not men and women, who changes situations."

Our faith in a liberator God requires that we reject this confrontation. The God proclaimed by Jesus in his messianic praxis has "killed" the "logic of the old human being," by which God and the human being are adversaries. God's liberating activity does not come in rivalry with the liberative efforts of human beings. Human beings, although not themselves God (there is an "infinite qualitative difference" between the human being and God), are nevertheless called to the task of re-creating and transforming history—*from beneath.* It is not a matter of choosing between "horizontalism" (history without grace) and "verticalism" (grace without history). Instead we have an analogy with the classic christological formulation of the mystery of the incarnation of the Word. We have human history and God's *oikonomia* in a relationship "without either separation or confusion." The God of the Bible is a God with a commitment to human history, a God who assumes the risks of the option for the poor who remains faithful to the task of re-creating life, and who thus invites us to enter into an alliance, a covenant to transform the world by humanizing life.

We have said no to a humanistic messianism, an immanentist reductionism that would posit human liberation *by* the human being *without* God. Here the human being would for all practical purposes be divinized, in an absolute self-assertion that would fly in the face of creaturely reality. Positing this exaltation of the human being would deprive the experience of God of any meaning: "The more I believe in the human being, the less I believe in God." Worse, this experience will be the opium of the people: "I do not believe in God, because God is an instrument for the exploitation and subjection of human beings."

We also say no to a *religious messianism*—a transcendentalistic reductionism positing the liberation of the human being *by* God *without* the human being. Confronted with this *deus ex machina,* this God without a history, the human beings ends up, for all practical purposes, dehumanized, reduced to an object: "The more I believe in God, the less I believe in human beings." Or worse, in view of the evil in the world, society, and humankind, the liberative effort of the human being in history is deprived of meaning and becomes an idolatrous illusion. Liberation becomes an individual affair, and indeed an eschatological one, something out beyond history.

The "logic" of the biblical bipolarity is very different. It is true that human beings are not God, but they are called to be the deputies, the vicars, of God. The true God does not replace human beings in the task of re-creating and transforming the world. God created the world and a humankind associated in the preservation and ongoing transformation of the world. To use the words of Methodist theologian José Míguez Bonino, God gave the human being "room to be person." That is, there is a space in which God has invited men and women to *act on their own.* God will never invade this space as a rival (*Espacio,* 23–36; *Fe en busca,* 124).

God assumes history not in order to replace human beings, but to open the way by which human beings can perform their task. Thereby God demonstrates the ultimate meaning of history—the kingdom—expresses the option for the lowly, the oppressed, and guarantees that justice and love will come to victorious realization, and that "there will be no love lost in this world" (Juan Luís Segundo). Our task is to make history.

God is self-revealed as demand—as an imperative of love, life, and justice, to be fulfilled by human beings. In response to this demand, faith achieves authenticity, and human beings discover themselves to be subjects capable of realizing themselves as subjects of their own history. God is not a power that "barges in" on us as some omni-predestining will. Human beings need not renounce their liberative historical initiatives in order to open themselves to God. On the contrary, a liberative praxis constitutes the surest way to the God of Jesus Christ. Far from wanting to subvert undertakings that seek to humanize life and generate new social relationships of greater fellowship, participation, and justice, God is absolute demand that the human be humanized "more and better." God wills that this life, in all its breadth, and including its material basis, may be truly worthy of the human being and in conformity with the aboriginal plan for humankind: *Gloria Dei, vivens homo.*

This is why God is revealed as guarantor of the possibility of realization of liberative undertakings in history above and beyond the limits of demonstrable human feasibility and hope. This is the meaning of eschatological plenification. The liberator God of the poor continues to be manifest in power, a power that vanquishes death, sin, and injustice, insuring the definitive triumph of life, justice, and a communion of sisters and brothers in God's utopia, the kingdom—that free gift of the Father and demand for fidelity to the historical practice of the gift of the kingdom.

Living according to the Spirit

History, as "room" for men and women, is the proper room and time for the experience of the Spirit. History, as locus of incarnation, as compass of struggle, and of personal and communitarian creativity on its way to the humanization of life and the creation of new relationships of fellowship, participation, and justice, is the space and time of the experience of the Spirit in the original biblical sense of living according to the Spirit. This enables us to recognize and acknowledge our freedom in the service of love (Gal. 5:13)—our freedom to be creative sons and daughters of the Father and sisters and brothers of one another.

If what is basic with the Spirit is the generation of life, and the ongoing generation of history, then to live according to the Spirit is to live in history in terms of an option for life, as demanded in Deuteronomy 30:15, and as befits a disciple of the Risen One.

To live according to the Spirit is to live in docility to the Spirit, which leads to the plenitude of an ethic of life that delivers us from the ethic of sin and death (Rom. 8:2). The plenitude of the ethic of life is resurrection—definitive victory over death. It is in an ethic of life that the fullness of corporeal life is achieved.[29] The ethic of life is an ethic of love and hope. Only love gives life. Not to love, not to have hope, is to live an ethic of sin and death. The ethic of life is actualized in struggle with whatever generates death, in ourselves and in society.

To live in the Spirit is to find the meaning of life in the struggle for the life of those who are deprived of it.[30] Such a one lives in continuous, renewed acceptance of the profound meaning of the life of Jesus, the one who, for love of others, arrives at total surrender of life in a sacrifice to the death. Whoever wishes to maintain an option for life must accept the fact that, for the sake of the life of others, one must be ready to give one's own life and live the paradox that the promotion of life can demand the surrender of life. The one who accepts this states in deeds—as Jesus did—that life is the most radically bestowed, the holiest and most unmanipulable, the most open and limitless, of gifts. Such a one actualizes, by the power of the Spirit, the radical experience of the God of life.

CONCLUSION

For the "third world" Christian there is no encounter with the Mystery of God the deliverer, God the lifegiver, without an efficacious decision to set out with God down the road to the liberating goals of history. God pays attention. God hears the cries of the Latin American people, who live in captivity in their own land. Only by hearing the same cries that issue from a great injustice that cries to heaven like the blood of Abel murdered by his brother Cain (Gen. 4:10), and by transforming these cries into a praxis of love and hope whose goal is the justice of the kingdom, shall we ever "correspond" to the reality of the God of the poor definitively revealed in Jesus of Nazareth.

The praxis of justice as an active concretion of love and hope affords us the possible and necessary "room" for our word on the sublimity of the *Mysterium Liberationis* to become real and historical, so that our "many abstract substantives" may become "few concrete substantives"—so that the good and glad news—coming from the God who bursts into history with the kingdom—may come to us today transformed into good *reality,* in a communion of love-in-solidarity and a participation in the fellowship of the land, bread, and joy for all—as tangible reality and collective enjoyment (Isa. 65:17–25). Then will God be all in all (1 Cor. 15:28).

I conclude this work strengthened and challenged by the biblical promise to Jesus' followers: Have no fear! Christ is risen! He is alive! And he has guaranteed us: "I have overcome the world. I am with you always, until the end of the world" (John 16:33; Matt. 28:20).

Notes

INTRODUCTION

1. The term "theology" originally had the strict sense of its etymology: the *logos* concerning God. It denoted the "doctrine of God," as contradistinguished from the doctrine of the "divine economy," which was that of the realization of the historico-salvific divine plan, beginning with creation ("protology") and ending with the final consummation ("eschatology"). Later in the history of Christian thought, the word "theology" was broadened to include the themes of the divine "economy" as well. Thus we speak of a "theology of creation," for example, or a "theology of grace," by virtue of the potential reference of any subject whatever to God. Considered *sub ratione Dei,* anything can be the object of "theology."

In the present study I propose to rehabilitate the original sense of the word "theology" as the "doctrine" or "science" *of God:* or, to express it tautologically, as the "theology of God." See Pannenberg, *Teoría,* 305ff. The Latin American theologians of liberation have coined no special term for the *logos* bearing upon the mystery of God specifically. Hence I prefer to hyphenate the word "theo-logy" when referring specifically to reflection on or understanding of God, in contradistinction from "theology"—theology in the broad sense.

2. This expression has become classic in contemporary theology since Gustavo Gutiérrez's "Theology from the Underside of History," written as a response-in-dialogue to German theologian Jürgen Moltmann's "Open Letter to José Míguez Bonino." The "underside of history" is "the other history: the history of the others," those who have no history, the ones "absent from history," the "wretched of the earth," the "exploited classes, oppressed cultures, and ethnic groups that suffer discrimination" (Gutiérrez, "Underside," 186, 190, 193, 201).

For me, Latin America, as the "underside of history"—as the other side of the coin of the historical development of the "first world"—does *not* constitute a "third world," a world separated and apart. It is part of the "first world"—the only world—of which Latin America is an impoverished, dominated, and underdeveloped part. Latin American underdevelopment is the "other face" of North Atlantic overdevelopment: development in that "world" is built on the underdevelopment of the "third world." The basic categories of historical understanding, then, according to Gutiérrez, are domination and dependency (*A Theology,* 81–99).

3. In my elaboration of the "meaning paradigm"—the hermeneutic framework—of theo-logy as the key to liberation, I shall attempt to mine this rich, demanding perspective; see below, pp. 20–24. See also Codina, "Irrupción."

4. In 1976, after an initial dialogue in Dar es Salaam, Tanzania, the Ecumenical Association of Third World Theologians (EATWOT) was founded. Orbis Books has published the papers of this conference (Torres and Fabella, *Gospel*) and of subsequent

EATWOT conferences. In 1977 the new association met in Accra, Ghana (Kofi Appiah-Kubi and Sergio Torres, eds., *African Theology en Route,* Orbis, 1979). In 1979 EATWOT met again, in Wennappuwa, Sri Lanka (Virginia Fabella, ed., *Asia's Struggle for Full Humanity,* Orbis, 1980). The fourth EATWOT conference was held in São Paulo, Brazil (Sergio Torres and John Eagleson, eds., *The Challenge of Basic Christian Communities,* Orbis, 1981). The fifth meeting was held in New Delhi, India, in 1981 (Virginia Fabella and Sergio Torres, eds., *Irruption of the Third World,* Orbis, 1983). The sixth conference—the first involving theologians representative of both the "first" and "third" worlds—was held in Geneva, Switzerland, in 1983 (Virginia Fabella and Sergio Torres, eds., *Doing Theology in a Divided World,* Orbis, 1985).

African theology takes its point of departure in the infrastructural dimension of a particular culture at the scene of a life-and-death struggle of so many oppressed peoples and races. Asians base their theology on a rereading of Christianity on the margin of the cultural tradition of the West, and in dialogue with the great religions of the East, especially those of India and China.

5. Theo-logy has certainly made itself heard here. James Cone has a chapter on God in black theology in his *Black Theology and Black Power,* as well as a more extensive treatment in his *God of the Oppressed.* See also his "Significado" and his *Spirituals and the Blues* (New York, Seabury, 1972).

6. The first congress was held in September 1981. Ignacio Ellacuría, of El Salvador, delivered an address entitled "Los pobres, lugar teológico en América Latina," later published in *Misión Abierta* (Madrid). The "message of the congress" said, in part: "The Christian community must always consider it a principal task of its mission to denounce poverty and inequality. In Spanish society, as in the international community, economic, cultural, and political misery and need exist side by side with wealth and ostentatious power. But these phenomena are not simply juxtaposed. The opulence of the few is the cause of the indigence of a great part of humanity, not only in our country, but especially in the Third World. . . . Faced with these facts, we here make a commitment to carry on our theological reflection, our witness to our faith, from a partisan option for the dispossessed and in identification with them" (*Misión Abierta,* 4–5 [1981] 301–2).

The second congress was held in September 1982. Its theme was that the hope of the poor is Christian hope. Jon Sobrino made a presentation entitled, "La esperanza de los pobres en América Latina," later published in *Misión Abierta.*

7. In his now classic *A Theology of Liberation,* which gave Latin American liberation theology a more defined, more systematic orientation, Gustavo Gutiérrez speaks of "encountering God in history" (chap. 10). Liberation theology, he says, is simply the experience of God rediscovered in liberation processes, rediscovered from the viewpoint of the poor, in light of what the Bible says about the God of the exodus, the God of Jesus Christ.

"In the appearance on our scene of the theology of liberation, there is certainly a political practice: a commitment of solidarity with the poor, and an unfaltering struggle for justice. . . . But the appearance of the theology of liberation is not the mechanical, spontaneous effect of this political practice. It is the effect of the *new experience of God* that we have had in political practice" (Richard, "Espiritualidad," 97–98). Still, liberation theology has developed no treatises *de Deo* of any breadth comparable with its elaboration of other themes, such as christology (Leonardo Boff's *Jesus Christ Liberator,* Jon Sobrino's *Christology at the Crossroads,* and more recently, Juan Luis Segundo's *El hombre de hoy ante Jesús de Nazaret*) or ecclesiology (see Víctor Codina,

"Eclesiología Latino-Americana de Libertação," REB, 165 [1982] 61-81; Quiroz Magaña, *Eclesiología*). The Latin American theology of liberation, by reason of the methodology peculiar to its theological effort, has not effectuated its theoretical articulation from a point of departure in the classic order of systematic theologies, governed from start to finish by a rigorous, all-embracing schema of exposition, proceeding from the "first things" (protology) to the "last things" (eschatological consummation). The theology of liberation, as a theology responding to the questions of the reality of its ambiance (the cry of the poor, the yearning for liberation), does not base its development on the theologian's arbitrary decision to handle this or that particular theme. As Enrique D. Dussel puts it, "The Latin American theological discourse never begins with the '*theological* state' of the question. It always begins with the '*real* state' of the question. Thus its 'point of departure' is not what theologians have *said* about reality, but what reality itself manifests to us" ("Dominación," 328).

8. There are works along these lines—e.g., José Míguez Bonino, *La fe en busca de eficacia,* an interpretation of Latin American theological reflection; Segundo Galilea, *Teología de la liberación,* an attempt to synthesize this theology; Julio Lois, "Teología de la liberación."

9. For such a discussion, see Richard, "Desarrollo"; Silva Gotay, *Pensamiento,* 29-72; Dussel, *History;* idem, *Desintegración,* 105-38.

10. The stratum of religiousness represented by the popular piety of the poor is one of the lines of investigation of the Centro Bartolomé de Las Casas in Lima, founded by Gustavo Gutiérrez in 1975.

11. See Gutiérrez, *Power,* chap. 2-4. See also Muñoz, *Conciencia,* a study of some 300 documents emanating from various Christian groups throughout Latin America from the close of the Second Vatican Council, in 1965, to 1970.

12. See Manzanera, *Teología* (bibliography of the works of Gutiérrez, pp. 428-32); Vidales, "Perfil." Gutiérrez was born in June 1928 in Lima. After five years at the University of Lima, during which he was involved with student activist groups, he broke off his study of medicine and began to study philosophy and theology in preparation for the priesthood. In 1959 he was ordained a priest in Lima. He received the licentiate in psychology at the University of Louvain in 1955, and the licentiate in theology at the Jesuit Theological Faculty of Lyons in 1959. From 1959 to 1960 he attended the Gregorian University, Rome. Since 1960 he has been living in Lima, where he has been chaplain and advisor of the National Catholic Student Union and professor in the departments of theology and social sciences at the Catholic University. He is a consulting editor of *Concilium.* In May 1979 the Catholic University of Nijmegen (Netherlands) conferred on him an honorary doctorate in theology and social sciences. He works with base ecclesial communities in Peru, and is an active member of EATWOT, the Ecumenical Association of Third World Theologians.

13. Originally published in Spanish, *Teología de la Liberación, Perspectivas* (Lima, CEP, 1971) as an expanded version of a November 1969 presentation to the SODEPAX meeting in Cartigny, Switzerland. This work was then published in Spain (Salamanca, Sígueme, 1972; 9th ed., 1980). It has been translated and published in ten other languages.

14. The collection was originally published in Spanish, *La fuerza histórica de los pobres* (Lima, CEP, 1979). It too was republished in Spain (Salamanca, Sígueme, 1982).

15. A presentation on God as portrayed in certain biblical themes, given as part of the Theological Reflection Days (XI) held at the Catholic University of Peru in February 1981, under the auspices of the Department of Theology.

16. It was in this address that, for all practical purposes, the expression "theology of liberation" was coined. On this occasion Latin American theology, according to Pablo Richard ("Desarrollo," 5), made a "quantum leap, and an explicit breach between a *Weltanschauung* bound to a 'developmentalistic' practice and one bound to a practice of 'liberation.' . . . The term, 'liberation,' is not an abstract, academic term, but one arising out of a very precise political practice, in Peru as throughout Latin America." Gutiérrez's address was published by MIEC, Montevideo, 1969. The same text appeared under the title "Apuntes para una teología de la liberación," in *Cristianismo y Sociedad* (Buenos Aires), 1970.

17. "In speaking of God, we are touching the very nerve of our theology. Ultimately all theology is a reflection on God" (Gutiérrez, "Comunidades," 25).

18. Sobrino is a Jesuit priest and naturalized Salvadoran. He was born in Orduña (Euskadi) in December 1938. He entered the Society of Jesus in 1956, was assigned to El Salvador for his noviceship and, except during his years of study, has resided in that country since 1957. He was ordained a priest in 1969, the year he received his licentiate in philosophy and M.S. in engineering from Saint Louis University in the United States. He was awarded the doctorate in theology by Sankt Georgen Institute, Frankfurt, his dissertation being a study of the christology of Wolfhart Pannenberg and Jürgen Moltmann. He has taught philosophy and theology at the Centro de Reflexión Teológica of José Siméon Cañas University in San Salvador. In 1979, he accompanied Archbishop Romero to Puebla, and in 1981 directed the compilation of the archbishop's writings.

Sobrino's theological contribution can be understood only in the light of a crucial antecedent of his theology: the history of oppression of the Salvadoran people. El Salvador is one of the smaller Central American republics, but its population is one of the densest: despite war casualties and thousands of refugees, an estimated 6 million Salvadorans (1985) (4.25 million in 1977) live on 21,394 square kilometers (8,260 square miles—approx. the size of Massachusetts). See Ricardo Sol, *Para entender El Salvador* (San José, Costa Rica, DEI, 1980); idem, *El Salvador: Un pueblo perseguido. Testimonio de cristianos* (Lima, CEP, 1981).

19. See Sobrino, "Iglesia de los pobres," idem, *True Church,* 228–52: "Theological Significance of 'Persecution of the Church' Apropos of the Archdiocese of San Salvador."

20. This expression, coined by Ignacio Ellacuría, points to "the existence of a great part of humanity literally and historically crucified by natural oppression, and by historical and personal oppression" (Ellacuría, "El pueblo crucificado," 49). This "historically crucified people" is a "sign of the times," and the historical continuation of the Servant of Yahweh (Ellacuría, "Discernir," 58).

21. I refer to Sobrino's three principal works (systematic reflections): *Christology at the Crossroads,* originally published in Spanish in 1975, with a second, corrected and expanded, edition appearing in Mexico in 1977; *The True Church and the Poor,* originally published in Spanish in 1981 and containing the principal, mainly ecclesiological, works of Sobrino from 1978 to 1980 (except that just cited); and more recently, *Jesús en América Latina.*

22. When I speak of "Latin American liberation theology," I am not referring to a compact and monolithic theological formulation, but to one that is open, and still growing. Nor do I speak of "theolog*ies* of liberation," as if I could distinguish radical differences among them such as would call for specifically distinct evaluations. It is true that one can distinguish, in the growth dynamics of this theology, various emphases or

accents—christological, hermeneutical, historical, and ecclesiological—converging in a rich "unity in diversity." But the common point of departure of all these emphases is the *perspective of the poor,* and the common formal object of their concrete methodology is faith realized in a liberative practice.

The milestones I consider important in the shaping of Latin American liberation theology are: 1971, publication of Gustavo Gutiérrez's *Teología de la liberación;* 1972, the El Escorial meeting (Spain); 1975, the first Latin American meeting, in Mexico City; 1978, the first Latin American meeting of theologians and social scientists, in San José, Costa Rica; 1979, the meeting in Puebla in connection with the third general CELAM conference; 1980, the International Ecumenical Congress of Theology, São Paulo. See L. Boff, *Periferia,* 67–83.

23. Alves: *Cristianismo: ¿opio o liberación?,* with its insights into "God's politics" as manifested in the exodus and the "suffering God."

Segundo: *Nuestra idea de Dios* (1970), vol. 3 of his *Teología abierta para laicos adultos,* with its "critical approach to the God of Western society" (125).

24. Miranda: *Marx and the Bible.* Miranda writes of the "God of the Bible," and of "God's intervention in history" in the form of a word that challenges and drives human beings to take the path of liberation and justice. See Pixley, "El evangelio paulino de la justificación por la fe: Conversación con José Porfirio Miranda."

L. Boff: His *La experiencia de Dios* (1974) is, in my opinion, the first specific work of theo-logy in liberation theology. Boff explains how the experience of God is lived at various levels of reality: how God appears within the modern technico-scientific world (chap. 5); how God appears within the oppressed world of Latin America (chap. 6); how God emerges along the pathway of personal history (chap. 7). Likewise important are his *Encarnación* and *The Lord's Prayer.* His interdisciplinary essay, *El Rostro materno de Dios,* on the feminine and its religious forms (the feminine as path to God and God's own path) falls outside the purview of my considerations: God is Mother, and not only Father. (Or, in the words of John Paul I, "God is Father, yes, but most of all she is Mother.") Boff goes in quest of a theology of the feminine as it is joined to the Holy Spirit, who willed to become "pneumatized" in the concrete person of a woman, Mary. "Like the only-begotten Son, the Holy Spirit, too, appears to have a peculiar mission and a full [human] personification" (Boff, *El Ave María: lo femenino y el Espíritu Santo,* 89). See also *Rostro,* 115. I know of nothing else of this tenor in the theology of liberation. Gutiérrez and Sobrino have a special place for Mary as a poor, committed woman, the Mary of the Magnificat, but no explicit development of her relationship with the Spirit in the divine motherhood, nor anything explicit about the feminine element of God. See Pikaza, *María y el Espíritu Santo,* 73–75, an early evaluation of Boff's approach.

Míguez Bonino: *Fe en busca* and *Espacio para ser hombre.* The latter is an interpretation of the biblical message for our times. Chap. 1, "Only an atheist can be a good Christian," has been of major help to me.

25. "Jesucristo, centro de la historia" is the work of a group of theologians serving as advisors to a considerable number of bishops at the Puebla conference, 1979. Among the bishops were those best known for their pastoral work from a point of departure in an evangelical option for the poor of the continent. See Cabestrero, *Teólogos,* 74–113.

The Idols of Death is the collective work of scripture scholars, theologians, and social scientists. It poses the problem of God in Latin America from the viewpoint of one of the most pervading traditions of the Bible, that of Yahweh's struggle with false gods. "The central question in Latin America today is not the problem of atheism. . . . [It] is *idolatry*—a worship of the false gods of the system of oppression. Even more tragic than atheism is the faith and hope that is put in false gods" (p. 1). This collection includes an essay by Jon Sobrino, in which he sets up an antithesis between the God of life and the false divinities of death (66–102).

The International Ecumenical Congress of Theology (IECT) was held under the auspices of EATWOT in São Paulo, Brazil, from February 20 to March 2, 1980 (papers and commentaries published in Torres and Eagleson, *Challenge*). Taking part were the best known Latin American theologians of liberation: Gustavo Gutiérrez, Jon Sobrino, Leonardo and Clodovis Boff, Hugo Assmann, Pablo Richard, Jose Míguez Bonino, Enrique D. Dussel, and many more. See Teólogos del Tercer Mundo, *Irrupción,* devoted to this congress, with commentaries by Teófilo Cabestrero.

It is precisely a text among the final documents of this congress—"Letter to Christians in Popular Christian Communities in the Poor Countries and Regions of the World" (Torres and Eagleson, *Challenge,* 247–50)—that has served as the point of departure for my own approach, providing me with a thesis that unifies a theo-logical vision under the formality of a "liberative key" (see below, pp. 33–37).

26. *Ideology and Utopia: An Introduction to the Sociology of Knowledge* (London and New York, Harcourt Brace Jovanovich, reprint ed., 1970) 268.

27. Xabier Pikaza helps us to understand *religious experience* as an openness on the part of the human being to radical mystery that cannot be closed in the name of positivistic science or rationalism without mutilating that human being. It is an *experience of meaning,* in which God is encountered at the very center. Thus religious experience may be defined as "that experience of meaning, at a specific depth, in which human beings cultivate their radical openness to, and gratefully acknowledge the fulfilling and salvific presence of, the Supreme Reality, which manifests itself by conferring a value and plenitude on their existence, the world, and history" (*Experiencia,* 130; see also 96–100).

28. It is noteworthy that Hans Küng, in his tightly reasoned study of the problem of God in modern European thought, presents faith in God so forcefully as "God-trust" *(Gott-vertrauen)*—that is, as a "trusting commitment to an ultimate ground, support, and meaning of reality" (*Existe,* 775).

29. Speaking of the "kairological today," from *kairos* in its meaning in biblical Greek, Boff says: "Faith testifies to a permanent, ongoing 'today' realized by God in behalf of human beings . . . a 'today' pregnant with salvation and the divine presence, transcending the category of linear time, and anticipating eternity. This 'today,' in virtue of its possession of the structure of the definitive and eschatological, abides as a constant present: it is neither swallowed up by the past nor outstripped by the future. In what does this 'now' consist? It consists in the testimony and proclamation that God, through the intermediary of the eternal Son, has intervened in history, to deliver it from its perversion, and carry it to its fullness of life, its realization. The eternal Son has become incarnate, in poverty and marginalization, in order that, from a point of departure in what is most interior, in what 'counts for nothing' (1 Cor. 1:18), he may save all that is anything at all—all that is. The resurrection has had the effect of confirming the joyous destiny of life, life's happy ending, despite the threats surrounding that destiny in history" (Boff, *Periferia,* 10). The "chronological today" designates linear, historical time, with its proper, specific content so challenging for human reflection. It is this challenge that renders necessary the mediation of the human and social sciences, which provide a more objective approach to the complex historical reality within which the discourse of faith must be articulated (ibid., 11–12).

30. The believer, like any other human being, is subject to the social dynamic, and one of the factors in the social dynamic is the existence of ideologies. Ideologies are socially conditioned and committed conceptions and lines of argumentation whose purpose is the justification or the denunciation of a determinate human situation. "Ideologies are schematic conceptions of reality, conditioned by the economic, social, and cultural situation of the groups maintaining them, and serving these groups as the theoretical basis for the planning of their activity with a view to maintaining or securing their interests" (Santa Ana, "Fe cristiana," 8). On the complementarity and difference between faith and ideology, see Segundo, *Hombre*, I, 149–77.

31. "As scandalous as such a proclamation may seem, one must affirm vigorously and without compromise that the experience of God implies in and of itself the notion of scandal. Many of the teachings of the faith point directly to it. That God became flesh, that the son humbled himself even unto death on the cross, that the wisdom of God was manifested in the cross, that the anguished cry of Jesus on the cross was met with silence, and that grace now overflows where sin used to abound: from the point of view of both philosophical and religious reason, these truths are not self-evident but scandalous" (Sobrino, *True Church*, 153).

32. See *Estudios Ecuménicos* (Mexico City), no. 39 (1980) *(Ecumenismo desde los pobres)*, esp. the articles by Jether Pereira Ramalho, "Ecumenismo que brota de las bases," and Javier Jiménez Limón, "Ecumenismo desde los crucificados." See also Jerez, "Ecumenismo."

33. "The union of Christians and the Christian churches will come about if we take as our starting point a historical practice based on the following of Jesus and if there is a real, effective commitment to the needs and longings of the vast majority of the human race, namely, the poor and the oppressed" (Sobrino, *True Church*, 39). See also the document published by the Comisión para la Participación de las Iglesias en el Desarrollo, *Iglesia*.

34. For an extensive bibliography on the theology of liberation, see Manzanera, *Teología*, 433–56. On the mystery of God generally, see the bibliographical appendix in J. Rovira Belloso, *Revelación*. See also the remarkable study by Xabier Pikaza, "Bibliografía trinitaria del Nuevo Testamento," in Pikaza et al., *Bibliografía trinitaria*.

CHAPTER 1

1. "From the beginning, the theology of liberation had two fundamental insights. Not only did they come first chronologically, but they have continued to form the very backbone of this theology. I am referring to its theological method and its perspective of the poor. . . . The second insight of the theology of liberation is its decision to work from the viewpoint of the poor—the exploited classes, marginalized ethnic groups, and scorned cultures. This led it to take up the great theme of poverty and the poor in the Bible. As a result the poor appear within this theology as the key to an understanding of the meaning of liberation and of the meaning of the revelation of a liberating God" (Gutiérrez, *Power*, 200).

2. See also Gutiérrez, "Itinerario," 56. In addition: "What is primarily at issue is not a theology, but popular liberation. Theology comes only later. . . . In order for theology to be a part of, and a service to, a concrete process of liberation, it has to be liberated— as do we also—from every restraint that impedes solidarity with the poor and exploited of this world. Only in this way can the effort of reflection escape being coopted by the system" (Gutiérrez, *Power*, 214). This means that theology must be liberated from the

socio-cultural world that marginalizes the poor as persons. It means that theologians themselves must be persons who are involved in the liberation process (ibid., 60).

3. L. Boff, *Teología,* 35. A view of the theology of liberation as just another of the "theologies of genitives" (such as the "theology of history," the "theology of work," and so on) leads to the misunderstanding of reducing it to social ethics. See Richard, *Iglesia,* 17–33.

4. Liberation—not as a theme, but as a method (liberation "as liberative")—in its theological elaboration (that is, in its effort to interpret God's word to us here and now), calls for a *permanent hermeneutic circle* as a condition for being liberative theology and not simply a discourse on liberation. "Here is a preliminary definition of the hermeneutic circle: it is the continuing change in our interpretation of the Bible which is dictated by the continuing changes in our present-day reality, both individual and societal. 'Hermeneutic' means 'having to do with interpretation.' And the circular nature of this interpretation stems from the fact that each new reality obliges us to interpret the word of God afresh, to change reality accordingly, and then go back and reinterpret the word of God again, and so on" (Segundo, *Liberation,* 8).

The indispensable conditions for keeping the hermeneutic circle in continuous function are two. First there is the richness and depth of our questions and suspicions concerning reality: "The first precondition is that the questions rising out of the present be rich enough, general enough, and basic enough to force us to change our customary conceptions of life, death, knowledge, society, politics, and the world in general. Only a change of this sort, or at the very least a pervasive suspicion about our ideas and value judgments concerning those things, will enable us to reach the theological level and force theology to come back down to reality and ask itself new and decisive questions" (ibid., 8–9).

The second condition is the richness and depth of a new interpretation of the Bible, which, by introducing new elements, the product of disciplines dealing with the past as well as with the present, enable theology to answer new questions by changing its accustomed interpretation of scripture. If interpretation fails to change as real problems change, not only is the circle broken, but the problems—provocative, general, basic questions—are left without an answer; "or worse, they will receive old, conservative, unserviceable answers." Without this hermeneutic circularity, theology cannot be liberative. It will continue to be a conservative way of thinking and acting (ibid., 9; see below, pp. 120–23, "Hermeneutic Mediation").

5. See also Vidales, *Tradición,* 6–56: "El método de la teología de la liberación"; Sobrino, *True Church,* 7–38: "Theological Understanding in European and Latin American Theology."

6. From its very inception, liberation theology has incorporated the mediation of the political and the data of the social and human sciences as data for theological reflection. See Silva Gotay, *Pensamiento,* 203–32. Hugo Assmann, who had always insisted upon this (*Theology,* 59–64, 111–25), noted years later: "It is incorrect to attempt to situate what is new and innovative in the theology of liberation in the theoretical sphere of methodological discussion, if what we mean by methodological discussion is the meticulous examination of 'epistemological mediations.' It is simply not true that the essential element in the theological 'method' of involved Christians is in the assumption of a determinate method of analysis of reality—for instance, the Marxist method. To make a statement like this is to give immediate occasion to all manner of questions that are actually 'secondary questions,' 'spin-offs,' logical consequences of a 'derived' type. *The 'methodological root' of the theology of liberation is to be found in an identifica-*

tion with the struggle of a people where its basic right to life is concerned. Anything else is 'overflow' " ("Tecnología," 32; emphasis added). For the "theoretical mediations" of the theology of liberation, see Clodovis Boff, *Teologia e prática.*

7. See Gutiérrez, *Power,* 169, 196–97.

8. On the sense of "people" in liberation theology it will be in order to notice that "people" is an *amplification of the concept of the "poor."* The life, struggles, and aspirations of a people are the life, struggles, and aspirations of the poor, of the poor as a collective subject. "Inasmuch as the vast majority of Latin Americans are poor, to speak of the poor is to speak of the people" (Segundo, "Teologías," 354).

9. See also Gutiérrez, *Power,* p. 219, n. 65. When Latin American theologians insist that they have "their own" theology, Hugo Assmann tells us, they are only referring to a "second act" with respect to praxis as "first act": "They are not referring to an abstract level of discussion on the epistemological relationship between theory and praxis (although the ultimate content of this discussion may be present, in a new form). What they are asserting is something extremely simple: 'What we have seen with our eyes, what we have looked at and what our hands have touched' concerning antilife in the 'word of life' of the system, 'this is what we make known. [Anti]life made itself known, we saw it and are witnesses . . .' (cf. 1 John 1:1–3). It is nonsense, then, to ask liberation theologians to give a better explanation of their concept of praxis. They are referring to something evident, to a reality that they have lived and experienced along with a people, although the people has experienced it in far more brutal forms than have those participating in the 'popular cause' " ("Tecnología," 31).

10. See also Gutiérrez, *Power,* 48–50. Human history is conflictual. But this is not enough to say. "One must insist on the necessity of a rereading of history. History, where God is revealed and where we proclaim God, must be reread *from the side of the poor.* The history of humanity has been written 'with a white hand' (Leonardo Boff's expression [see his *Teología,* 146ff.]), from the side of the dominators. History's losers have another outlook. History must be read from a point of departure in their struggles, their resistance, their hopes" (Gutiérrez, *Power,* 201).

11. Gustavo Gutiérrez has concerned himself with this theme in several of his writings. See *Power of the Poor,* pp. 20–21 ("The Subversion of History"), 48–50 ("Transforming History with a Liberating Love"), 58–59 ("Theory and Praxis"), 171–85 ("Theology and the Modern Spirit"). See also his *A Theology,* 6–11.

12. This historical process has led to a change in *our way of knowing,* in the manner in which human beings approach truth and relate it to their historical practice. The whole process has revealed a special trait in the profile of contemporary consciousness: that knowledge is bound up with transformation. Praxis is the matrix of an authentic cognition, and the test of its validity, so that we speak of "veri-fication." See Gutiérrez, *Power,* 58–59.

13. When I speak of a "Latin American theology," thus modifying "theology" with a geographical designation, I am not suggesting a mere "application"—that key word in the religious language of the Evangelical tradition—of a generic truth to the determinate situation (in Latin America). "Christian faith has no structure of application, of adaptation of generic truths, of syllogistic deduction. What it does have instead is a *concretion* of its truth. Christian faith is a *concrete universal,* which continues to appear in various forms all down through history. The truth of that concretion is verified only within the hermeneutic circle" (Sobrino, "Significado," 34; see also Segundo, *Liberation,* chap. 1; Ellacuría, *Freedom,* 3–14).

14. See Sobrino, "Dios," 110. See also the Puebla Final Document, no. 1209 (in Eagleson and Scharper, *Puebla,* 273).

15. See Vidales, "Sujeto histórico de la teología de la liberación." Gutiérrez's "Theology from the Underside of History" is enlightening on this point. Gutiérrez makes a comparative analysis of two theological outlooks, the European and the Latin American, from a starting point in their *distinct* and *contradictory* historical subject. (The contradiction has its roots in social reality.) See also Gutiérrez, *Power,* 93–94.

16. See Gutiérrez, *Power,* 185–86. The irruption of the poor in the church has its roots in the peculiar, waxing dynamic of the popular movement itself. In Latin America, from the 1960s onward, we have a process of peaking, of climax and maturation, in the popular movement (see the IECT Final Document, no. 10). Increasingly, the popular base of the Latin American church lives and celebrates its faith within that movement. An ecclesial and popular current is arising, with different forms of expression in life and in Christian community (ibid., nos. 19–20). An understanding of this irruption stamping the life of the Latin American church demands an analysis of the historical processes of the period beginning in the 1960s. The task is a broad one, and goes beyond the limits of my study. See Richard, *Iglesia,* 59–74.

17. See Gutiérrez, "Comunidades," 14; *Power,* 77–90.

18. See Míguez Bonino, "El descubrimiento de nuestra realidad," in his *Fe en busca,* 43–61.

19. Some manifestations of the worsening living conditions of the great Latin American majorities are "the lack of decent housing, an accelerating increase in the rate of unemployment and underemployment, a decrease in the purchasing power of the popular classes, the unsatisfied demand for services such as education, health, social security, and so on, the spread of chronic malnutrition, infant mortality. . . . Some 40% of the population of Latin America, or about 113 million persons, live in conditions of poverty, and almost half of them in outright destitution. By 1990 those below the poverty line will number 120 million (25% of the population), and by the year 2000 they will number 128 million (21%), according to data supplied by the World Bank and the Economic Council for Latin America" (Gorostiaga, *Entender,* 18).

With prophetic vision, Medellín declared in 1968 that "in many parts of Latin America we find a situation of injustice that can be called *institutionalized violence.* Because of structural failings in industrial and agricultural undertakings, in the national or international economy, and in cultural and political life, 'whole nations lack the bare necessities of life and are under the thumb of others. They cannot act on their own initiative; they cannot exercise personal responsibility; they cannot work toward a higher degree of cultural refinement or a greater participation in social and public life' (*Populorum Progressio,* 30). This situation . . . violates fundamental rights" ("Medellín Document on Peace," in Peruvian Bishops' Commission, *Honesty,* 206).

20. See IECT, "Final Document," nos. 12–17: "Structures of Domination" (in Torres and Eagleson, *Challenge,* 233–34). Liberation theology places great emphasis on this point (see Míguez Bonino, *Fe en busca,* 177).

21. See Assmann, "Tarea." Speaking from the nations of the poor, in defense of the *right to life,* EATWOT theologians in their New Delhi meeting in 1981, called attention to the threat to life constituted by the arms race promoted by war industrialists, and the imminent danger of nuclear destruction that places us before the choice between survival and destruction as never before in history ("Final Statement," no. 25, in Fabella and Torres, *Irruption,* 195).

22. Puebla offers a clear and meaningful description of the poverty of the Latin American majorities. "This situation of pervasive extreme poverty takes on very

concrete faces in real life. In these faces we ought to recognize the suffering features of Christ the Lord, who questions and challenges us" (Puebla Final Document, no. 31 [in Eagleson and Scharper, *Puebla*, 128]). Puebla then offers a broad description of these "faces," including those of indigenous peoples and Afro-Americans, peasants, laborers, the marginalized and overcrowded urban populations, the underemployed and unemployed, disoriented youth, children struck down by poverty, and the marginalized elderly (ibid., nos. 32–39 [pp. 128–29]). For a commentary on the poor in the Puebla Final Document, see Gutiérrez, *Power,* 125–65.

23. Cited in L. Boff, *Periferia,* 87.

24. On the question of what politics is—an area in which so much confusion exists, especially among Christians—I think it will be helpful to cite the following remarks of Gustavo Gutiérrez, in spite of their length.

"For a long time, the area of the political seemed an area apart, a sector of human existence subsisting alongside of, but distinct from one's family, professional, and recreational life. Political activity was something to be engaged in during the time left over from other occupations. Furthermore, it was thought, politics belonged to a particular sector of society specially called to this responsibility. But today, those who have made the option for commitment to liberation look upon the political as a dimension that embraces, and demandingly conditions, the entirety of human endeavors. Politics is the global condition, and the collective field, of human accomplishment. Only from a standpoint of this perception of the global character of politics, in a revolutionary perspective, can one adequately understand the legitimate narrower meaning of the term—orientation to political power.

"All human reality, then, has a political dimension. To speak in this way not only does not exclude, but positively implies, the multidimensionality of the human being. But this conception rejects all socially sterile sectarianism that diverts our attention from the concrete conditions in which human existence unfolds. For it is within the context of the political that the human being rises up as a free and responsible being, as a truly human being, having a relationship with nature and with other human beings, as someone who takes up the reins of his or her destiny, and goes out and transforms history" (*Power,* 46–47). See also L. Boff, *Periferia,* 87–89.

25. The defense of human rights has come to be tantamount to the defense of the basic right to life where the poor majorities of Latin America are concerned. This basic right to life includes the right to the *material means* of life. Human rights ought to be viewed primarily as the rights of the oppressed. Only by doing justice to the rights of the oppressed classes as collective subject will it be possible to conduct a quest for the authentic common good, and for certain genuinely universal rights. See Ellacuría, "Historización."

26. The terms "social class" and "social conflict" designate analytical categories (theoretical instruments) for an attempt to explain social reality from a *dialectico-structural* reading. (See chap. 4, below, pp. 115–17, "Reading the Reality of the Poor.") This analytical approach perceives history as primordially conflictual, rather than as a linear evolutionary development. The conflictual constant among various groups and social classes arises out of the economic element—means of production, social relationships of production—by reason of the nonconvergence (antagonism) of the interests of these social classes. Society organized in a capitalistic mode of production presents a basic contradiction: it is "based on private profit and private ownership for profit" (Gutiérrez, *Power,* 47). All members of a capitalistic society contribute to the production of the material goods of life. But, in virtue of the concentration of the means of

production in the hands of a few, as the private property of the owners of the means of production and of capital, it is these few who receive most of the benefits of everyone's labor. In a word, social classes "are large social groups, distinguished from one another by the place they occupy in a determinate social system; one of these groups, solely by reason of the place it occupies in the relationships of production, appropriates a part of the fruit of the toil of the other, and has the power to maintain this state of affairs. . . . Accordingly, each of these groups has basic social interests that are distinct and antagonistic. They can gradually become conscious of these interests, and organize to defend them" (Arroyo, "Classes," 24). From this outlook, the poor cannot be considered apart from the social class to which they belong. They are members of a social class despoiled of the fruit of its labor, openly or subtly, by another social class. See Gutiérrez, *Power,* 44–45.

27. For a wider discussion of this theme in Latin American liberation theology, see Míguez Bonino, *Fe en busca,* 131–60 ("love, reconciliation, conflict").

28. See also Sobrino, *True Church,* 306. It is important to emphasize this, in the face of the temptation to "dogmatic idolatry" proper to all theological fundamentalism, which unconsciously and naively comes to identify the word of God with the word of the theologian. "I firmly believe," says Roger Garaudy, "in what Barth said about everything that I can say about God being said by a human being" (interview in *Vida Nueva,* 1065 [1977] 27). It is this humility that makes it possible for the theologian to speak the whole truth at the particular time at which he or she happens to be living and working. "No theology can monopolize theology, and attempt to present itself as theology *simpliciter.* In whatever is said, there remains what is unsaid. Reason—including theological reason—is finite. Consequently no generation of Christians can pose and solve all of the problems that faith presents. We may conclude from this that every theological tendency ought to know its scope, and above all, its limits" (L. Boff, *Iglesia,* 30).

29. It seems to me a good idea to recall the warning of José Ignacio González Faus: "To speak of God is always a little blasphemous, a little idolatrous. It always involves a bit of taking the name of God in vain. Indeed it is always a useless undertaking, because God cannot be spoken of. Only an idol, a false image of God, can be spoken of. St. Thomas used to say that the final word that the human being can pronounce on God consists in asserting that all the words pronounced until that moment have been a lie, even the most profound of them—that nothing has been said with them. . . . Despite all this, it may be that, today more than ever, we must speak of God" (*Acceso,* 158–59).

30. See Echegaray's book, *The Practice of Jesus,* in which he synthesizes the message of the words and deeds of Jesus' life, of his historical humanity.

31. See Jon Sobrino on the matter of the theological mood or tone (modality) common to the theology being done in Latin America (*True Church,* 4–5).

32. The processes of liberation, says Sobrino, place us squarely before the basic question for Christians and for the church: Do we really believe in God? In what God do we believe? ("Dios," 114).

33. See Muñoz, *Consciencia,* 133–47, where the author examines the "theo-logical dimension" (the faith affirmation in the liberator God) that took shape in the new Latin American ecclesial consciousness from 1965 to 1970.

34. "Theologians do not waft about in the air. They are social agents, they are situated in a determinate place in society, they develop cognitions and significations by utilizing the instruments offered and allowed them by their situation, and they have definite addressees. They are, then, inserted into the social context" (L. Boff, *Jesucristo,* 13–14).

35. See also Gutiérrez, *Power,* 212. Gutiérrez's "Theology from the Underside of History" (ibid., 169–221) begins with an attempt to understand contemporary theology from the social processes to which it is bound (171–85). His analysis yields a view of the Christian theology of the "center" as intimately bound up with a culture (Western), a race (the white), a mode of production (the capitalist), an ideology (liberalism, or "modern liberties"), and an interlocutor (the bourgeois class, the dominant class in the current mode of production). From the eighteenth century up to our day, the great challenge for Western Christianity has been the *economic, political, and cultural revolution* of the bourgeoisie, which has so radically re-created human and natural history alike (cf. Richard, *Iglesia,* 35–36). On the historical, socio-political, ecclesial, and ideological conditioning of *sub*versive theology—theology that comes "from beneath," or "from the underside of history," see the second part of this same article by Gutiérrez (in *Power,* 185–214). See also Segundo, "Condicionamientos."

36. For a theoretical exploration of the "social ubication" proper to all theological discourse, see Clodovis Boff, *Teologia e prática,* 281–95. The theme is of paramount importance for the theology of liberation. Without attempting to convey Boff's detailed treatment in the space at disposal here, I must nevertheless call attention to the distinct but inseparable "regimens" of theology—its *internal* regimen of *autonomy* (by reason of its methodologico-epistemic locus) and its *external* regimen of *dependency* (by reason of its social locus, object of the sociology of knowledge) (see ibid., 57–62). The former regimen, springing from the *epistemic* locus, consists of the autonomy of theological practice with respect to the development of a discourse in conformity with its proper methodology. That is, theology has its own manner of theoretical practice, which it has no need of justifying before another "tribunal," seeing that it possesses its own internal epistemological legitimacy (its own criterion of truth). In virtue of their internal character, these determinations do not constitute theoretical instruments capable of judging the value of a theological production as such. A theology is not epistemologically or methodologically better or worse for having emerged from the "center" or from the "periphery." The second regimen of theology, springing from its *social* locus, revolves about the social character of theological practice. Theologians do not live in the clouds. They are social agents, and they necessarily have a determinate "ubication" in concrete social reality. For the selection and accent of their theological thematic they depend on this social locus, and on the importance they ascribe it in their reflection on their own historico-religious concretion, the importance they ascribe their social ambit.

In light of all this, it seems to me that what Leonardo Boff has to say of liberative christological reflection is valid as well for *liberative theo-logical reflection.* To paraphrase Leonardo Boff: "The accents and the [theo-logical] subject matter are defined by what emerges as relevant from surrounding reality. Thus we must deny that there is, indeed that there can be, a neutral [theo-logy]. All [theo-logy] is *partisan,* or *engagé.* Willy-nilly, its reflection has repercussions on its situation, with the conflictive interests that permeate it. . . . All [theo-logy] manifests in its own way the relationship of functionality that it maintains with the historico-social situation: thus it is always 'committed.' Let us, then, retain this basic proposition: [Theo-logy], as the developed and systematized knowledge of faith in God, springs forth at a determinate moment of history, develops under determinate modes of material, ideal, cultural, and ecclesial production, and is articulated in function of determinate interests of which it is not always aware. Therefore the real question is: To whom is this type of theology committed? What cause does it seek to serve? A theology proclaiming a liberator God (acting in the midst of history on the side of the poor) seeks to be committed to the economic, social, and political liberation of oppressed and dominated groups" (cf. L. Boff, *Jesucristo,* 14).

37. The liberation theologian's "suspicion is that anything and everything involving ideas, including theology, is intimately bound up with the existing social situation in at least an unconscious way. . . . [He or she] feels compelled at every step to combine the disciplines that open up the past with the disciplines that help to explain the present. And he [or she] feels this necessity precisely in the task of working out and elaborating theology, that is to say, in the task of interpreting the word of God as it is addressed to us here and now" (Segundo, *Liberation,* 8). See C. Boff, *Teologia,* 96-100.

38. Two factors have contributed to this *prise de conscience.* The first is a Christianity that, over the course of many centuries, in our Western culture, has acquired forms of a "sociological Christianity," and been "usurped by the establishment as its ideological legitimation" (L. Boff, *Experiencia,* 48). The second factor is the sociological weight of religion in the Third World, especially that of Christianity in Latin America, a continent of peoples at once oppressed and believing.

39. Consider the following passage, written in 1908. In its simplistic formulation we see the profound symbiosis, centuries old, existing between Christian language and the social consciousness of the bourgeoisie (a sociological Christianity domesticated by domination). "Human society, as established by God, is composed of unequal elements. Consequently it is in conformity with the order established by God that human society have princes and subjects, lords and proletariat, rich and poor, wise and ignorant, noblemen and plebeians" (cited by Roger Garaudy, *Anatema,* 97). See also Assmann, "Iglesia," 283.

40. "The most terrible thing about oppression is the multiplicity of means it employs to see that the oppressed do not change, do not struggle to be free . . . especially the effort to tame the oppressed by offering them false 'liberations' with the object of preventing them from struggling to deliver themselves historically. The kernel of the Marxist critique of religion prevails, wherever theologies of oppression continue to prevail and block the fulfillment in the poor of their biblical privilege, which is theirs only on condition that they battle for their freedom" (Assmann, "Tercer Mundo," p. A-8).

41. See Juan Luís Segundo's commentary on the declaration of Vatican II concerning the genesis of contemporary atheism (*Gaudium et Spes,* no. 19, in *Liberation,* 45-47).

42. Compare the theo-logy of Dietrich Bonhoeffer, who states that to know God is to share in the suffering of God in the life of the world (Letter of July 18, 1944; in *Resistencia,* 211-14). See also Gutiérrez, "The Limitations of Modern Theology: On a Letter of Dietrich Bonhoeffer" (in *Power,* 222-34).

43. See L. Boff, *Jesucristo,* 423. At the roots of liberation theology "we find the experience of open veins, and passion for the oppressed joined to passion for God. More than wonder, it is suffering that makes one think—*and especially that obliges one to act"* (L. Boff, *Periferia,* 69; emphasis added).

44. Those seeking justice and liberation, even though not professed Christians, are closer to the living and true God than those who profess their faith in God and accept the whole of Christian orthodoxy, yet close their eyes and harden their hearts to the excruciating exploitation of millions of men and women. See L. Boff, *Experiencia,* 48.

45. Apropos of language about God, it would seem appropriate to report something here about what José I. González Faus designates as the "biblical norm for speaking about God." The New Testament, says González Faus, gives us a basic recommenda-

tion: "No one has ever seen God. But the Only-Begotten, who lives in union with the Father, has told us about the Father. That is, God cannot be spoken of as an object, as something that has been seen, and in being seen, possessed. God cannot be spoken of *in se.* Only God's works can be spoken of. What God has done, and that alone, can be "told," or narrated, and something of God be allowed to shine through in this narration. Language about God must therefore become infinitely modest, infinitely simple, and infinitely reverent, and thus is transformed into the last chapter of a narrative theology (*Acceso,* 159).

46. See Sobrino, *True Church,* 144–48: "The Experience of the Greater God"; ibid., 148–53: "The Experience of the Lesser God."

47. "God did not remain closed up in indecipherable mystery, but emerged from inaccessible light and entered human darkness. God did not remain in everlasting almightiness, but penetrated the fragility of creation. God did not draw humanity godward, but deigned to be drawn to the heart of humanity. God willed to come to what was different from the divinity; God *willed to become what, in all eternity, God had not been"* (L. Boff, *Encarnación,* 11; emphasis added).

48. "The *humanity* of God, properly understood, signifies God's relationship of self-donation to humankind . . . the free grace of God . . . the God of humankind. . . . The *divinity* of God, correctly understood, includes the humanity of God" (Karl Barth, "La humanidad de Dios" [1956], in *Ensayos teológicos* [Barcelona, Herder, 1978], 9, 17).

49. González Faus's expression (*Acceso,* 176).

50. Alves, *Cristianismo,* 146. This is not true only of the Old Testament. "The consciousness of the New Testament communities does *not* deviate from this context. This consciousness is rather a new expression of the historical consciousness and language-consciousness of the Old Testament. When Jesus began to preach, saying 'This is the time of fulfillment. The reign of God is at hand! Reform your lives and believe in the gospel!,' he was not speaking a foreign language. He was addressing a community determined by a history, and with a historical hope. . . . The gospel, then, is the proclamation of the historical reality of *God's actually operative policy, which does not manifest itself as a philosophical or mystical experience, but as a force that invades history"* (Alves, *Cristianismo,* 146–47; emphasis added).

51. N. J. Snaith's expression, cited by Alves, *Cristianismo,* 144. Consequently, special attention to history as the primordial sphere of God's revelation means that "the focus of our attention will be the *objectivity* of the historical deeds of God, not the subjectivity of internal, emotional, diffuse, and mystical experience" (Wright, *Dios,* 75).

52. See Sobrino, "Dios," 120–28; idem, *True Church,* 53–63. On the theo-logical sense of "mystery," Sobrino closely follows Karl Rahner's thought. For Rahner, Christianity basically says only one thing: that mystery remains eternally mystery. See Rahner, "Sobre la posibilidad de la fe hoy," in *Escritos de Teología,* V, 14; also, *Nuovi Saggi,* III, 182. "The concept 'God' is not an apprehension of God whereby the human being takes hold of mystery, but an apprehension of the human being by an ever present mystery that eludes us. This mystery remains mystery even when it opens itself to the human being, and this is precisely how it grounds the human being lastingly" (Rahner, *Curso,* 76).

53. This is the case with mystical religions. See Pikaza, *Experiencia,* 289.

54. "This silence *(first act)* is the condition and necessary mediation for speaking of the Lord, for doing theo-logy, for doing discourse *(second act)"* (Gutiérrez, *Dios,* 7).

55. The expression is that of José María González Ruíz, in his book with this same title.

56. A Basque priest born in Orozko (Vizcaya) in 1941 and a member of the Order of Mercedarians, Pikaza has for a number of years been a professor of theology and exegesis at the Pontifical University of Salamanca. He has a doctorate in theology and philosophy and a master's degree in biblical sciences. He is well known for his biblical studies, among them being: *La Biblia y la teología de la historia; La teología de los evangelios de Jesús; Los orígenes de Jesús: Ensayos de cristología bíblica; Hermanos de Jesús y servidores de los más pequeños (Mt. 25:31–46); Anunciar la libertad a los cautivos.*

57. The three fundamental types of religious experience correspond to the three primordial routes of human experiential openness (*Experiencia,* 110–26): openness to the *world* (cosmic experience), openness to *interiority* (self-awareness), and openness to *history* (human existentiality as becoming). In each of these types—on each of these routes—the human being expands toward the future: of the world, of the interior, of history. They are the routes of our "tendency toward mystery." At the point of departure of Pikaza's religious typology are: (1) his reliance on the historical and descriptive data of phenomenology (in contradistinction to the evolutive genetic model); (2) an element of historical advance represented in Karl Jasper's hypothesis of the time-axis (transition from sacred objectivity to creative subjectivity) (ibid., 264–65); (3) complementing the first two elements, the key importance of transcending the myth of the eternal recurrence (ibid., 264–66); (4) the symbolic medium—that is, the hierophanic mediation that cements the various ways of realizing the religious encounter.

58. Between God and the human being, "a *locus communis* of encounter has formed. Out beyond their differences, yet with these differences altogether intact, dialogue ensues. This means that being a human being does not consist in being bathed in the divine, but in something more profound: being a human being means dialoguing as a person with a God who is personal. As field of dialogue, history is at once theophany and anthropophany" ("Tipificación," 295).

59. Pikaza distinguishes three principal elements in the nature religions. (1) *Cosmic sacrality:* The cosmos appears as a divine totality embracing and basing all life. The cosmos as a whole, like its root, has a sacred character. (2) *The salvific character of nature:* Human beings live immersed in cosmic sacrality. They must live their lives and come to self-realization in rhythm with the cosmos. In this immersion is their salvation. They are a part of the great whole. To know this and live it is their destiny. (3) *The symbolic value of myth:* Myth is the language proper to nature religions. Thus, for example, in the Syro-Canaanite religious schema as found in Ugarit, we have the divine strife between Baal (lord of vegetation and life), Yamm (the great original chaos), and Mot (death) ("Tipificación," 268–70).

60. This religious approach was "reflected in late Hellenism, [but] triumphed mainly in India. When the rhythm of reincarnations subjecting human beings to the life-chain of the cosmos is seen to be the effect of sin and the expression of suffering, these human beings seek another exit, one leading to mystery. They discover it along the lines of their own interior life. The unfathomable abyss of one's own interiority, then, is the radical locus of the sacred. They then move to a second level, that of cosmic contemplation and ritual participation. The creative capacity of the human being in history is ignored or given short shrift. The divine is defined as depth, religion is defined as *en-stasis,* 'enstasy.' Involution with one's Self, or interior quest—the quest for the Atman—is the field of encounter with the absolute, with Brahman. Transcendence of the desire for life translates into the emergence of mystery, translates into the nirvana of Hinduism and Buddhism" ("Tipificación," 263).

61. "The twin columns of the Israelite faith take the form of a double responsibility: human beings are responsible for the cosmos, and human beings are responsible for one another. That is to say, the religious condition of the Jewish people is basically radicated in its 'promissory' vocation to dominate and transform the cosmos (Gen. 1:26). The Hymn of the Six Days is only a projection of this collective vocation of all human beings: they are called to be 'stewards' at once of the cosmos and of society (Gen. 1:5, 6, 10). The Genesis narrative exhibits the human being as possessed of a mighty and effective transformative capacity. Hence a 'magical' attitude vis-à-vis the cosmos will be roundly condemned, and any desire to use a pseudo-religious shortcut to attain what must be the achievement of a labor of normal historical maturation will be radically excluded. In other words, the religious condition of the people, far from leading the people away from its task of worldly building, consists precisely in this task" (Vidales, "Vida-trabajo," 96).

62. This is where the timely word of the prophet comes into play. The prophet's eyes scrutinize the signs of history (which in turn is the "sign of the times," in order to discern the perennial newness of the manifestation of a God acting in history. See Croatto, *Liberación*, 88–90; Sobrino, *Monseñor Romero*, 2–7).

63. See Pikaza, *Experiencia*, 233–34.

64. See Pikaza, *Dimensiones*, 100–110.

65. See Vidales, "Vida-trabajo," 97.

66. "Once a people has discovered its responsibility before God, and once God has been grasped by this people as the one who acts in history, all possible temptations to intimistic or cosmic escapism are closed off. Only the advance of history expresses the sign and fullness of the divine" (Pikaza, "Tipificación," 293).

67. See Pikaza, *Dimensiones*, 97–100; Moltmann, *Teología*, 123–80.

68. See Gutiérrez, *Power*, 6–7.

69. See Gutiérrez, *Power*, 7. This is a "biblical constant." Croatto says: "To tell the truth, this is nothing but the other side of the coin of the liberation kerygma, the key idea of the Israelite 'creed' and soteriological hopes. The God who delivers from oppression in Egypt is identified as liberator from all oppression. Genesis itself serves as conceptual and anthropological backdrop here in proclaiming that every human being, and not just the king, as in Egypt or Mesopotamia, is the 'image' of God, thereby creating a society of brothers and sisters, a society of equality, among all. This is why God hears the cry of the poor. The prophets emphasize this anthropological dimension with reference to minorities or individuals, in the traditional kerygmatic context: Yahweh is the God of Israel, but Yahweh is also—and by the same token—*defender* of the poor, of the orphan, and of the widow, a formula that became a stereotype (as long ago and far away as the ancient Middle East) for the salvific will of God or for God's representatives acting in behalf of the marginalized" ("Liberar," 21).

70. "Both texts transmit the memory of a kind of religious judgment in which the existence of Israel as a people consecrated to Yahweh is at stake. The former expresses the crucial alternative posed on the occasion of the conquest of the land of Canaan: to serve the gods of fertility, or to keep trust with Yahweh, God of the covenant. The people's answer is defined in its confession of faith: 'Yahweh is our God,' 'We shall serve Yahweh because he is our God.' 1 Kings 18:39 propounds the crisis symbolized by Elijah. The people's fidelity vacillates between Baal and Yahweh; the prophet intervenes, God's judgment is pronounced, and now the people repeatedly proclaims, 'Yahweh is the true God.' Enlightened by God's presence, in a sort of juridical gesture, the people responds with a free commitment to accept Yahweh, to live by the covenant" ("Tipificación," 299).

71. "The origin and principle of this creed is God's revelation, God's deed of historical creativity, his word of assistance and promise. All of this is contained in the profession of Yahweh as the one God. The people's response comes in light of this revelation, as a response to a demand for total love" (p. 300).

72. See Pikaza, *Experiencia,* 331. See also L. Boff, *Periferia,* 58–63: "El mensaje liberador de la Biblia para las opresiones de nuestro tiempo."

CHAPTER 2

1. "To believe in God is ever to believe in the possibility of something new. A God who does not seem evident and clear, who is not always to be found in the same place, will burst in before us each time in different, unforeseen ways, making unheard-of demands, inspiring us with new forms of reverence in genuine worship, creating approaches to God that have never been charted before. Is this meaning and experience not the same as that of the Psalmist's insistent, ongoing exhortation, 'Sing to the Lord a new song'? Granted, the novelty can be frightening. But it does not frighten those who have faith. It frightens those who, in a certain sense, do not have faith, or who have what the Gospel of Matthew calls 'little faith.' Faith is incompatible with attitudes of apprehension. Faith can be lived in the dark (or in the 'bright dark,' as the classic expression goes), but not in fear. Jesus' oft-repeated 'fear not' means 'Have faith,' or 'Have courage' (Matt. 8:26). Cowardice in the face of the new is contrary to faith. The encounter with God 'according to the scriptures' implies openness to the new, to what is capable of revealing to us God's presence/absence along unexpected paths. The God of the Bible is a God who is revealed, who is discovered, who comes to evidence,without ceasing to be a hidden God, and a God who is revealed in what is new. 'See, I make all things new!' (Rev. 21:5). God is the one who has been, who is, and who *will be"* (Gutiérrez, *Dios,* 60–61).

2. Jesus "certainly does meet death because of his fidelity to the Father's will, but historically his death is the result of a specific love that leads to a specific practice. From the historical standpoint Jesus was put to death by unjust authorities who saw him as a threat" (Sobrino, *True Church,* 49–50). See also Sobrino, *Christology,* 201–17; Ellacuría, "Muere," 91–101.

3. See Gutiérrez, *Power,* 12–16. "Acknowledging God as Father implies acceptance of the fact of God as origin of all, as beginning, as creative principle, as Alpha (Rev. 22:13). The 'first initiative' comes from God. A second notion, which renders the sense of the first more precise, preventing it from becoming excessively, even exclusively, philosophical is that God is Father because God communicates life. In the Bible, the statement that God is Father means those two things: that God is the origin of all else, and that God is the transmitter of life. Both concepts, however, are but dimensions of a single revelation about God" (Gutiérrez, *Dios,* 9). The fatherhood of God wins the attention of the liberation theologians in connection with the experience of human fellowship and divine adoption. To profess God as Father is to profess the gift of filiation bestowed by the Father, a gift that can be received only along with the task of creating a world in which an authentic communion of brothers and sisters in history, and the divine filiation, come to coincide (see Gutiérrez, *Power,* 66–68; L. Boff, *Prayer,* 24–28).

4. See Gutiérrez, *Power,* 21–26. "It is unnecessary to insist on the intimate relationship, from the viewpoint of biblical revelation, between a reflection on Jesus Christ and a reflection on the God he reveals. It will suffice to recall two verses. The first: 'No one

knows the Father but the Son' (Matt. 11:27), a gospel statement implying a great deal more than mere intellectual cognition. In the Bible, to know means to love. The meaning of this verse, then, is actually, 'No one loves the Father but the Son.' It is the Son, it is from the Son, that we love the Father. The second verse is: 'Whoever has seen me has seen the Father' (John 14:9)" (Gutiérrez, *Dios,* 1–2).

5. To study the reality of God from a starting point in Jesus has two meanings, says Sobrino: a *historical* meaning (the God of Jesus) and a *pistic* ("believing") meaning (God-for-us). Here I am not dealing with the pistic meaning, viewing Jesus in his primordial relationship with his Father, Jesus as participating in the very reality of God as Son of God. Pistic reflection dwells on the fundamental *normativity* of the mediator and his mediations. "Thus the Father of Jesus, through the Son's journey, and in a history that diffuses the Spirit, becomes God-for-us." The *historical* meaning is the consideration of Jesus as a historical figure, in his concrete life (as we would consider, for example, Moses or Jeremiah), in order to understand who God was for Jesus. That is, I am undertaking a historical analysis of how God appears in the mediator and his mediations. This analysis of the historical Jesus must take into account both the notions Jesus had of God, and especially his praxis and fate, which demonstrate the concrete reality of these notions (Sobrino, "Epiphany," 91–94). The abundant bibliography on Jesus' theo-logical experience along his life's journey is an indication of contemporary interest in the subject. See Sobrino, ibid., p. 101, n. 66.

6. "Tradition and scholastic theology insist on a basic point: the Word will never lay aside the humanity that he has assumed. That is, he has made our history his forever" (Espeja, *Jesucristo,* 284).

7. The Old Testament has it that anyone who seeks to see God will die. On God's invisibility, see Ps. 104; Dan. 7:9; Exod. 24:10–18, 33:23; Ezek. 1:4–28, 8:1–18. See also Pikaza, *Experiencia,* 236.

8. "God's union with human beings in Jesus Christ is historically a union undertaken by an 'emptied' God—the God of the *kenosis*—in his absolutely basic turning to the world of the poor" (Ellacuría, "Iglesia," 717).

9. "The scriptures teach us that the God of the Bible irrupts in history. But at the same time they show us that God, in historical becoming, is not diluted. This is why we can still say that the Holy God is . . . the Utterly Other, the Holy One" (Gutiérrez, *Dios,* 25). On God's ongoing vivifying assumption of the socio-historical, see L. Boff, *Periferia,* 60.

10. "The early fathers of the church themselves said that the Trinity is the Father, the Son, and ourselves. By not naming the Spirit, but 'ourselves' they were making the most profound statement about God and the Spirit that they could have made. For they were saying that the trinitarian God is not something extraneous to history, not even some reality that reveals itself to history, but one that assumes history. . . . And if the Spirit, within the Trinity, is what joins the Father to the Son, in history the Spirit is divinity inasmuch as it joins history to God and God to history" (Sobrino, "Fe en el Espíritu," 153–54).

11. "Neither the mountain, nor the ark, nor the temple, nor any single reality or social dimension, nor indeed any experience or historical occurrence, can set limits to the presence of God. This is one reason for the Old Testament opposition to the fashioning of images: they cannot depict God. And so, at the very moment when the Jewish people, having recalled the presence of the Lord on the mountain and the experience of God's company in the wilderness, built a temple, a fixed place for God

to dwell, the prophets had to engage in a bit of mind-stretching. Standing before the beautiful temple, fashioned of cedar of Lebanon, the prophets retort: God's dwelling is the heavens. 'Listen to the petitions of your servant,' they cry to the Lord, 'and of your people Israel which they offer in this place. Listen from your heavenly dwelling and grant pardon' (1 Kings 8:30) . . . . [God] abides above any attempt to limit the scope of the divine presence, as happens with the establishment of an immovable, unequivocal place of residence for God" (Gutiérrez, *Dios,* 53–54).

12. Gutiérrez offers an important clarification here: "It would be erroneous, surely, to state that nothing contains God, not even Jesus, Son of God and God in person. Thus the New Testament, in speaking of Christ, speaks of the coming of the fullness of time, or the moment of God's total habitation" (*Dios,* 55–56).

13. See Sobrino, *True Church,* 2,77, 112. On the God of the Bible who takes sides with the poor, José Comblin writes: "We can say that God has already taken sides with the poor and the oppressed. God knows no abstract, generic human being. God does not come to save humankind in general or the abstract totality of individuals in which the human essence is realized. There is a religion that knows of relationships between a universal God and a universal humanity: the religion of the bourgeois. But the religion of the Bible is the religion of the poor. In the Bible there are no 'human beings'—only oppressors and oppressed, rich and poor, dominators and subjected, learned and ignorant. God has made a choice, and it falls on the ignorant, the poor, and the subjugated. God does not shape a people out of just any class of human beings. God accepts some persons and rejects others. There is a heaven and a hell" ("Humanidad," 266).

14. "The 'Nicaraguan Peasant Mass' ranks among the best, most successful, and most concrete (from the standpoint of expressing real situations experienced by the people and communication with the people) of all that liberation theology has produced in Latin America. Here, that theology assumes the most consistent and concrete forms" (Assmann, "Faith," 228). See also Arnaldo Zenteno, "Tú eres el Dios de los pobres: la Misa Capesina Nicaragüense," *Christus,* 559–560 (1982) 61–70.

15. As Gutiérrez observes, the proclamation of God must be enfleshed in history, must become history, must take the form of deeds, in the practice of solidarity with the poor. In a society marked by injustice and oppression, the proclamation of God "to the exploited, the laborers and *campesinos* of our lands, will lead them to perceive that their situation is contrary to the will of the God who makes himself known in events of liberation. It will help them come to a consciousness of the profound injustice of their situation" (*Power,* 18).

16. Gutiérrez, *Teología de la liberación* (Salamanca, Sígueme, 1972) 11. See also Gutiérrez, *Power,* 19, 106. "I think José María was right," says Gutiérrez elsewhere. "In this dialogue [between the priest and the sacristan] there is a deep, rich, and actually beautiful focus on the liberator God. . . . The God of the dominators, who plunder and murder the people, is not the god of the poor. God is 'something else,' 'not the same thing' " ("Itinerario," 65). (See also Gutiérrez, *A Theology,* 195.) "Ultimately the dominator is one who does not really believe in the God of the Bible" (Gutiérrez, *Power,* 204).

17. "Here the two essential, ongoing dimensions of faith are inextricably intertwined"—the contemplative and the historical, the mystical and the political (*Power,* 8–9).

18. For a brief critical observation on the notion of God as frequently presented in our Western culture, basically as a God who is provident in history, see *Power,* 123–24: "Religion as Tranquilizer."

19. I take the liberty of referring to some other authors who expand on Gutiérrez's ideas: see L. Boff, *Teología,* 314–15 ("Jesús, el rico que se hizo pobre"). On the poverty of Jesus' social milieu, see Echegaray, *Práctica,* 145–54. On the poor as the addressees of Jesus' gospel, see Sobrino, *Jesús,* 102–4), and Echegaray, *Práctica,* 155–73. On the rich in Jesus' message, see Santa Ana, *Desafío,* 28–50, and Gonzáles Faus, "Jesús."

20. "In talking here about Jesus' notion and experience of God, I am obviously referring to the impact of the Father on the *human* consciousness of Jesus. I am not going into the eternal relationship between the Father and the Son within the Trinity" (Sobrino, *Christology,* p. 177, n. 10). On the consciousness of Jesus with respect to the Father, see ibid., 70–74.

21. "First of all, Jesus did make use of the *prophetic* tradition. There God is seen as one who is partial to the poor and the defenseless. He is clearly opposed to the historical sinfulness that creates a situation of injustice. He wants to establish justice on the earth. This God also wants the inner, personal conversion of the individual. He is responsible for the vocation of the prophet, from whom he demands everything— perhaps even his life. He is a God of conflict precisely because he is partial to the oppressed.

"Jesus also made use of the *apocalyptic* tradition. It stresses the renewal of reality by God at the end of time. It is a gratuitous act on his part, which is carried out by his power and which will be preceded by a worldwide cataclysm.

"Jesus also made use of the *sapiential* tradition. There the emphasis is on a creating, provident God who allows both the just and the unjust to grow up together in history. Only at the final judgment will he impart justice. He is a kind and good God in whom we should trust, for his providence extends even to our daily needs.

"Finally, toward the end of Jesus' life in particular, we find another tradition about God at work. According to this tradition, we are faced with the silence and seeming absence of God, as Jesus was in the garden and on the cross. We find earlier strains of this tradition in some of the Psalms, in the book of Lamentations, and in the book of Ecclesiastes.

"All of these traditions, with their somewhat different conceptions of God, had some influence on Jesus' life. On the conceptual level, at the very least, they reveal a certain amount of tension. God is glimpsed in *day-to-day* life, in the natural rhythm of living; but he is also seen as *eschatological,* as one who will reveal himself at the end of history. God seems to impose an *obligation* on us, to call for clear-cut action on behalf of the oppressed; but he also seems to be something or someone who is wholly *gratuitous* in his approach to us because he lies at the absolute beginning and in the final future of the kingdom. God seems to be someone *near* who can be called "Father"; but he also seems to be an *impenetrable* mystery who must ever remain God for us. Toward the end of Jesus' life God seems to be both a *presence* and an *absence,* both *power* and *impotence.*" (Sobrino, *Christianity,* 160–61; emphasis added in last paragraph).

22. See ibid., 158–76: "The God of Jesus as the Basis of His Prayer."

23. "We get much closer to [Jesus'] notion of God when we realize that for him God is grace. This point is made in parable after parable: the parable of the importunate friend (Luke 11:5–8); the identification of God with a human father, who would not give his child a stone instead of bread; and so forth. At this level the gratuitous goodness of God is presented in terms of criteria that are normal and comprehensible to human beings. However, Jesus is simply preparing people to realize that the grace of God is something absolutely unimaginable. That point is brought out in the parable of the prodigal son, for example (Luke 15:11–24)" (*Christology,* 163).

24. "The unfolding pageant of [Jesus'] life is not a lineal development, with the end implicit in the beginning. When Jesus uses the word 'God' at the start of his public life (Mark 1:15), his conception of God is different from that which he has when he pronounces that same word on the cross (Mark 15:34). Jesus' life went through different stages, stages that are distinct not only on the external, descriptive level but also on the level of his interior life. His conception of God changes, and the transition from one stage to the next does not take place without temptations, crises, and areas of ignorance being involved. That is the concrete way in which Jesus allows God to be God in his life. The reality of a transcendent God, of a God who remains ever greater than human beings and even than Jesus' own reflections on him, is what explains the life of Jesus with its transitions and ruptures" (Sobrino, *Christology*, 164-65).

25. On the aspect of tenderness in "God is love," see González Faus, *Acceso,* 172-177: "Qué Dios se nos revela en Jesucristo."

26. Sobrino studies passages in which Jesus speaks of worship, the Sabbath, and the twofold great commandment (*Christology,* 167-71). "It will not be out of order to recall the well-known fact that the first Christian theologians defined God as love (1 John 4:8, 16), and proclaimed love for one's neighbor as the fundamental commandment (1 John 4:11; John 13:34, 15:12, 17; Gal. 5:14; Rom. 13:8-10)" (Sobrino, "Epiphany," 92-93).

27. See Sobrino, *True Church,* 51-52; Richard, "Significado," 123; L. Boff, *Experiencia,* 73, 89.

28. Boff has also devoted attention to this, in the work just cited, *Jesucristo y la liberación* (in the study entitled, "Pasión de Cristo y sufrimiento humano" from which our extended extract comes, two paragraphs above). Gutiérrez does not handle this theme *in recto,* but apropos of Dietrich Bonhoeffer's question as to how one ought to speak of God in an adult world. One should speak of a God who suffers in Jesus, Bonhoeffer holds, and saves us not through domination but through suffering. The cross is the place where we may see, and so powerfully, God's weakness as an expression of God's love for an adult world (Bonhoeffer, *Resistencia,* 209-10). Gutiérrez approves of this approach (which, he points out, has reappeared in contemporary theology in Moltmann and Kitamori), and observes that the theme of suffering in Bonhoeffer, to which his analysis of the modern world had led him, indicates another doorway: the outlook "from beneath" (*Power,* 228-33).

29. See also Sobrino, *Christology,* 232. On the death of Jesus, see *Christology,* 179-81, 191. For a more extensive discussion of the "cry of Jesus," see Pikaza, *Orígines,* 142-49.

30. On the suffering of God, see Sobrino, *Christology,* 221-22. The concept has become familiar through the work of the Japanese Lutheran theologian Kazo Kitamori, *Theology of the Pain of God.*

31. See Gutiérrez, *Dios,* 3; Sobrino, *Christology,* 197; Moltmann, *Dios,* 382-94.

32. This expression became familiar with the appearance of Moltmann's work of the same title in 1972. See *Concilium,* 76 (1972) 336-47. Sobrino acknowledges Moltmann's influence on his own work (see *Christology,* 179, 235, n. 1).

33. For the sake of clarity, Sobrino puts his "more important points and formulations" here "in the form of theses," observing that "they will deal with the hard content of a theology of the cross as well as with its presuppositions and consequences" (*Christology,* 182). He posits thirteen "theses." Theses 1-5 refer to the "postresurrection view of Jesus' death" (ibid., 184-98). Theses 6-9 are on "Jesus' cross as the historical consequence of his life" (ibid., 201-15). Theses 10-14 focus on "the presence of God on Jesus' cross" (ibid., 217-29).

34. The cross bestows credibility not only on *God's love,* as we see that God delivers up Jesus out of love, but also on God's power. "On Jesus' cross," observes Sobrino, "in a first moment, what comes to light is *God's helplessness.* This helplessness, this powerlessness, does not of itself cause hope. But it lends credibility to the power of God that will be manifested in the resurrection. The reason is that *God's helplessness is the expression of utter nearness to the poor,* and of the fact that God shares their lot to the very end. If God was on Jesus' cross, if God has shared the horrors of history in this way, then what God did in the resurrection of Jesus becomes credible, at least to those who have been crucified. God's silence on the cross, which has so scandalized natural reason and the modern mind, does not scandalize the crucified, for what they would really like to know is whether God was present on the cross of Jesus. If God was, then that nearness of God to human beings that was begun in the incarnation, then proclaimed and rendered present by Jesus during his earthly life, is consummated. What the cross says, in human language, is that nothing in history has managed to set any limits to God's proximity to humankind. Without this nearness, God's power in the resurrection would remain pure 'otherness'—ambiguous, then, and, for anyone crucified, historically threatening. But with this nearness, the crucified are enabled really to believe that God's power is good news, because it is love. *The cross of Jesus is the abiding, plenary, assertion, in human language, of God's measureless love for those who have been crucified.* Jesus' cross says, in credible language, that God loves human beings, that God is pronouncing a word of love and salvation, and that God, in self-utterance, and self-donation, is love and is salvation. Jesus' cross—if we may so speak—says that God has passed the test of love, so that now we may believe in God's power as well" (*Jesús,* 178; emphasis added).

35. Along these same lines, Gutiérrez wonders: "Is not this the experience as well of a great part of the Latin American people today? It would seem to be, especially in those places where Christians have no other way of expressing their life but through their death—that is, by surrendering their lives—lives that are negated, snatched away, in so many different ways. I should say that this death passage is the passover, the paschal sacrifice, the final stage in preparation for the revelation of an authentic life" (Gutiérrez, *Dios,* 24).

36. "We discover the distinctive nature of Jesus' death by considering three elements: his message concerning the imminent approach of God, his cry on the cross, and his abandonment by the Father. Moltmann sums up the point: 'Jesus preached God's approaching nearness in grace as no one ever had before in Israel. He preached it to those without God, to the violators of the law, the alienated, and the rejects of society. Someone who had lived and acted in that way, who was wholly conscious of the nearness of God, could not experience death on the cross as confirmation or as mere misfortune. He could only experience it as hellish abandonment by the very God whose loving nearness he had proclaimed. For the experience of being abandoned by God can only be rooted in the realization that God is not far away but near, that his action is grace rather than judgment' " (Sobrino, *Christology,* 218, citing Jürgen Moltmann, *Umkehr zur Zukunft* [Hamburg, Siebenstern, 1970] 137).

37. Accordingly, Sobrino continues, "alongside the notion of God as a 'process,' then, we have Christian existence as a 'way' based on the following of Jesus. When we view Christian existence as the following of Jesus, we are not simply viewing it in ethical terms that flow from a prior faith. Strictly speaking, we are viewing it as a participation in the very life of God. . . . We are not made children of God by some expression of intent or by some mysterious supra-historical reality (akin to what has traditionally been

called the 'supernatural'). We are made children of God by participating in the very process of God. Following Jesus means taking the love that God manifested on the cross and making it *real* in history" (*Christology,* 226-27).

38. "In Latin America the cross has traditionally been the main focus of popular festivity. For peasants and oppressed groups in general, their great Christian feast has been Good Friday, not Easter Sunday or Christmas. A profound insight underlies that emphasis, but it has been counterbalanced by the utilization of Good Friday as a substitute for responsible effort in the cause of liberation. Popular intuition has rightly grasped the authentic element of Christian faith in Good Friday, but it has often grasped it in very passive terms. The present-day situation in Latin America has brought out a somewhat different focus, particularly among groups more deeply involved in the effort for social change. This new Christian focus on the cross is much more activist in character" (Sobrino, *Christology,* 180).

39. See also L. Boff. "¿Cómo predicar hoy la cruz de Cristo?" in his *Jesucristo,* 437-41.

40. See also L. Boff, *Jesucristo,* 422-36: "El sufrimiento que nace de la lucha contra el sufrimiento."

41. The expression is Xabier Pikaza's. See his *Experiencia,* 247, where he identifies God's activity in history as salvific praxis in behalf of the human being.

42. See also Alves, *Cristianismo,* 157. The term "liberation," observes Gutiérrez, contains three levels of meaning, all interpenetrating, and each functioning as part of a single complex process whose profound sense and full realization is in God's salvific activity (or praxis): (1) the liberation of oppressed peoples and groups; (2) the liberation of humankind throughout history in the acquisition of a real, creative freedom; (3) liberation from sin, the ultimate root of all breach of friendship with God and of the community of sisters and brothers among human beings (by injustice and oppression). See Gutiérrez *A Theology,* 36-37; and *Power,* 61-63; Cosmao, "Salvación."

43. See Hinkelammert, *Armas,* 268-317: "La orientación teológica hacia la vida: la teología de la liberación": Vidales, *Cristianismo,* 94-131: "Teología de la liberación: teología de la vida."

44. Gutiérrez's concept (*A Theology,* 155-57). See also Miranda, *Marx,* 77-108: "God's Intervention in History," esp. 77-88: "The God of the Bible"; Richard, "Exodo"; IECT, "Final Document," no 94. Rubem Alves, in his reflection on liberation and hope ("Lenguaje del humanismo mesiánico"), studies the exodus as a paradigm. The Israelite experience of the exodus reflects a divine policy, manifested as a force for liberation that subverts the status quo by creating a future of freedom for the human being. A future objectively and subjectively closed by the oppressive power of Egypt, and the "slave mentality" of the people, are smashed to smithereens by a God who appears as free of all historical determinism, free to make history. Thus this God makes possible a human politics (one of "rendering and maintaining human life human") that does not cancel human creative activity. God, as the future of freedom, as freedom for the future (over against an absolute determination by the past that would render the movement of history superfluous), makes self-initiated human betterment possible, however much history in a given moment may incline to the negative side of the balance sheet in terms of oppression and despair, for human liberation is the beginning, middle, and end of God's activity—its principle, its means, and its goal. See also Míguez Bonino, Foreword to the first edition of Alves, *Cristianismo,* vi-vii.

On the exodus as the archetypal, structuring event in Israel's religious consciousness, see Croatto, "Liberación," 219; see also Alves, "Pueblo," 136-39. For a commentary on Exodus from a Latin American perspective, see Pixley, *Exodo.*

45. On the eschatological promises as central to the theology of liberation, see Gutiérrez, *A Theology,* 160-68. On the reign of God as likewise of key importance in liberation theology, see Sobrino, "Jesús y el Reino." For the centrality of the cross in liberation theology, see Sobrino, *Christology,* 179-235: "The Death of Jesus and Liberation in History"; idem, *Jesús,* 185-91. Finally, on the privileged place of Jesus' resurrection in that theology, see Sobrino, *Christology,* 258-72; *Jesús,* 173-83.

46. "The *go'el* is the liberator, the rescuer, redeemer, protector, the blood avenger. We find its original meaning in the biblical history of Israel—for example, in Lev. 25:23-49 and Num. 35:19-27. The *go'el* is the nearest relative of the victim of murder or dispossession, and has the obligation of avenging the murder victim, or of rescuing or redeeming goods or persons fallen into the hands of strangers or foreigners" (Gutiérrez, *Dios,* 26-27).

47. Bartolomé de Las Casas's expression, with reference to the spoliation and death brought upon the indigenes of Indoamerica by the lust for gold at the beginning of the colonial domination of the sixteenth century. See Gutiérrez, "En busca," 150.

48. Unlike the nature religions, the Israelite religion did not divinize death. God is life. Therefore there is no identification of the divine with death. See Pikaza, "Muerte," 687-91.

49. Sobrino comments: "In the gospels, Jesus *argues* from the Torah as from an irrefutable authority for it is there that one finds the basic norms of God's original will. The few passages in which this argumentation appears refer to the observance of the second part of the Decalogue (Mark 10:19 and parallels). That is, they refer to respect for human life in its various aspects: they may stress assistance to one's parents in need (Mark 7:10; Matt. 15:4), or the equivalency of love for God and love for one's neighbor (Mark 12:28-34 and parallels). . . . But besides citing the Law, Jesus *deepens* it, in at least two areas, the *better* to safeguard human life. In the matter of marriage, one must return to the origins of God's true will (Mark 10:6, referring to Gen. 1:27), by which man and woman become one, and by which a person will leave his or her family (Mark 10:7, referring to Gen. 2:24). Jesus defends marital cohabitation, radicalizing adultery (Matt. 5:27-32) and extracting the deeper implications of the Law (Exod. 20:14). Jesus' *radicalization* of the Law along lines of life is still more evident when he speaks of life itself. He extends the 'You shall not kill' of Exodus 20:13 to anger and insult (Matt. 5:21-26). Not only life, but its roots, are to be defended and secured. The *lex talionis,* which included even 'life for life' (Exod. 21:23), is abolished (Matt. 5:38-42). In other passages, not directly concerned with the law, but nevertheless with life, the Synoptics omit important elements, with a view to showing God to be the God of life. In the passage in which Jesus answers John's envoys (Matt. 11:2-6; Luke 7:18-28), he cites the positive signs of life: the blind see, the lame walk, and so on, but he omits the next lines of the passage from Isaiah to which he is referring, where the prophet speaks of the extermination of evildoers (Isa. 29:20). The same sort of omission occurs in Jesus' citation of Isaiah 61:2 in his presentation of his program in Luke. He ends with the mission 'to announce a year of favor from the Lord' (Luke 4:19, referring to Isa. 61:2). . . . Clearer still is this intent when Jesus criticizes the Halakah, the 'oral Torah'—that is, the interpretation of the Law. In Mark 7:8-13 (cf. Matt. 15:3-9), Jesus shows how clearly human traditions, seemingly arising in God's name, contravene God's original intention. . . . And more generally, this critique of human traditions as contravening God's primordial will appears in the famous passage about 'man and the Sabbath' (Mark 2:23-28 and parallels). In various ways, Jesus takes a stance contrary to that of

the Halakah, citing the case of David (Mark 2:25-28, referring to 1 Sam. 21:2-7), who, because of a real need, gathered and consumed the loaves of offering, the showbread. Jesus also cites the activity of the priests in the temple on the Sabbath (Matt. 12:5). Finally, he argues *ad hominem,* citing the practice of the very ones who are criticizing him (Matt. 12:11). But the basic argumentation he uses—the principle on which he bases his argumentation—is the will of God itself: 'The Sabbath was made for man' (Mark 2:27). The Sabbath is God's creation, but God did not create it for the divinity. God created it for the benefit of human life, in this case through rest and repose (Deut. 5:14)" ("Dios," 84-86).

50. See also Sobrino, *Jesús,* 95ff.: "Jesús, Reino de Dios y vida de los pobres."

51. "It is not that the universality of Jesus' hearers is an incorrect notion per se. There are in the gospels sufficient symbols of that universality in Jesus' contacts with Martha, Mary, Lazarus, Zaccheus, the Roman centurion, Nicodemus, and others. This does not mean that the universality of the hearers should be ignored on the basis of the gospel. What it means is that such a view is not the primary or the most correct one for understanding the fullness of life of the God of Jesus.

"The most correct view is gained rather from a different standpoint. Jesus announced the kingdom of God to the poor; he announced life to those who had it least. That God is God must undergo a historical verification, which is nothing but the giving of life to those deprived of it for centuries: the poor and oppressed majorities. And therefore, together with the announcement of the coming of the kingdom of God (Mark 1:15; Matt. 4:17), the poor appear as its privileged recipients (Matt. 5:3; Luke 6:20)" (Sobrino, "Epiphany," 74-75).

52. See chap. 3 below, pp. 97-103, where I summarize Sobrino's analysis of Jesus' anti-idolatric practice in terms of a choice between the God of life and the false divinities of death.

53. The theme of life is central to the Gospel of John. See Mateos and Barreto, *Vocabulario,* 296-302.

54. Sobrino: "Jesus' resurrection is not just a symbol of God's omnipotence, as if God had decided, arbitrarily and without any connection with Jesus' life and fate, to demonstrate the divine omnipotence. Rather Jesus' resurrection is presented as God's response to the unjust, criminal actions of human beings. God's responding action, therefore, can be understood only against the background of the action of human beings that is at the origin of this response: the murder of a just person. Looked at in this way, Jesus' resurrection directly demonstrates the triumph of justice over injustice. It is the triumph not only of God's omnipotence but of God's justice as well—although, to be sure, in order to manifest this justice God calls on power. Jesus' resurrection thus becomes good news, and the essential element in this good news is that, once and for all, justice has triumphed over injustice. The 'victim has triumphed over the executioner' " (*Jesús,* 174-75).

55. See Acts 2:24, 3:13-15, 4:10, 5:30, 10:39, 13:28-37; Rom. 4:24, 10:9. "In the first Christian preaching, although we have it only in stereotyped form, Jesus' resurrection was presented as follows: 'You even made use of pagans to crucify and kill him. God freed him from death's bitter pangs, however, and raised him up again' (Acts 2:23-24; cf. the same schema in Acts 3:13-15, 4:10, 5:30, 10:39, 13:28ff.). In this proclamation, a basic importance attaches to the fact that someone has been raised from the dead; but a no less basic importance attaches to the identity of the one raised up by God—Jesus of Nazareth" (Sobrino, *Jesús,* 174).

56. IECT, "Letter," 249; Sobrino, *Jesús,* 176-77, 179ff.

57. Archbishop Oscar Romero: "We know that offending God is death for humans. We know that such a sin really is mortal, not only in the sense of the interior death of the person who commits the sin, but also because of the real, objective death the sin produces. Let us remind ourselves of a fundamental datum of our Christian faith: sin killed the Son of God, and sin is what goes on killing the children of God.

"We see that basic truth of the Christian faith daily in the situation in our country [El Salvador]. It is impossible to offend God without offending one's brother or sister. And the worst offense against God, the worst form of secularism, as one of our Salvadoran theologians has said, is 'to turn children of God, temples of the Holy Spirit, the body of Christ in history, into fodder for political repression. The worst of these forms of secularism is the denial of grace by the objectivization of this world as an operative presence of the powers of evil, the visible presence of the denial of God' " (*Voice*, 183, citing Ignacio Ellacuría, "Entre Medellín y Puebla," ECA, 353 [1978] 123).

58. See Sobrino, "Epiphany," 67. This positive statement of life is borrowed from the mystical formulation of the second-century Christian thinker Irenaeus of Lyons: *Gloria Dei vivens homo, vita autem hominis visio Dei:* "The glory of God is a living human being; but the life of a human being is the vision of God."

59. IECT "Final Document," nos. 28–38; Míguez Bonino, "Reino."

60. Gutiérrez cites three biblical texts, each propounding a different form of the absence of God—in the Temple, in the leaders of the people, and in religious actions—but all pointing in the same *theo*-logical direction: "God is not there because God's reign does not come, because human beings are not feeding on God's will" (*Dios*, 50). (1) In the temple (see Jer. 7:1–7): God is absent because his kingdom is not being built in the nation—justice is not being practiced. (2) In the leaders of the people (see Mic. 3:9–12): God is absent by the fault of those in power, who shed innocent blood, detest justice, and twist the law to their own advantage, and hence are guilty of idolatry (the idolatry of Mammon—bribery, graft, money)—"while they still rely on the Lord" (Mic. 3:11)—that is, they manipulate the presence of God for the legitimation of unjust behavior. (3) In religious actions (see Matt. 7:21–23): God is absent because religious actions have been converted into rights and gestures that are empty of concrete love for one's brother and sister, concrete love for the poor (ibid., 47–50).

61. See also IECT, "Final Document," no. 47; Ellacuría, "Fe y justicia," 16.

CHAPTER 3

1. See Sobrino, *True Church,* 52–53. For the historical meaning of praxis—of the human being as the "practical being" who transforms history and is self-transformed in the process—see pp. 16–18, above. The meaning of praxis for belief—the praxis of faith as practice of love, practice of justice, and anti-idolatry practice—will be considered in this chapter. For the ecclesial level of this praxis—hearing, acceptance, service—see pp. 139–43, below.

2. See Sobrino, *Jesús,* 110; *True Church,* 317–28; IECT, "Final Document," nos. 46–52. Sobrino, in his *Christology at the Crossroads,* sets forth his reflections on the discipleship of Jesus more *in extenso* (108–145). "The central idea of my christology is that faith in Christ must become real in the following of Christ. . . . It emerges as credible and real only to the extent that we seek to do the same thing as Jesus did" (Sobrino, "Martirio: el nuevo nombre del seguimiento," 471).

3. See Míguez Bonino, *Fe en busca,* 111–30.

4. "God is unknown, unless the human being shares in God's concrete life by way of

the active exercise of love. There is no question of a minimization of the historical revelation in Jesus; on the contrary—for me this revelation is a decisive proof. But this revelation is not abstract theoretical knowledge. It is concrete existence—existence in love" (Míguez Bonino, *Fe en busca,* 116); see also Díez Alegría, *Credo,* 68–87.

5. See Gutiérrez, *Power,* 53–55. In this perspective, sin is in those persons who do not open out to God, who is their definitive realization, but remain turned in upon themselves and, thus subject to the power of selfishness, come into hostile confrontation with others in a refusal of fellowship. See Gutiérrez, *A Theology,* 151–52; Sobrino, *True Church,* 107–8.

6. "Evangelical conversion *(metanoia)* implies a rupture with our mental categories, our social group (culture, class, ethnos), our affective and emotional inclinations, our secret complicities with a world in which the poor do not have the place assigned them by the preferential and gratuitous love of God for them. The social dimensions of conversion to God—for each Christian and for the whole church—become perfectly clear from the moment we recognize that conversion necessarily involves solidarity with the poor and oppressed" (Gutiérrez, "Beber," 358).

7. "God's 'lasting' name, the name with which God is to be invoked 'from generation to generation,' establishes an indissoluble link between the 'I am who am' and the 'Lord God of your fathers'—that is, between the God of tradition and the God who transcends history. This double aspect is expressed from a starting point in mission—concretely, the liberation of the Jewish people in its confrontation with the pharaoh, the oppressor. In this liberation, God is self-revealed as the 'I am,' but not only as the 'I am,' for God is also the 'God of your fathers'—a clear, very precise reference to the history of the people. This 'I am,' the absolute principle, the beginning of all, is at the same time the God of the past, the God of those who have preceded the ones to whom Moses is sent. Consequently, we might say that although 'I am' has no past—God is absolute—faith in God does have a past. Faith in God is always historical. 'I am' is principle, origin, Father. Faith in the Father, faith in Yahweh, has a history. From mission, it becomes possible to understand who God is as absolute principle, as Lord, and at the same time as a God of the past, the God of the patriarchs" (Gutiérrez, *Dios,* 12). Gutiérrez's diagram may help clarify these relationships:

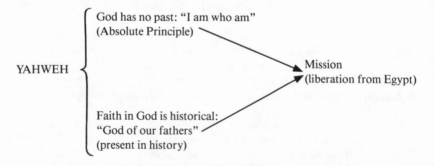

YAHWEH

God has no past: "I am who am"
(Absolute Principle)

Mission
(liberation from Egypt)

Faith in God is historical:
"God of our fathers"
(present in history)

8. "This formula and content of the covenant, reiterated with almost an obsessive intensity, becomes a key element in the national identity of the Jewish people. It is important to realize this. Faith in Yahweh enables Israel not only to recognize itself 'religiously,' but also to assert itself as a people, a human community. Israel is a nation that has *its* Lord, that belongs to *its* God. Israel is a people having made a pact with the

Lord. And this 'attitude of pact' will be the definitive, indelible mark of biblical faith" (Gutiérrez, *Dios,* 19–20).

9. On the personal nature of the act of faith, Sobrino has this to say: "In Christian revelation it clearly appears that faith is an act of an individual person. It is an act by which a person places himself or herself before God to hear and receive God's manifestation, to respond to it by surrendering wholly to God, and thus to correspond to the reality of God. This act is profoundly personal. Responsibility for this act cannot be delegated to someone else" (Sobrino, "Conllevamos," 173). At the same time, in the words of Xabier Pikaza, we must say that "no one experiences God on the basis of their own forces. No one has encountered God in virtue of their own individual quest. God is discovered out of the witness of a praying community (a church, a family) that hands on its faith, and in continuity with a believing tradition that lives and celebrates that faith *(Experiencia,* 201).

10. See also L. Boff, *Teología del cautiverio,* 256–89, where he attempts to identify the praxic concretion of the church in its capactiy as prophetic sacrament-sign-instrument. See also Ellacuría, "La Iglesia de los pobres, sacramento histórico de liberación."

11. The experience of the grass-roots ecclesial communities of the church in Latin America—a church that, under the impulse of the Spirit, deepens its roots in an oppressed, believing people—demonstrates this historical "irruption" of the poor. See IECT, "Final Document," nos. 19–26; C. Boff, "Fisonomía de las comunidades eclesiales de base"; L. Boff, *Eclesiogénesis. Las comunidades de base reinventan la iglesia.*

Jon Sobrino speaks of a "resurrection of the true church"—the original title of his *The True Church and the Poor:* "The term *resurrection* means that the Church of the poor breaks away from traditional ways of being Church. In this Church of the poor the Church attains a greater fullness and authenticity.

"The application of the metaphor of 'resurrection' to the Church may scandalize or seem extreme, as though implying that the Church had been dead and were now beginning to live again in the Church of the poor. That is not what I mean by speaking of the Church as experiencing a 'resurrection' in the Church of the poor. If I use the term (as I do) in a way that is more than purely metaphorical, then I am acknowledging that in the Church of the poor there is, first, a newness in substance and a historical break from other ways of being the Church and, second, that in this new situation the Church is returning to life—a life seriously threatened with destruction and irrelevance and even with betraying its own reason for existence if it does not become a Church of the poor" *(True Church,* 84).

With reference to the church of the poor, Sobrino develops an important "ecclesio-*theo*-logical" thesis. In the church of the poor we have, today, concretely, a "better"—though not unique—historico-structural channel for a concretization of the experience of God. (The church of the poor has no monopoly on the experience of God.) See *True Church,* 129. This means that if we take seriously the importance of the *place* from which we approach the experience of God, asserting that the poor furnish us with a special locus for approaching Mystery (ibid., 91), then a church of the poor furnishes the best opportunity for the experience of God (ibid., 126)—furnishes the "channel and epistemology for giving belief in God a meaning—a determinate meaning" (Sobrino, "Resurrección," 146).

12. This ecclesial conversion implies a passage by way of the demanding mediation of the "other"—the poor and oppressed—and their evangelizing potential. Gutiérrez points out: "Indeed, the acquisition of self-awareness implies a passage by way of the

mediation of the other, without which we fail to perceive ourselves as what we are—persons in relationship with others. During the time of the Second Vatican Council one heard a great deal about the church having to become aware of itself. But obviously it could not do so without passing by way of the mediation of the other, of the world—otherwise it would have fallen into the very ecclesiocentrism from which the Council sought to dislodge it. How, then, will the church in Latin America today acquire an ecclesial awareness—thus having to pass by way of the mediation of the poor and oppressed world—without what we might call a 'bad conscience,' the bad conscience of knowing that it is still a stranger to the world of the poor today? . . .

"After Vatican II, under the impulse of Medellín, the gospel expression 'evangelizing the poor' [from Luke 4:18, 'to bring glad tidings to the poor'—*euangelisasthai ptochois,* Jesus' citation of Isaiah 61:1], became an important one again, and with a creative meaning. The option for the oppressed and solidarity with them encouraged a series of rich and promising experiments the length and breadth of Latin America. But . . . the gradual conversion of the popular sectors—at great cost to them in their role as the protagonists of history—forced us to delve more deeply into the question. The practice of evangelization in the midst of poor, exploited peoples afforded us the following lesson. . . . *In the effort to carry the good news to the oppressed, we have the experience of being evangelized by them.* Here the popular Christian communities have played a capital role, as Puebla has pointed out, speaking of the discovery—made by the church in its commitment to the poor sectors, and in these communities—of the 'evangelizing potential of the poor.' This is something that is gradually coming to dominate our work and our manner of regarding the church. This experience has brought us to understand that it is the poor who do the evangelizing, just as it has brought us to understand, in new terms, that God is *revealed in history through the poor*" (Gutiérrez, "Comunidades," 16–17, 23, emphasis added; see also Sobrino, *True Church,* 52; and pp. 125–28, below).

13. *The Discovery of God* (Chicago, Regnery, 1967) 106–7.

14. "When the Pharisees are scandalized by the fact that Jesus breaks the cultic rules by eating with sinners and not observing the Sabbath, Jesus quotes Hosea to them: 'It is mercy I desire and not sacrifice' (Hos. 6:6; see Matt. 9:13; 12:7). To those who are angry with their fellows he says: 'If you bring your gift to the altar and there recall that your brother has anything against you, leave your gift at the altar, go first to be reconciled with your brother, and then come and offer your gift' (Matt. 5:23–24). To anyone who would pray he says: 'When you stand to pray, forgive anyone against whom you have a grievance so that your heavenly Father may in turn forgive you your faults' (Mark 11:25–26)" (Sobrino, *Christology,* 166).

15. Following M. E. Boismard, Sobrino calls our attention to a datum of scriptural analysis: "It may seem scandalous enough that Jesus seems to correlate and equate love of God with love of neighbor. What is even more scandalous is the possibility that love of God as the chief commandment may not have been in the original version of Mark's gospel at all! This view is regarded as highly probable by some scholars. Boismard, for example, offers the following reconstruction of the text in its most primitive form (see Pierre Benoit and M. E. Boismard, *Synopse des Quatre Evangiles* [Paris, Cerf, 1965] 350–51): 'And one of the scribes said to him, "Well, Master," and asked him: "Which is the greatest commandment of all?" Jesus replied: "It is this: You shall love your neighbor as yourself; there is no greater commandment." And no one dared to ask him anything further' " (Sobrino, *Christology,* 169–70). See also Sobrino's commentary on this reconstruction of the original text, ibid., 170.

For the parallel in Hellenistic Judaism with the doctrine of the Markan pericope, see Quell and Stauffer, *Caridad*, 88–89.

16. For the relationship between faith and justice in biblical theology, see also Alonso Díaz, "Buenas obras." For the same relationship in the gospel message, see also *La vida religiosa a partir de la congregación general XXXII de la Compañía de Jesús* (Panama City, CICA, 1978) 49–70; Sobrino, *True Church*, 64–76.

17. *"Faith is certainly an act elicited by a subject, but if it is to be a reality, the subjective act as such is not enough.* Nor is Christian perseverance in faith accomplished simply by an intention of the will to preserve faith subjectively. If through faith as a subjective act we accept God along with the meaning that such an acceptance imposes on our life, then this faith can exist only in conjunction with something historical and objective. This historical, objective reality is (though not exclusively) the practice of justice as the historical way of proclaiming the reign of God and making this reign real" (Sobrino, *True Church*, 62).

18. The demand for the fuller humanization of everything human is a demand for what the New Testament calls the "new man." Here is how Sobrino describes this ideal new man and woman: "The new human beings are those who are able to learn, change, and be converted and thus to be honest with themselves; persons whose values are those of the Sermon on the Mount, whose eyes and heart are pure, who show mercy, are devoted to justice and ready to run the risks that this devotion entails, who prefer peace to needless struggle; those who are ready to forgive their enemies, are generous in victory, and always give their adversary another chance. They are, finally, disposed to be thankful for life and to celebrate it; they believe in life and continue to hope" (*True Church*, 188).

19. "This is precisely the temptation we see at work at the beginning of the Church's history in the form of the docetism, gnosticism, and enthusiasm that are condemned in the theologies of John and Paul: the temptation to look for fulfillment and salvation outside history instead of finding it by penetrating more deeply into the historical" (Sobrino, *True Church*, 188).

20. "An unqualified readiness for death is a mediation of the experience of God. . . . Those who are disposed to give their own life in order that others may have life are in a radical way experiencing the God of life. . . . Those who are ready to abide by the paradox that the unconditional promotion of life may demand the surrender of their own life are confessing *in actu* the sovereign demand of life. For a Christian, such a confession is an affirmation of the mystery of God" (Sobrino, *True Church*, 58).

21. See Segundo, *Nuestra idea,* 13. "Our falsified, inauthentic ways of dealing with our brothers and sisters form a close alliance with our falsifications of the idea of God" (ibid.).

22. Archbishop Romero spoke repeatedly of this idolatry in his homilies, and specified some of its idols: the absolutization of wealth and the absolutization of power in national security regimes. See Sobrino, *Monseñor Romero,* 9–13.

23. For analysis of fetishism in general as a key to political economics (Marx and other currents), see Hinkelammert's study on the discernment of fetishes, *Armas,* 7–159; on the fetishism of money, see ibid., xiv-xv, 22–32.

24. Along these same lines Sobrino calls our attention to how, in ancient Israel (in the northern kingdom), where land monopoly was the order of the day, the prophet Amos observed and denounced the social configuration established there: that between the monopolizers and the dispossessed, the poor. Theoretically, Sobrino points out, both groups invoked the God of Israel—but the prophet "denounces the religion of the

former as idolatry, for the people are perishing. The 'monopolizers' are not rendering worship to the God of life, but to the gods of death—hence the critical distinction made by God through the mouth of the prophets: 'you,' the monopolizers, and 'my people,' the 'helpless,' the 'poor' " ("Dios," 112). See also the linguistic and exegetical study by José Luís Sicre, presenting the anti-idolatric dimension of the preexilic prophets from a point of departure in two concrete forms of idolatry: political power and wealth: *Los dioses olvidados: Poder y riqueza en los profetas pre-exílicos.*

25. "We must not see this as a call to evade our own responsibilities, or as a depreciation of human deeds and the necessary means for their realization. The same passage ends by emphasizing that we should 'seek first [the Father's] kingship over you, his way of holiness' [Matt. 6:33]—'seek' it, obviously, by putting it into practice. The gospel summons us to avoid a confusion of hierarchies and, in particular, to accept the radical demand of gratitude imposed by God's love. It would be simplistic and mistaken to see an exclusive contradistinction here between abandonment to providence and the acceptance of historical responsibilities" (Gutiérrez, *Dios,* p. 41, n. 18).

26. Many are the biblical passages testifying to this. For example, Ezek. 22:27, 29.

27. "The dimension of basic alternatives runs through the synoptic gospels in various forms. . . . On the anthropological level, it is affirmed in the Beatitudes and the denunciations (Luke 6:20–26), and in saving and losing life (Mark 8:35 and parallels). On the christological level, it is asserted that one must be with Jesus or against him (Matt. 12:30). And on the level of divinity—the most important one for our present purposes—the alternative is expressed clearly: 'No servant can be a slave to two masters; for either he will hate the first and love the second, or he will be devoted to the first and think nothing of the second. You cannot serve God and Money' (Matt. 6:24; Luke 16:13)" (Sobrino, "Epiphany," 84–85).

28. "It has been rightly claimed that *temptation* was the atmosphere in which all of Jesus' life took place, and that it related to true messianism—that is, to the true will of God concerning him. But it is also a fact that *persecution* was the atmosphere in which his mission took place, at least as of a certain date. Although it is difficult to determine the various periods of Jesus' life exactly, 'the gospels are faithful to history when they state that successes and failures, sympathy and hostility, were the fabric of Jesus' life from the beginning' " (Sobrino, "Epiphany," 85, citing Günther Bornkamm, *Jesus of Nazareth* [London/New York, Hodder & Stoughton/Harper, 1960] 153).

29. " 'Alas for you who are rich' is the comment in the first denunciation (Luke 6:24). There is here an absolute condemnation of wealth, primarily because of its results for the rich person per se: 'You have had your time of happiness' (Luke 6:24), and it will do that person no good on the day of judgment (Luke 12:13–21). But, in particular, there is condemnation of the intrinsic root of the evil of wealth, which is relative: wealth is unjust. The moderate Jerusalem Bible comments: 'It is called "unjust," not only because those who possess it have acquired it by evil means, but also, in a more general way, because there is some injustice in the origins of nearly all fortunes.' Hence wealth is not merely the possession of goods, which makes it extremely difficult to open one's heart to God (Matt. 19:13–26; Mark 10:23–27), but rather an accumulation of goods, which deprives others of the goods to which they are entitled. For that reason, the rich are the oppressors of the poor, according to Luke. Thus the conversion of Zaccheus is not praised only because of the giving away of riches, but also because of the proper distribution of them to others (Luke 19:8). Therefore, the rich are 'oppressors of the poor' [Escudero Freire, *Devolver,* 273], and states of poverty are 'caused by the oppressor' [ibid., 315]. The rich deprive others of what is necessary for life, and that is why

Jesus anathematized them" (Sobrino, "Epiphany," 77).

30. Recall the well-known reproaches and anathemas directed at the Pharisees and scribes in Matthew 23 and Luke 11. Jesus condemns hypocrisy (a false subjective attitude) and its objective consequences oppressive of others (Mark 12:38-40; Matt. 12:4; Luke 11:46). "What is particularly emphasized in these passages is the conceit and hypocrisy of the scribes and Pharisees. That hypocrisy evokes severe judgment from Jesus: 'They will receive the severest sentence' (Mark 12:40; Luke 20:47). But the fundamental flaw was not the overweening malice of their hypocritical subjective attitude, but rather the fact of oppressing others, imposing heavy burdens on them and taking over the property of widows. That is the fundamental sin, and the fundamental negation of the will of God, subjecting it to hypocritical pride" (Sobrino, "Epiphany," 77).

31. "Jesus' castigation of the priests reaches a peak in the expulsion from the temple (Mark 11:15-59 and parallels). These narratives, plus those that follow, on Jesus' authority (Mark 11:27-33 and parallels), have been highly theologized in christology and in Jewish eschatology—that is, the future of the Jewish people as the chosen people. But the original core of the narrative appears to be in Mark 11:15-16. The priests have committed the horrendous crime of defiling the essence of the temple. But, once again, their crime does not entail a religious wickedness alone, but a human one as well. 'The priests have converted the temple into a den of thieves, a den from which evildoers continually emerge to commit their evil deeds. The priests misuse their vocation, which is to conduct worship for the glory of God. Instead, they engage in business, and accrue profits' (Joachim Jeremias, *New Testament Theology* [New York, Scribner's, 1971], 145). Although not in the form of anathemas, these harsh rebukes by Jesus have the same logical structure: fellow human beings are being oppressed in areas of their human existence, and with the overbearing wickedness that makes it possible in the name of an institution willed by God" (Sobrino, "Epiphany," 79).

32. "Jesus rebukes 'those with political power,' saying that 'the recognized rulers lord it over their subjects, and their great men make them feel the weight of authority' (Mark 10:42 and elsewhere). This is certainly a general rebuke, unlike the other, detailed ones, although it is confirmed by Jesus' harsh words about the ruler Herod (Luke 13:32). Once again, the point lies in the relational aspect of political power. Regardless of the fact that, in a given era, power may have grandeur and honor, and even God's blessing, Jesus condemns a power whose historical consequences are oppression and deprivation of life—here, in the realm of political rights" (Sobrino, "Epiphany," 79).

33. Sobrino studies the controversies that Mark places near the beginning of Jesus' public activity (Mark 2:1-3:6; cf. Luke 5:17-6:11), which Matthew divides into two series (Matt. 9:1-17, 12:1-4). These controversies concern: (1) the cure and forgiveness of the paralytic; (2) Jesus' eating with sinners; (3) the question of fasting; (4) the ears of grain gleaned on the sabbath; and (5) the healing of the person with the withered hand.

34. "The controversies do not essentially involve different religious explanations of the reality of God, which would also entail different legal requirements. They involve different understandings of the reality of God, which will naturally come out in religious explanations. And, because what one understands as the reality of God can differ, from person to person, discussion therefore emerges. And, because the realities compared are not only different but conflicting, controversy emerges" (Sobrino, "Epiphany," 82).

35. Both levels of controversy—the human (the social fact) and the religious (the miracles)— although they can be distinguished, are combined; "and hence it is possible

to make a human controversy the substratum of a religious controversy" (Sobrino, "Epiphany," 82).

36. That Jesus' argumentation is theo-logical becomes clear when he takes advantage of the controversy to offer a new image of true worship, in Matthew's double reference to Hosea 6:6 at the meal with the publicans (Matt. 5:11-13), and in the account of the gathering of the ears of grain (Matt. 12:7)—an image in conformity, as it happens, with the Matthean view of Christian worship (Matt. 5:23). All this appears more clearly in Jesus' declaration on the Sabbath.

37. Matt. 22:34-40 and parallels. Sobrino's analysis: "In his teaching on the love for God, Jesus touches on the human tendency to manipulate not only certain provisions of the law, but even the greatest and most sacred of commandments—love for God— precisely to disregard the express will of the God whom one must love: love for one's neighbor. Hence, Jesus exposes the use of religious law because in its name disregard is shown for what God, in fact, wills for human life" ("Epiphany," 84).

38. The passage is the synoptics' classic example of the matter under discussion here. The situation is simple: the disciples take their meals without washing their hands—in other words, with impure hands (Mark 7:2)—thereby violating the tradition of the elders, to which the Pharisees hold tenaciously. "Such traditions abounded, particularly regulations for legal purity. And according to the synoptic gospels, Jesus and his disciples broke them unabashedly (Mark 1:41, 5:41; Luke 7:14, 11:38)" (Sobrino, "Epiphany," 82).

39. Sobrino provides a summary of the provocation and persecution to which Jesus was subjected during his public ministry, until the moment of the betrayal by Judas ("Epiphany," 85–86).

40. So it is recorded in the primitive kerygma, in its more historical versions (2 Thess. 2:15) as well as in its more theologized versions (Acts 2:23, 3:13, 15, 4:10, 5:30, 10:39) in Peter's discourses, and Acts 13:28 in a discourse of Paul. Sobrino comments: "The fact that in these texts the Jews are held responsible for Jesus' death, and their blame is emphasized—because the initial Christian polemic took place in Jerusalem—does not detract anything from the underlying truth. Jesus was a victim of the oppression he had preached against, and a victim of the most acute form of oppression—death" ("Epiphany," 88).

41. "According to John, the interrogation before Annas related to the teachings of Jesus and his disciples (John 18:19). But in the accusation before the Sanhedrin it related to two key points concerning Jesus as a mediator and the mediation of the God of Jesus. The cause of the conviction appears in the charge that Jesus has blasphemed by declaring himself the Christ (Matt. 26:24; Mark 14:62; Luke 22:67). But, in addition to this cause, which probably comes from redactional sources, we must consider the other cause, which relates not so much to Jesus' claims about himself, as to the claims of a new mediation of God, and not only new, but different and contrary: the temple (Matt. 26:61; Mark 14:58; John 2:19). Only by understanding what the temple meant in the religious, political, and economic spheres can one understand the totality that Jesus offers as an alternative to the temple. Jesus offers not a change in, but an alternative to, the temple. The destruction of the temple implies the surpassing of the law, as the leaders of the people interpreted it, and even as it appeared in some of the prophetic and apocalyptic traditions; and it implies no longer making the temple the center of a political, social, and economic theocracy" (Sobrino, "Epiphany," 89–90).

42. See Hans Küng, *Does God Exist? An Answer for Today,* for an exhaustive consideration of the theme for our own day in the European philosophico-theological tradition.

43. See Sobrino, in Ellacuría et al., *Cruz,* 147. For a believing, oppressed people, confronted with the misery of reality, "the equivalent to the temptation of atheism or agnosticism in other climes is the temptation to fatalism" (ibid.). "The persistence of a reality of poverty and suffering poses difficult questions. An evasive reply may end in an acceptance of, even a resignation to, evil and injustice that is contrary to faith in the God of liberation" (Gutiérrez, *Dios,* 66–67). This is not to deny the fact of processes of secularization and unbelief in intellectual or revolutionary circles, nor the fact that, for committed, radicalized believers, God has ceased to be a positive experience. See Terán Durati, "Ateismo."

44. The expression is that of Sergio Arce Martínez, Presbyterian theologian and professor in the seminary of Matanzas, in Cuba, from his typology of atheism. Arce Martínez lists three types of atheism: (1) the atheism of *disbelief* ("There is no God"—from an "unwillingness to believe"); (2) the atheism of *despair* ("There is no God"—from the "nonrationality of hope"; and (3) the atheism of *injustice* ("There is no God"—from the "nonjustice of love") (Arce Martínez, "Teología," 141ff.).

45. See Míguez Bonino, *Espacio,* title of chap. 1: "Only an atheist can be a good Christian." The origin of this curious expression is in an exchange between philosopher Ernst Bloch and theologian Jürgen Moltmann. Bloch made the paradoxical assertion of Míguez's chapter title—whereupon Moltmann responded, "But only a Christian can be a good atheist" (ibid., 11). See also Dussel, *Método,* 258: "El atheísmo de los profetas."

46. See Assmann, "El Tercer Mundo evangeliza a las Iglesias," 1; Dussel, "Acceso ético al Absoluto: el discurso ateo como condición de la afirmación de Dios," in Dussel, *Religión.* Also in *Christus,* 484 (1976).

47. Bonhoeffer, *Resistencia,* 189ff., 206ff. (letters of June 8 and July 16, 1944).

48. "There are not two histories, one profane and one sacred, 'juxtaposed' or 'closely linked.' Rather there is only one human destiny, irreversibly assumed by Christ, the Lord of history. His redemptive work embraces all the dimensions of existence and brings them to their fullness. The history of salvation is at the very heart of human history" (Gutiérrez, *A Theology,* 153). See also Ellacuría, *Freedom,* 3–19). This unitary conceptualization of history is illustrated and developed by Gutiérrez on the basis of two biblical themes: the relationship between creation and salvation, and the eschatological promises (*A Theology,* 153–68).

49. See also Sobrino, "Martirio," 468–69; Hernández Pico, "Martirio." "When our church does not consent to live a life generously surrendered for the cause of God in the cause of today's exploited and oppressed classes, when it allows itself to be paralyzed with fear and does not remember its martyrs in solidarity with the people, we have the right to ask if it has new eyes to recognize the crucified Lord in the disfigured faces of the impoverished people of the Third World" (IECT, "Final Document," no. 71, p. 243).

50. Consider the implications of a like assertion for the Christian notion of holiness (Sobrino, *True Church,* 107, 109).

51. Cited by Míguez Bonino, *Espacio,* 58.

52. See Gutiérrez, *A Theology,* 168–72: "Temporal Progress and Growth of the Kingdom."

CHAPTER 4

1. The Latin American theology of liberation has not taken its point of departure for a reflection on the Mystery of God in an analysis of classic dogmatic formulations, like the Apostles' Creed or the Nicaeo-Constantinopolitan Creed. But this does not

mean that it ignores them, and still less that it takes its distance from them or denies them. The thrust of the contribution of liberation theology is precisely to show how these formulas can have sense and meaning in ongoing history. What is really at stake is the *real content* implied in a dogmatic formulation, rather than the formulation itself in its formal content. As Jon Sobrino writes, "The locus where the content of dogmatic statements functions is not in the dogmatic statements themselves, but in something antecedent to them: the manner of existence that gives them their meaning" ("Resurrección," 143).

2. Sobrino has correctly insisted that the ultimate meaning of "Ortho*doxy*" is *"dox*ology." See *Christology,* 323–28.

3. See pp. 132–33, below.

4. Liberation theology frequently uses the term "Spirit of Jesus" (Acts 16:7; cf. Rom. 15.5; Phil. 1.19). See Sobrino, "Resurrección," 151ff. We must not lose sight of the fact that the "Spirit of Jesus" is the Spirit not only of Jesus, but also "of the Father" and "of the Son."

5. "The fact that the theology of liberation takes risks, as theology must, and that it has perhaps sometimes contained ambiguities or oversimplifications, does not destroy its basic legitimacy or diminish its importance and urgency. It calls for sympathy and support. There is another type of ambiguity that is more to be feared: that of a polemical attitude in its regard, leading to a harmful outcome for something more important than theology—the Christian commitment to fellowship and justice, and thus to the liberation of the oppressed" (Alfaro, "Notas," 600).

6. The basic thesis that liberation theology will indeed propose is that "only in solidarity with the life, struggles, and aspirations of the oppressed is faith in the God of the poor expressed" (Gutiérrez, "Itinerario," 60).

7. "The analogy of poverty," as Sobrino has emphasized, "broadens tragically. In theological language, the poor are transformed into the *suffering Servant of Yahweh.* Like the latter, the poor have striven to implant right and justice among the nations, and, again like the latter, their thanks has been death. The poor today are without human face or shape, and others turn away from them in disgust. They are impoverished and annihilated by the sin of the powerful, and bear the burden of that sin. Many times have they been driven to the slaughter—recall the massacres—like sheep without a voice to raise in complaint. Then they are taken and buried as malefactors, subversives, godless miscreants, so that not only their bodies, but their dignity is put to death, and their reality perverted utterly. The poor today are the crucified people, then" ("Esperanza," 116; see also *Jesús,* 186–88: "The Servant of Yahweh and the Crucified People").

8. This does not mean "a return to theologies of creation that pay no heed to the sin that objectively cuts across creation and that promote a linear development based on the dynamic 'seeds' present in the created world. Such a return would amount to an endorsement of developmentalist socioeconomic theories. The point is rather to see creation as the (logically) first mediation of the being of God. It is to see in creation the first manifestation of the God of life. . . . The issue, then, is not to fall into the trap of turning too quickly to eschatology but rather to turn soberly to protology. The real problem in Latin America is not that the eschaton has not come but that the realities and values present at the beginning have not achieved their full being" (Sobrino, *True Church,* 164).

9. In the Evangelical tradition, in virtue of the biblical specificity of its "principistic" framework (its formation on the basis of biblical "principles," its "fundamentalism"), we have the epistemological obstacle that Leonardo Boff denominates

"theologism," which in our case would be better called *biblism*. "Theologism expects to be able to explain all problems, even political ones, and furnish all solutions, in terms of theology [or the Bible]. The legitimacy and contributions of other discourses are not acknowledged. Theology [or the Bible] is substituted for social analysis" (Boff and Boff, *Salvation*, 49).

10. Juan Luís Segundo is surely on the mark when he says of the "hermeneutic circle": "The last systematic obstacle for any theology committed to human liberation . . . is a certain type of academicism which posits ideological neutrality as the ultimate criterion: which levels down and relativizes all claims to absoluteness and all evaluations of some ideas over others. This is the theological equivalent of another great ideological adversary of liberation: the so-called quest for the death of ideologies or their suicide on the altars of scientific and scholarly impartiality" *(Liberation,* 25, citing Gutiérrez, *A Theology,* 21–42).

11. Poverty proclaimed more or less generally as a "Christian ideal" has become an *equivocal* proclamation. "In the Bible, material poverty is a subhuman situation, the fruit of injustice and sin. This poverty should not be a Christian ideal. This would mean aspiring to something considered demeaning for a human being. Further, it would place the gospel demands at cross-purposes with humanity's great desire and striving—to break free of subjection to nature, to eliminate human exploitation, and to create better conditions of life for everyone. It would likewise—and no less gravely—mean the justification, however unintentional, of the situation of injustice and exploitation that is the basic cause of poverty—real poverty, which the great majority suffer in Latin America" (Gutiérrez, *Power,* 54). On the meaning of poverty in the religious life, see Sobrino, *True Church,* 302–37: "Religious Life in the Third World"; Cussianovich, *Desde los pobres.*

12. This is one of the objectives of the *Historia general de la Iglesia en América Latina,* being written under the auspices of the Comisión de Estudios de Historia de la Iglesia en Latinoamérica.

13. Juan Luís Ruiz de la Peña, professor of theological anthropology and eschatology in the Pontifical University of Salamanca, has suggested the term *analogia praxeos.*

14. See Barth, *La revelación como abolición de la religión.* See also Leuba, "Dios salvador según Karl Barth."

15. This distinction was suggested to me by the Spanish theologian José María Castillo, on the basis of Clodovis Boff's distinction between "the real" and "awareness of the real" *(Teología de lo político,* 185). "We must never forget that God has been revealed to human beings *not in a humanly neutral situation,* but in a situation of profound, crying injustice, a situation in which some are rich precisely because others are poor. Now if, in such a situation, God were to be revealed as the God of everyone, then it would be clear that God is not the God of everyone, but the God of the favored and privileged, the God of the rich and powerful of this world. Instead, God is self-revealed as the God of the poor, so as to say to the rich and the poor alike that God is the Father of everyone. And because God is the Father of everyone, God is unwilling that some dominate others. That is, God does not wish that there be rich and poor" (Castillo, "Teología," 154; emphasis added).

16. In theology, the term "economic," from the Greek *oikonomia,* "administration," "management," refers to the actualization of God's salvific plan in history, as distinguished from the being of God *in se,* "immanent" activity. The economic Trinity, then, is the Trinity manifested in the manifestation of salvation. See Rahner, "Dios

Trino," 370–71; see also Rahner, ed., *Encyclopedia of Theology: the Concise Sacramentum Mundi* (New York, Crossroad, reprint ed., 1984) 1758–64.

17. For the distinction and antagonism between Christendom and the church, see Richard, *Muerte de la Cristiandad—Nacimiento de la Iglesia.* "Christendom" denotes a specific historical mode of the insertion of the church into society, in which it has utilized, as mediation for the realization of its mission, the political power (political society) and hegemonic power (civil society) of the dominant sectors, which power is concentrated in the state and in the organs of civil society: schools, universities, communications, media. The church of Christendom holds that it has more evangelizing (or better, "christianizing") force to the extent that its presence and power are greater in all the organisms of the dominant political and civil society, and in the measure that these organs defend the church. Today, however, breach with Christendom does not mean breach with the church. Indeed, a breach between the church and the dominant political power, which has led to the "crisis of Christendom," has made church renewal possible. The death of Christendom permits the rebirth of the church. See Richard, *Mortes das cristandades;* idem, "Situación," 101–4. The following of Jesus as discernment, says Sobrino, involves the discernment of the truth of a God who hears the cry of the oppressed, calls for justice, and proclaims liberation, in *contradistinction and opposition* to the idea of God presented by so-called Western civilization and the culture of Christendom. Christians exercise this discernment "by denying the reality of a *God who is power,* who historically has been seen to be an oppressor, either subtly, often through religious and church traditions, or grossly, in the image of divinity concealed in prevailing systems, be they called capitalism, national security, the multinationals, or trilateralism. We believe that this discernment has been exercised inasmuch as the Spirit has placed Christians not at the center of power, but on the periphery of poverty" (*Jesús,* 160). (For trilateralism, see L. Boff, *Periferia,* 201–5; Hinkelammert, *Armas,* 101–29.)

18. That love necessitates historical mediations has been abundantly emphasized and analyzed by liberation theology. See Sobrino, "Seguimiento," 526–29.

19. See Sobrino, "Aporte," 123–27.

20. See Archbishop Romero's third pastoral letter (*Voice,* 85–113).

21. Gutiérrez writes: "The place of the mission of the church is where the celebration of the Lord's supper and the creation of human brotherhood are indissolubly joined. This is what it means in an active and concrete way to be the sacrament of the salvation of the world. . . . Without a real commitment against exploitation and alienation and for a society of solidarity and justice, the Eucharistic celebration is an empty action, lacking any genuine endorsement by those who participate in it. . . . 'To make a remembrance' of Christ is more than the performance of an act of worship; it is to accept living under the sign of the cross and in the hope of the resurrection. It is to accept the meaning of a life that was given over to death—at the hands of the powerful of this world—for love of others" (*A Theology,* 262, 265).

22. See Pablo Richard and Diego Irarrázaval, *Religión y política en América Central* (San José, Costa Rica, DEI 1981). See also Irarrázaval's study, *Religión del pobre y liberación* (Lima, CEP, 1978), based on studies and surveys carried out in Chimbote.

23. See Sobrino, *Christology,* 70–74, 146–78 ("The Prayer of Jesus"), 217–35 (on Jesus' death), 259–62 (on his resurrection), and 362–66 ("The Consciousness of Jesus").

24. Vincent Cosmao's *Changing the World* has been very enlightening to me in this matter.

25. It has been commonplace, since the Renaissance, and especially since the seven-

teenth century, to vaunt the human capacity to know and to transform nature and society—that is, to take them into its own hands and transform history (see Gutiérrez, *Power,* 171–76). But an important nuance is to be observed. Human toil, science, technology, and development, in their historical concretion, are *not a neutral reality.* They have served to create instruments and relationships of the domination of some countries over others, and one social class over another. Thus we must keep account that the assumption and transformation of history will have to be effectuated *from beneath,* from among "the crucified of history."

26. Sobrino posits a "verification" of God in history as penultimate reality. This verification can be undertaken "by showing that, with God, the totality of history is better explained—or, more 'trinitarily,' by showing that, with God, history gives more of itself. . . . The eschatological reservoir functions not only as negative criterion of the 'not yet,' but *as a positive principle, as genuine reservoir of history,* upon which human beings seize in order to make history give more of itself" ("Abordar," 23–24; emphasis added).

27. See Rubem Alves, "La función ideológica y posibilidades utópicas del protestantismo latinoamericano," in *De la Iglesia y la Sociedad* (Montevideo, Tierra Neuva, 1971) 13–21.

28. For the religion of the Bible as an ethico-prophetical religion of hope, see Díez Alegría, *Creo,* 60–67.

29. See Richard's study on spirituality in Bonnín, *Espiritualidad,* 92–101. See also Gutiérrez, *We Drink.*

30. In the Bible the spiritual is never set in opposition to material life or the social. "The spiritual, as we say, is not opposed to the social. The real opposition is between bourgeois individualism and the spiritual in the biblical sense" (Gutiérrez, *Power,* 203).

Reference Bibliography

Alfaro, Juan. "Notas preliminares para una teología de la liberación." *Salmanticensis*, 3 (1977) 589–600.

Alonso Días, José. "Las 'buenas obras' (o la 'justicia') dentro de la estructura de los principales temas de teología bíblica," in Alonso Días et al., *Fe*, 13–59.

——, et al. *Fe y justicia.* Salamanca, Sígueme, 1981.

Alves, Rubem A. *Cristianismo ¿opio o liberación?* Montevideo, Tierra Nueva, 1972.

——. "El lenguaje del humanismo mesiánico," in Richard et al., *Cristianismo*, 140–59.

——. "El pueblo de Dios y la búsqueda de una nueva ordenación social," in Assmann et al., *Religión*, 136–139.

Araya Guillén, Victorio. "Interpretación en clave liberadora del principio bíblico 'Dios es Amor': Estudio en Jon Sobrino." *Vida y Pensamiento*, 1 (1982) 3–18.

Arce Martínez, Sergio. "La teología y el ateismo contemporáneo," in Arce Martínez et al., *Cristo*, 141–60.

——, et al., *Cristo vivo en Cuba: Reflexiones teológicas cubanas.* San José, Costa Rica, DEI, 1978.

Arroyo, A. "Classes sociales." *Christus*, 534 (1980).

ASET. *Teología desde el Tercer Mundo: Documentos finales de los cinco congresos internacionales de la Asociación Ecuménica de Teólogos del Tercer Mundo.* San José, Costa Rica, 1982.

Assmann, Hugo. "Aspectos básicos de la reflexión teológica en América Latina," in Assmann et al., *Teología negra*, 83–97.

——. "The Faith of the Poor in Their Struggle with Idols," in Richard et al., *Idols*, 194–229.

——. "Iglesia de los pobres," in Ellacuría et al., *Cruz*.

——. "Tecnología y poder en la perspectiva de la teología de la liberación," in Comisión para la Participación, Tecnología, 29–44.

——. "El Tercer Mundo evangeliza a las Iglesias," in PRODIADIS, *Lectura*, 1–10.

——. "La tarea común de las ciencias sociales y de la teología en el desenmascaramiento de la necrofilia del capitalismo" en Varios, *Capitalismo: violencia y anti-vida*, San José, DEI-EDUCA, 1978.

——. *Theology for a Nomad Church.* Maryknoll, N.Y., Orbis, 1975.

——, et al. *Religión ¿instrumento de una nueva liberación?* Barcelona, Fontanella, 1973.

——, et al. *Teología negra y teología de la liberación.* Salamanca, 1974.

Avila, Rafael. *Teología y política.* Bogotá, Presencia, 1977.

Bandera, Armando. *La iglesia ante el proceso de liberación.* Madrid, Católica, 1975.

Barth, Karl. *The Humanity of God.* Richmond, Va., John Knox, 1960.

——. "The Mercy and Righteousness of God," in *Church Dogmatics* (Edinburgh, Clark, 1957) 2/1, 368–406.

———. *La revelación como abolición de la religión.* Madrid, Marova, 1973.

Baum, Gregory, et al. *Vida y reflexión: Aportes de la teología de la liberación al pensamiento teológico actual.* Lima, CEP, 1983.

Bernardini, Eugenio. *Communicare la fede nell'America oppressa: Storia e metoda della Teologia della liberazione.* Turin, 1982.

Boff, Clodovis, "Fisonomía de las comunidades eclesiales de base." *Concilium,* 164 (1981) 90–98.

———. *Teologia e prática: Teologia do político e suas mediações.* Petrópolis, Vozes, 2nd ed., 1982. Span. trans., *Teología de lo político, sus mediaciones* (Salamanca, Sígueme, 1980). Engl. trans., *Theology and Praxis* (Maryknoll, N.Y., Orbis Books, 1987).

———. "Teología e prática." REB, 144 (1976) 789–810.

Boff, Leonardo. *El Ave María: Lo femenino y el Espíritu Santo.* Santander, Sal Terrae, 1982.

———. *Eclesiogénesis. Las comunidades de base reinventan la iglesia.* Bogotá, CLAR, 1981. Engl. trans., *Ecclesiogenesis: The Base Communities Reinvent the Church* (Maryknoll, N.Y., Orbis, 1986).

———. *Encarnación: La humanidad y jovialidad de nuestro Dios.* Santander, Sal Terrae, 1980.

———. *De la espiritualidad de la liberación a la prática de la liberación.* Bogotá, CLAR, 1981.

———. *La experiencia de Dios.* Bogotá, CLAR, 1977.

———. *La fe en la periferia del mundo: El caminar de la Iglesia con los oprimidos.* Santander, Sal Terrae, 1981.

———. *Iglesia: Carisma y poder. Ensayos de eclesiología militante.* Santander, Sal Terrae, 1982. Engl. trans., *Church: Charism and Power* (New York, Crossroad, 1985).

———. *Jesucristo y la liberación del hombre.* Madrid, Cristiandad, 1981.

———. *The Lord's Prayer: The Prayer of Integral Liberation.* Maryknoll, N.Y., Orbis, 1983. Translated from the Portuguese original, *O pai-nosso: a oração da libertação integral* (Petrópolis, Vozes, 1979).

———. *Desde el lugar del pobre.* Bogotá, CLAR, 1984.

———. *El rostro materno de Dios.* Madrid, Paulinas, 1980.

———. "Salvación en Jesucristo y proceso de liberación." *Concilium,* 96 (1974) 375–88.

———. *Teología del cautiverio y de la liberación.* Madrid, Paulinas, 2nd ed., 1978.

———. *Way of the Cross—Way of Justice.* Maryknoll, N.Y., Orbis, 1980.

———, and Boff, Clodovis. *Salvation and Liberation.* Maryknoll, N.Y./Melbourne, Orbis/Dove, 1984. Translated from the original Portuguese, *Da libertação: O sentido teológico das libertações sócio-históricas* (Petrópolis, Vozes, 1979).

Bonhoeffer, Dietrich. *Resistencia y sumisión.* Barcelona, Ariel, 1969.

Bonnín, Eduardo, ed. *Espiritualidad y liberación en América Latina.* San José, Costa Rica, DEI, 1982.

Cabestrero, Teófilo. *Diálogos sobre la Iglesia en América Latina.* Bilbao, Desclée, 1978.

———. *Los teólogos de liberación en Puebla.* Madrid, PPC, 1979.

Casalis, Georges. *Les idées justes no tombent pas du ciel.* Paris, Cerf, 1977. Engl. trans., *Correct Ideas Don't Fall from the Skies: Elements for an Inductive Theology* (Maryknoll, N.Y., Orbis, 1984). Span. trans., *Las buenas ideas no caen del cielo* (San José, Costa Rica, EDUCA, 1979).

———. "Jesus—Neither Abject Lord nor Heavenly Monarch," in Míguez Bonino, ed., *Faces,* 72–76.

Castillo, José María. "Teología y pobreza." *Misión Abierta*, 4–5 (1981) 151–63.

Centro de Estudios y Publicaciones. *El credo de los pobres*. Lima, CEP, 1978.

Chenu, Marie-Dominique. "Una realidad nueva: teólogos del Tercer Mundo." *Concilium*, 164 (1981) 37–46.

Codina, Víctor. "Eclesiologia Latino-Americana da libertação." REB, 165 (1982) 61–81.

———. "La irrupción de los pobres en la teología contemporánea." *Misión Abierta*, 4–5 (1981) 203–12.

———. *Renacer a la solidaridad*. Santander, 1982.

Comblin, José. "Humanidad y liberación de los oprimidos." *Concilium*, 175 (1982) 264–75.

———. "A Missão do Espírito Santo." REB, 35 (1975) 288–325.

Comisión para la Participación de las Iglesias en el Desarrollo (Consejo Mundial de Iglesias). *Hacia una iglesia solidaria con los pobres*. Lima, CPID/CELADEC, 1979.

———, and Asociación de Economistas del Tercer Mundo. *Tecnología y necesidades básicas*. San José, Costa Rica, Editorial Universitaria Centroamericana, 1979.

Cone, James H. *A Black Theology of Liberation*. Philadelphia, Lippincott, 1970.

———. *God of the Oppressed*. New York, Seabury, 1975.

———. "El significado de Dios en los espirituales negros." *Concilium*, 163 (1981) 390–94.

Consejo Episcopal Latinoamericano. *Dios: problemática de la no-creencia en América Latina*. Bogotá, Secretariado General del Consejo Episcopal Latinoamericano, 1974.

———, Segunda Conferencia General. *Medellín*. Bogotá, Secretariado General del Consejo Episcopal Latinoamericano, 9th ed., 1976.

———, Tercera Conferencia General. *Puebla*. Madrid, 1982.

Cosmao, Vincent. *Changer le monde: Une tâche pour l'Eglise*. Paris, Cerf, 1979. Span. trans., *Transformar el mundo: una tarea para la Iglesia* (Santander, Sal Terrae, 1981). Engl. trans., *Changing the World: An Agenda for the Churches* (Maryknoll, N.Y., Orbis, 1984).

———. "La salvación a la luz de la teología de la liberación." *Selecciones de Teología*, 70 (1979) 179–83.

Croatto, J. Severino. *Liberación y libertad: pautas hermenéuticas*. Lima, CEP, 1978. Engl. trans., *Exodus: A Hermeneutics of Freedom* (Maryknoll, N.Y., Orbis, 1981).

———. "Liberación y libertad: Reflexiones hermenéuticas en torno al Antiguo Testamento," in Croatto et al., *Pueblo*.

———. "Liberar a los pobres: aproximación hermenéutica," in Instituto Superior Evangélico, *Pobres*, 15–28.

———, et al. *Pueblo oprimido. Señor de la historia*. Montevideo, Tierra Nueva, 1972.

Cussianovich, Alejandro. *Desde los pobres en la tierra. Perspectivas de vida religiosa*. Salamanca, Sígueme, 1977.

Díez Alegría, José María. *¡ Yo credo en la esperanza!* Bilbao, Desclée, 1972. In English, *I Believe in Hope* (Garden City, N.Y., Doubleday, 1974).

Dillenberger, John, and Welch, Claude. *Protestant Christianity Interpreted Through Its Development*. New York, Scribner's, 1958. Span. trans., *El cristianismo protestante* (Buenos Aires, La Aurora, 1958).

Duquoc, Christian, *Dios diferente: Ensayo sobre la simbólica trinitaria*. Salamanca, 2nd ed., 1982.

———. "El Dios de Jesús y la crisis de Dios en nuestro tiempo," in Vargas Machuca, *Jesucristo*, 39–50.

Dussel, Enrique D. "Acceso ético al absoluto: El discurso ateo como condición de la afirmación de Dios." *Christus*, 484 (1976). Also in Dussel, *Religión*, 15–66.

——. "Coyuntura de la praxis cristiana en América Latina," in Pixley and Sebastian, *Praxis*, 204–8.

——. *Desintegración de la cristiandad colonial y liberación.* Salamanca, Sígueme, 1978.

——. "Dominación-liberación: Un discurso teológico distinto." *Concilium*, 96 (1974) 328–352.

——. *A History of the Church in Latin America: Colonialism to Liberation (1492–1979).* Grand Rapids, Eerdmans, 1981.

——. *De Medellín a Puebla: Una década de sangre y esperanza.* Mexico City, 1979.

——. *Método para una filosofía de la liberación.* Salamanca, Sígueme, 1974.

——. "El Reino de Dios y los pobres." *Servir*, 83–84 (1979) 521–50.

——. *Religión como supra e infra-estructura.* Mexico City, Edicol, 1977.

——, et al. *Liberación y cautiverio: Debates en torno al método de la teología en América Latina.* Mexico City, Comité Organizador del Encuentro de Teología Latinoamericana, 1976.

Eagleson, John, and Scharper, Philip, eds. *Puebla and Beyond: Documentation and Commentary.* Maryknoll, N.Y., Orbis, 1979.

Eagleson, John, and Torres, Sergio, eds. *Theology in the Americas* (Maryknoll, N.Y., Orbis, 1976).

EATWOT. "The Irruption of the Third World—Challenge to Theology: Final Statement of the Fifth EATWOT Conference, New Delhi, August 17–29, 1981," in Fabella and Torres, *Irruption*, 191–206.

Echegaray, Hugo. *Apurando la historia.* Lima, Comisión Evangélica de Educación, 1980.

——. The Practice of Jesus. Maryknoll, N.Y., Orbis, 1984. Translated from the Spanish original, *La práctica de Jesús* (Salamanca, 1982).

Ellacuría, Ignacio. "Las bienaventuranzas como carta fundacional de la Iglesia de los pobres," in Romero et al., *Iglesia*.

——. *Conversión de la iglesia al reino de Dios.* San Salvador, 1985.

——. "Discernir 'el signo' de los tiempos." *Diakonía*, 17 (1981).

——. "Fe y justicia en la historia de salvación," in Ellacuría et al., *Fe*, 13–78.

——. *Freedom Made Flesh: The Mission of Christ and His Church.* Maryknoll, N.Y., Orbis, 1976.

——. "Historización del bien común y de los derechos humanos en una sociedad dividida," in Tamez and Trinidad, *Capitalismo*, II, 81–94.

——. "La iglesia de los pobres, sacramento histórico de liberación." ECA 348–49 (1977) 707–22.

——. "Los pobres, lugar teológico en América Latina." *Misión Abierta*, 4–5 (1981) 225–40.

——. "¿Por qué muere Jesús y por qué le matan?" in Ellacuría et al., *Temas*, 91–101.

——. "El pueblo crucificado: ensayo de soteriología histórica," in Ellacuría et al., *Cruz.*

——. "El Reino de Dios y el paro en el Tercer Mundo." *Concilium*, 173 (1982) 588–96.

——. "Tesis sobre posibilidad, necesidad y sentido de una teología latinoamericana," in Vargas Machuca, *Teología*, 325–50.

——, et al. *Cruz y resurrección: Presencia y anuncio de una Iglesia nueva.* Mexico City, CRT, 1978.

———, et al. *Fe, justicia y opción por los oprimidos*. Bilbao, Desclée, 1980.

———, et al. *Temas para reflexión teológica*. Managua, Universidad Centroamericana, 1982.

Equipo SELADOC. *Panorama de la teología latinoamericana*. Salamanca, Sígueme, 1975.

Escudero Freire, Carlos. *Devolver el evangelico a los pobres*. Salamanca, Sígueme, 1978.

Espeja Pardo, Jesús. *Jesucristo palabra de libertad*. Salamanca, San Esteban, 1979.

Fabella, Virginia, and Torres, Sergio, eds. *Irruption of the Third World: Challenge to Theology* (papers from the fifth EATWOT conference, Aug. 1981, New Delhi, India). Maryknoll, N.Y., Orbis, 1983.

Feiner, Johannes, and Löhrer, Magnus, eds. *Mysterium Salutis*. Madrid, Cristiandad, 1969.

Fernández, Bonifacio. "Lugares humanos del Espíritu: de la salvación perdida a la salvación realizada." *Misión Abierta*, 2 (1981) 65–75.

Floristán, Casiano, and Tamayo, Juan José, eds. *Conceptos fundamentales de pastoral*. Madrid, Cristiandad, 1983.

Freire, Paulo. *Las iglesias, la educación y el proceso de liberación humana en la historia*. Buenos Aires, La Aurora, 1974.

Fries, Heinrich, ed. *Conceptos fundamentales de teología*. Madrid, 1966.

Galilea, Segundo. *Teología de la liberación: Ensayo de síntesis*. Bogota, Indo-American Press Service, 1976.

García-Murga, José R. "El rostro liberador de Dios," in Vargas Machuca, *Teología*, 89–114.

Garaudy, Roger. *Del anatema al diálogo*. Salamanca, Sígueme, 2nd ed., 1980. In English, *A Marxist Challenge to the Christian Churches* (New York, Vintage, 1968).

———. *Palabra de hombre*. Madrid, Cuadernos para el diálogo, 2nd ed., 1976. French original, *Parole d'homme* (Paris, Laffont, 1975).

Geffré, Claude. "La conmoción de una teología profética." *Concilium*, 96 (1974) 301–12.

Gibellini, Rosino, ed. *Frontiers of Theology in Latin America*. Maryknoll, N.Y., Orbis, 1979.

González, Justo. *Encarnación y revolución*. San Juan, La Reforma, 1965.

González Faus, José Ignacio. *Acceso a Jesús*. Salamanca, Sígueme, 2nd ed., 1979.

———. "Dios, problema político." *Razón y Fe*, 975 (1979) 387–95.

———. *Este es el hombre: Estudios sobre identidad cristiana y realización humana*. Santander, Sal Terrae, 1980.

———. *La humanidad nueva*. Madrid, EAPSA, 2nd ed., 1974.

———. "Jesús de Nazaret y los ricos de su tiempo." *Misión Abierta*, 4–5 (1981) 45–71.

———. *La teología de cada día*. Salamanca, Sígueme, 1976.

González Montes, Adolfo. "Las aporías de la teología critica." *Salmanticensis*, 3 (1982) 425–42.

———. *Razón política de la fe cristiana: Un estudio histórico-teológico de la hermenéutica política de la fe*. Salamanca, Universidad Pontifícia, 1976.

González Ruiz, José M. *Dios está en la base: Aproximación a una teología de la base*. Barcelona, 1973.

Gorostiaga, Xabier, ed. *Para entender América Latina: Aporte colectivo de los científicos sociales en Puebla*. San José, Costa Rica, Editorial Universitaria Centro-Americana, 1979.

Greinacher, Norbert. "La teología de la liberación, desafío a las iglesias del primer mundo." *Selecciones de Teología*, 85 (1983) 44–54.

Gutiérrez, Gustavo. "Apuntes para una teología de liberación." *Cristianismo y Sociedad*, 24–25 (1970) 6–22.

———. "Beber en su propio pozo." *Concilium*, 179 (1982) 351–63.

———. "En busca de los pobres de Jesucristo," in Richard, *Materiales,* 137–63.

———. "Caminando con el pueblo." *Pasos* (Santiago), 25 (1979) 1–11.

———. "Comunidades cristianas de base: Perspectivas eclesiológicas," *Cristianismo y Sociedad*, 64 (1980) 14–25.

———. *El Dios de la vida.* Lima, Universidad Católica, 1981. Also in *Christus*, 556 (1982) 28–50. Engl. trans., forthcoming, Orbis Books.

———. "Evangelio y praxis de liberación," in Instituto Fe y Secularidad, *Fe cristiana,* 231–45.

———. "El fenómeno de la contestación en América Latina." *Concilium*, 68 (1971) 193–207.

———. "Finding Our Way to Talk about God," in Fabella and Torres, *Irruption*, 222–34.

———. "Freedom and Salvation: A Political Problem," in Gutiérrez and Richard Shaull, *Liberation and Change*, Atlanta, John Knox, 1977, 3–94.

———. "The Historical Power of the Poor," in Gutiérrez, *Power*, 75–107.

———. "Itinerario eclesial: de Medellín a Puebla." *Moralia* (Madrid), 314 (1982) 51–66.

———. "Liberation and the Poor: The Puebla Perspective," in Gutiérrez, *Power*, 125–65.

———. "The Limitations of Modern Theology: On a Letter of Dietrich Bonhoeffer," in Gutiérrez, *Power,* 222–33.

———. *Lineas pastorales en América Latina.* Lima, Centro de Documentación, MIEC-JECI, 5th ed., 1970.

———. "Lyon: Debate de la tesis de G. Gutiérrez." *Páginas* 10, nos. 71–72 (1985).

———. "Marxismo y Cristianismo." *Pasos* (Santiago), 13 (1972) 1–27.

———. "Movimientos de liberación y teología." *Concilium*, 93 (1974) 448–56.

———. "Los pobres en la iglesia." *Concilium*, 124 (1977) 103–9.

———. *Power of the Poor in History.* Maryknoll, N.Y. 1983. Spanish original, *La fuerza histórica de los pobres* (Lima, CEP, 1979).

———. "Praxis de liberación: Teología y anuncio." *Concilium*, 96 (1974) 353–74.

———. "Statement by Gustavo Gutiérrez," in Eagleson and Torres, *Theology*, 309–13.

———. *Hacia una teología de la liberación.* Bogotá, Indo-American Press Service, 1971.

———. "Teología y ciencias sociales." *Páginas* 9, nos. 63–64 (1984).

———. *A Theology of Liberation: History, Politics, and Salvation.* Maryknoll, N.Y., Orbis, 1973. Spanish original, *Teología de la liberación, Perspectivas* (Lima, CEP, 1971).

———. "Theology from the Underside of History," in Gutiérrez, *Power*, 169–221.

———. "Two Theological Perspectives: Liberation Theology and Progessivist Theology," in Torres and Fabella, eds., *Emergent Gospel*, 227–55.

———. "La violencia de un sistema." *Concilium*, 160 (1980) 565–75.

———. *We Drink from Our Own Wells: The Spiritual Journey of a People.* Maryknoll, N.Y., Orbis, 1984. Spanish original, *Beber en su propio pozo: En el itinerario espiritual de un pueblo* (Lima, CEP, 2nd ed., 1983).

Hanks, Tomás. *Opresión, pobreza y liberación: Reflexiones bíblicas.* San José, Costa Rica, Caribe, 1982. Engl. trans., *God So Loved the Third World* (Maryknoll, N.Y., Orbis Books, 1983).

Hernández Pico, Juan. "El hombre nuevo y la nueva sociedad según la fe cristiana hoy en Centroamérica." *Christus,* 542 (1981) 41–54.

———. "El martirio hoy en América Latina: scándalo, locura y fuerza de Dios." *Diakonía,* 23 (1982) 37–54.

Hinkelammert, Franz Josef. *Las armas ideológicas de la muerte.* San José, Costa Rica, DEI, 2nd ed., 1981. Engl. trans., *The Ideological Weapon of Death* (Maryknoll, N.Y., Orbis Books, 1983).

Hortal, Jesús. "Experiencia de Dios: Su lugar en la teológia actual," in Equipo. SELADOC, *Panorama,* I, 13–26.

IECT. "Final Document," in Eagleson and Torres, *Challenge,* 231–46.

———. "Letter to Christians in Popular Christian Communities in the Poor Countries and Regions of the World," in Eagleson and Torres, *Challenge,* 247–50.

Iglesia y Sociedad en América Latina (ISAL). *Pueblo oprimido, Señor de la historia.* Montevideo, Tierra Nueva, 1972.

Instituto Fe y Secularidad. *Fe cristiana y cambio social en América Latina.* Salamanca, Sígueme, 1973.

Instituto Superior Evangélico de Educación Teológica. *Los pobres: Encuentro y compromiso.* Buenos Aires, 1978.

Internacional Comisión Teológica, *Teología de la liberación.* Madrid, BAC, 1978.

Jerez, César. "Ecumenismo desde los pobres." *Diakonía,* 19 (1981) 74–88.

———. "Jesucristo, centro de la historia." *Servir,* 85 (1980) 123–43.

Jiménez Limón, Javier. "Ecumenismo desde los crucificados." *Estudios Ecuménicos* (Mexico City), 39 (1980) 36–48.

———. "Meditation on the God of the Poor," in Richard, *Idols,* 150–58.

———. "Opción cristiana por los oprimidos y acción política, hoy." *Christus,* 487 (1976) 42–54.

Kirk, J. Andrew. *Liberation Theology: An Evangelical View from the Third World.* Atlanta, John Knox, 1979.

Kitamori, Kazo. *Theology of the Pain of God.* Richmond, Va., John Knox, 1965.

Küng, Hans. ¿*Existe Dios?* Madrid, 1979. Engl. trans., *Does God Exist? An Answer for Today.* (New York, Vintage, 1981).

Latin American Bishops' Conference. "Evangelization in Latin America's Present and Future: Final Document of the Third General Conference of the Latin American Episcopate [Puebla]," in Eagleson and Scharper, *Puebla,* 122–285.

Leuba, Jean-Louis. "Dios salvador según Karl Barth: Un modelo de soteriología protestante," in Leuba et al., *Dios,* 113–35.

———, et al. *El Dios de nuestra salvación.* Salamanca, Secretariado Trinitario, 1977.

Leuridan, Juan, comp. *Justicia y exploitación en la tradición cristiana antigua.* Lima, CEP, 1978.

Libânio Cristo, Carlos Alberto. *¡Creo desde la cárcel!* Bilbao, Desclée, 1976.

Lois, Julio. "Teología de la liberación," in Rossi and Valsecchi, *Diccionario,* 1391–1405.

Lotz, J. B., et al. "Dios," in Fries, *Conceptos,* I, 404–42.

de Lubac, Henri. *The Discovery of God.* Chicago, Regnery, 1967.

Lucchetti Bingemer, María. "A pregunta por Deus e a realidade latinoamericana." REB, 165 (1983) 273–91.

Malvido, Eduardo. *El Jesús histórico y el Jesús resucitado: Bases de una cristología catequista.* Madrid, San Pio X, 1983.

Manzanera, Miguel. *Teología y salvación-liberación en la obra de Gustavo Gutiérrez.* Bilbao, Universidad de Deusto/Mansajero, 1978.

Marion, Jean-Luc. *L'idole et la distance.* Paris, Grasset, 1977.

Mateos, Juan, and Barreto, J. *Vocabulario teológico del Evangelio de Juan.* Madrid, Cristiandad, 1980.

Metz, Johannes, B. *La fe en historia y la sociedad.* Madrid: Christiandad, 1979. Engl. trans., *Faith in History and Society: Toward a Practical Fundamental Theology* (New York, Seabury, 1980).

Miguélez, Xosé. *La teología de la liberación y su método: Estudio en Hugo Assmann y Gustavo Gutiérrez.* Barcelona, Herder, 1976.

Míguez Bonino, José. *Christians and Marxists: The Mutual Challenge to Revolution.* Grand Rapids, Eerdmans, 1976.

———. "El compromiso cristiano ante la liberación." *Acción Ecuménica,* 1 (1973) 18–30.

———. *Espacio para ser hombre.* Buenos Aires, 1975. In English, *Room to Be People: An Interpretation of the Message of the Bible for Today's World* (Geneva, World Council of Churches, 1979).

———. *La fe en busca de eficacia.* Salamanca, Sígueme, 1977.

———. "Nuestra fe y nuestra tiempo." *Cristianismo y Sociedad,* 4 (1974) 1–12.

———. "El Reino de Dios y la historia," in Padilla, *Reino,* 75–95.

———. *Toward a Christian Political Ethics.* Philadelphia, Fortress, 1983.

———, ed. *Faces of Jesus: Latin American Christologies.* Maryknoll, N.Y., Orbis, 1984.

Miranda, José Porfirio. *El comunismo en la Biblia.* Mexico City, Siglo XXI, 1981. Engl. trans., *Communism in the Bible* (Maryknoll, N.Y., Orbis, 1982).

———. *Hambre y sed de justicia.* Mexico City, n.p., 1972.

———. *Marx y la Biblia, Crítica a la filosofía de la opresión.* Salamanca, Sígueme, 1971. Engl. trans., *Marx and the Bible: A Critique of the Philosophy of Oppression* (Maryknoll, N.Y., Orbis, 1974).

———. *El ser y el Mesías.* Salamanca, Sígueme, 1973. Engl. trans., *Being and the Messiah: The Message of St. John* (Maryknoll, N.Y., Orbis, 1977).

Moltmann, Jürgen. "Crítica teológica de la religión política," in Moltmann et al., *Ilustración,* 11–45.

———. *The Crucified God.* New York, Harper & Row, 1974. Span. trans., *El Dios crucificado* (Salamanca, Sígueme, 1975).

———. "El 'Dios crucificado': El moderno problema de Dios y la historia trinitaria divina." *Concilium,* 76 (1972) 335–47.

———. *El experimento esperanza.* Salamanca, Sígueme, 1976. In English, *The Experiment Hope* (Philadelphia, Fortress, 1975).

———. "Open Letter" [to José Míguez Bonino]. *Christianity and Crisis,* March, 1975.

———. *Teología de la esperanza.* Salamanca, Sígueme, 1978. In English, *A Theology of Hope* (New York, Harper & Row, 1967).

———, et al. *Ilustración y teoría teológica.* Salamanca, Sígueme, 1973.

Muñoz, Ronaldo. *Nueva conciencia de la iglesia en América Latina.* Salamanca, Sígueme, 1974.

Nygren, Anders. *Eros y ágape.* Barcelona, 1969.

Oliveros, Roberto. *Liberación y teología: Génesis y crecimiento de una reflexión 1966–1977.* Lima, CEP, 1977.

Padilla, René. "La teología de la liberación: una evaluación crítica." *Misión*, 2 (1982) 16–21.

———, ed. *El Reino de Dios y América Latina*. El Paso, Casa Bautista, 1975.

Pannenberg, Wolfhart. *Teoría de la ciencia y teología*. Madrid, Cristiandad, 1981. In English, *Theology and the Philosophy of Science* (Philadelphia, Westminster, 1976).

Pereira Ramalho, Jether. "Ecumenismo que brota de las bases." *Estudios Ecuménicos* (Mexico City), 39 (1980) 24–25.

Peruvian Bishops' Commission for Social Action. *Between Honesty and Hope: Documentation from and about the Church in Latin America*. Maryknoll, N.Y., Maryknoll Publications, 1969.

Pikaza, Xabier. *Anuciar la libertad a los cautivos*. Salamanca, Sígueme, 1985.

———. *La Biblia y la teología de la historia*. Madrid, Fax, 1972.

———. "Conocimiento de Dios y pecado de los hombres: Rm 1, 18–32." *Cultura Bíblica*, 265 (1976) 245–67.

———. *Las dimensiones de Dios: La respuesta a la Bíblia*. Salamanca, Sígueme, 1973.

———. *Evangelio de Jesús y praxis marxista*. Madrid, Marova, 1977.

———. *Experiencia religiosa y cristianismo: Introducción al misterio de Dios*. Salamanca, Sígueme, 1981.

———. *Hermanos de Jesús y servidores de los más pequeños (Mt 25: 31–46)*. Salamanca, Sígueme, 1984.

———. "El lugar de la experiencia de Dios." *Diálogo Ecuménico*, 14 (1979) 71–100.

———. *María y el Espíritu Santo*. Salamanca, 1981.

———. "Mateo 25, 31–46: Cristología y liberación," in Vargas Machuca, *Jesucristo*, 220–28.

———. "La muerte en el pensamiento bíblico." *Sal Terrae*, 10 (1977) 687–98.

———. *Los orígenes de Jesús: Ensayos de cristología bíblica*. Salamanca, Sígueme, 1976.

———. "Postscriptum: Carta de un dogmático a un catequeta," in Malvido, *Jesús*, 229–53.

———. *Presupuestos filosóficos de la exégesis de R. Bultmann y J. Moltmann*. Madrid, 1972.

———. *La teología de los evangelios de Jesús*. Salamanca, Sígueme, 1974.

———. "Tipificación de la experiencia religiosa," in Pikaza, *Experiencia*, 256–300.

———. "Trinidad y ontología, reflexiones en torno al planteamiento sistemático del misterio trinitario." *Estudios Trinitarios*, 2 (1974) 189–236.

———, et al. *Bibliografía trinitaria*. Salamanca, Secretariado Trinitario, 1978.

Pixley, Jorge. "El evangelio paulino de justificación por la fe: conversación con José Porfírio Miranda." *Revista Bíblica* (Buenos Aires), 171–72 (1979) 57–74.

———. *Exodo: Una lectura evangélica popular*. Mexico City, Casa Unida, 1983. English trans., *On Exodus* (Maryknoll, N.Y., Orbis, 1987).

———, and Bastian, Jean-Pierre, eds. *Praxis cristiana y producción teológica*. Salamanca, Sígueme, 1979.

PRODIADIS. *Lectura política de la Biblia*. San José, Costa Rica, 1979.

Quell, Gottfried, and Stauffer, Ethelbert. *Caridad*. Madrid, Fax, 1974. In English, *Love* (London, Black, 1949).

Quiroz Magaña, Alvaro. *Eclesiología de la teología de la liberación*. Salamanca, Sígueme, 1983.

Rahner, Karl. "Amor," in Rahner, *Sacramentum*, I, 114–33.

———. *Curso fundamental sobre la fe: Introducción al concepto de cristianismo*. Barcelona, Herder, 1979.

————. "El Dios Trino como principio y fundamento transcendente de la historia de la salvación," in Feiner and Löhrer, *Mysterium*, 2/1, 360–449.

————. *Escritos de Teología*. Madrid, Taurus, 1964.

————. "Per una 'formula breve' della fede cristiana," in Rahner, *Nuovi saggi,* III, 175–89.

————. *Foundations of Christian Faith*, New York, Crossroad, 1982.

————. *Nuovi saggi*. Rome, Paoline, 1969.

————, ed. *Sacramentum Mundi*. Barcelona, Herder, 1972.

Ramm, Bernard. "Fundamentalismo." *Diccionario de Teología Contemporánea*. El Paso, Casa Bautista, 1969.

Ramos Regidor, José. *Jesús y el despertar de los oprimidos*. Salamanca, Sígueme, 1984.

Ratzinger, Joseph, et al. *Teología de la liberación: Documentos sobre una polémica*. San José, Costa Rica, DEI, 1984.

Richard, Pablo. "Biblical Theology of Confrontation with Idols," in Richard et al., *Idols*, 3–25.

————. "Desarrollo de la teología latinoamericana: 1968–1978." *Serie reflexiva bíblico-teológica*, 1 (1979) 1–18.

————. "La ética como espiritualidad liberadora en la realidad eclesial de América Latina." *Moralia* (Madrid), 13–14 (1982), 101–14.

————. "El Exodo: la búsqueda de Dios en la lucha política liberadora," in Richard et al., *Cristianismo*, 67–82.

————. *La Iglesia latinoamericana entre el temor y la esperanza*. San José, Costa Rica, DEI, 1980.

————. *Mortes das cristandades e nascimento da igreja*. São Paulo, Paulinas, 1982. Engl. trans., *Death of Christendoms and Birth of the Church* (Maryknoll, N.Y., Orbis Books, 1987).

————. *Muerte de la cristiandad—Nacimiento de la iglesia*. Paris, 1979.

————. "La razón de nuestra esperanza: nuestra teo-logía de la liberación." *Spiritus*, 90 (1983) 49–50.

————, ed. *Materiales para una historia de la teología en América Latina*. San José, Costa Rica, DEI, 1981.

————, ed. *Raíces de la teología latinamericana*. San José, Costa Rica, DEI, 1985.

————. "El significado de Jesucristo para un proceso revolucionario," in Richard et al., *Fe cristiana*.

————. "Situación religiosa y eclesial de América Latina," *Moralia* (Madrid), 13–14 (1982).

————, et al. *Cristianismo, lucha ideológica y racionalidad socialista*. Salamanca, Sígueme, 1975.

————, et al. *Fe cristiana y revolución sandinista en Nicaragua*. Managua, IHC, 1979.

————, et al. *The Idols of Death and the God of Life: A Theology*. Maryknoll, N.Y., Orbis, 1983.

————, and Meléndez, Guillermo, eds. *La Iglesia de los pobres en América Central: Un análisis socio-politico de la Iglesia centroamericana 1960–1982*. San José, Costa Rica, DEI, 1982.

Romero, Oscar A. *The Church, Political Organisation and Violence: The Third Pastoral Letter of Mgr. Oscar Arnulfo Romero, Archbishop of San Salvador, and the First of Mgr. Arturo Rivera Damas, Bishop of Santiago de María*. London, CIIR, CAFOD, and Trocaire, 1980.

————. "La dimensión política de la fe desde la opción por los pobres." *Servir*, 87 (1980) 431–50. Engl. trans. in Romero, *Voice*, 177–87.

————. *Romero, Martyr for Liberation: The Last Two Homilies of Archbishop Romero of San Salvador.* London, CIIR, 1982.

————. *Voice of the Voiceless: The Four Pastoral Letters and Other Statements.* Maryknoll, N.Y., Orbis, 1985.

————, et al. *Iglesia de los pobres y organizaciones populares.* San Salvador, UCA, 1978.

Rossi, Leandro, and Valsecchi, Ambrogio, eds. *Diccionario enciclopédico de teología moral.* Madrid, Paulinas, 4th ed., 1980.

Rovira Belloso, José M. *Revelación de Dios, salvación del hombre.* Salamanca, Secretariado Trinitario, 1979.

Ruíz, Gregorio. "El Magnificat: Dios está por los que pierden." *Sal Terrae,* 68 (1980) 781–90.

de Santa Ana, Julio. *El desafío de los pobres a la Iglesia.* San José, Costa Rica, EDUCA, 1977.

————. "Fe cristiana e ideología," *IS,* 3 (1963) 3–15.

————. *Good News to the Poor: The Challenge of the Poor in the History of the Church.* Maryknoll, N.Y., Orbis, 1979.

Scannone, Juan Carlos. "La teología de la liberación: caracterización, corrientes, etapas." *Stromata* (Buenos Aires), 1–2 (1982) 3–40.

Schillebeeckx, Edward. "Presentación de Gustavo Gutiérrez en la Universidad de Nimega." *Servir,* 82 (1979) 462–66.

Segundo, Juan Luís. "Condicionamientos actuales socio-políticos, eclesiales e ideológicos para la reflexión teológica en América Latina," in Segundo et al., *Liberación,* 91–102.

————. *El hombre de hoy ante Jesús de Nazaret.* Madrid, Cristiandad, 1982, 3 vols. Engl. trans., *Jesus of Nazareth Yesterday and Today* (Maryknoll, N.Y., Orbis, 1984–87), 5 vols.

————. *The Liberation of Theology.* Maryknoll, N.Y., Orbis, 1976.

————. *Nuestra idea de Dios.* Buenos Aires, Lohlé, 1970. Engl. trans., *Our Idea of God* (Maryknoll, N.Y., Orbis, 1984).

————. "Las teologías de liberación." *Pastoral Misionera* (Madrid), 4 (1982) 352–65.

————, et al. *Liberación y cautiverio: Debates en torno al método de la teología en América Latina.* Mexico City, ELT, 1976.

Sicre, José Luís. *Los dioses olvidados: Poder y riqueza en los profetas pre-exílicos.* Madrid, Cristiandad, 1979.

Silva Gotay, Samuel. *El pensamiento cristiano revolucionario en América Latina y el Caribe.* Salamanca, Sígueme, 1980.

————. *El Salvador: Un pueblo perseguido, testimonio de cristianos.* Lima, CEP, 1981.

Sobrino, Jon. "El aporte de la Iglesia a la esperanza de los pobres." *Misión Abierta,* 4–5 (1982) 123–27.

————, et al. *Apuntes para una teología nicaragüense.* San José, Costa Rica, DEI, 1980.

————. *Christology at the Crossroads: A Latin American Approach.* Maryknoll, N.Y., Orbis, 1978. Spanish original, *Cristología desde América Latina: Esbozo a partir del seguimiento del Jesús histórico* (Mexico City, 2nd ed., 1977).

————. "¿Como abordar pastoralmente el tema de Dios?" Mimeographed (San Salvador, 1982) 1–25. Engl. trans. in Floristán and Tamayo, eds., *Conceptos,* 248–64.

————. "Conllevamos mutualmente: Análisis teológico de la solidaridad cristiana." *ECA,* 401 (1982) 157–78.

————. "Cristianos y desarrollo." *ECA,* 402 (1982) 279–84.

———. "Dios y los procesos revolucionarios," in Sobrino et al., *Apuntes*, 105–29. Also in *Christus*, 556 (1982) 15–27.

———. "Los documentos de Puebla: Serena afirmación de Medellín." *Puebla* (Petrópolis), 4 (1979) 197–217.

———. "The Epiphany of the God of Life in Jesus of Nazareth," in Richard et al., *Idols*, 66–102.

———. "La esperanza de los pobres en América Latina." *Misión Abierta*, 4–5 (1982) 112–27.

———. "Espiritualidad de Jesús y de la liberación." *Christus*, 529–30 (1979) 59–63.

———. "Experiencia de Dios en la iglesia de los pobres," in Bonnín, *Espiritualidad*, 133–52.

———. "La fe en el Hijo de Dios desde un pueblo crucificado." *Concilium*, 173 (1982) 331–40.

———. "La fe de la Iglesia de los pobres," in Ellacuría et al., *Cruz*.

———. "La fe en el misterio de Dios Padre," in Ellacuría et al., *Cruz*.

———. "La fe en el Espíritu de Jesús," in Ellacuría et al., *Cruz*.

———. "La iglesia ante la crisis política actual: Recordando a Monseñor Romero." ECA, 390–91 (1981) 349–66.

———. "La iglesia de El Salvador: Interpelación y buena noticia." ECA, 411 (1983) 27–36.

———. "La Iglesia de los pobres en El Salvador," in Richard and Meléndez, *Iglesia*, 45–133.

———. "Jesús de Nazaret," in Floristán and Tamayo, eds., *Conceptos*, 480–513.

———. "Jesús y el Reino de Dios: Significado y objectivos últimos de su vida y misión." *Christus*, 540 (1980) 17–27. Also in *Jesús en América Latina*, 95ff.

———. *Jesús en América Latina: Su significado para la fe y la cristología.* San Salvador: UCA, 1982. Engl. trans., *Jesus in Latin America* (Maryknoll, N.Y., Orbis Books, 1987).

———. "La lucha por la justicia y el mensaje evangélico." *Selecciones de Teología*, 82 (1982) 83–90.

———. "Martirio: el nuevo nombre del seguimiento." *Sal Terrae*, 6 (1981) 465–73.

———. "El mayor servicio, carisma de la Compañia de Jesús." *Diakonía*, 22 (1982) 5–41.

———. "Monseñor Romero y la Iglesia salvadoreña: Un año despues." ECA, 389 (1981) 127–50.

———. *Monseñor Romero, verdadero profeta.* Managua, IHC/CAV, 1981.

———. "La oración de Jesús y del cristiano," in Sobrino et al., *Oración*, 55–125.

———. "Perfil de una santidad política." *Concilium*, 183 (1983) 335–44.

———. "Presupuestos teológicos de la tercera carta pastoral de Monseñor Romero," in Romero et al., *Iglesia*, 125–45.

———. "Reflexiones sobre el documento de cristología de Puebla," *Puebla* (Petrópolis), 4 (1979) 237–47.

———. "Relación de Jesús con los pobres y desclasados." *Concilium*, 150 (1979) 461–71.

———. "El resucitado es el crucificado: Lectura de la resurrección de Jesús desde los crucificados del mundo." *Sal Terrae*, 3 (1982) 181–94.

———. "Resurrección de una Iglesia popular," in Ellacuría et al., *Cruz*, 83–159.

———. "Sacramento: Conceptos útiles en teología," *Christus*, 534 (1980) 59–61.

———. "El seguimiento de Jesús como discernimiento." *Concilium*, 139 (1978) 517–29.

———. "El significado histórico del celibato en América Latina." *Christus*, 546 (1981) 34–42.

———. "Theological Analysis of His Life and Work," in Romero, *Martyr.*

———. "A Theologian's View of Oscar Romero," in Romero, *Voice,* 22–51.

———. *The True Church and the Poor.* Maryknoll, N.Y./London, Orbis/SCM, 1984. Spanish original, *Resurrección de la verdadera Iglesia: Los pobres, lugar teológico de la eclesiología* (Santander, Sal Terrae, 1981).

———. *La vida religiosa.* Panama City, 1978.

———, et al. *Oración cristiana y liberación.* Bilbao, Desclée, 1980.

Tamez, Elsa. *Bible of the Oppressed.* Maryknoll, N.Y., Orbis, 1982.

———, and Trinidad, Saúl, eds. *Capitalismo: violencia y anti-vida: La opresión de las mayorías y la domesticación de los dioses.* San José, Costa Rica, CSUSA, 2 vols., 1978.

Teólogos Latinoamericanos. *Iglesia que nasce del pueblo: Reflexiones y problemas.* Mexico City, CRT, 1978.

Teólogos del Tercer Mundo. *La irrupción del pobre en la sociedad y en la Iglesia: Documentos finales del IV Congreso Internacional Ecuménico de Teología.* Bilbao, Departamento Ecuménico de Investigaciones, 1982.

Terán Durati, J. "El ateísmo en América Latina: Reflexiones para un estudio inte-grado," in Vargas Machuca, *Teología,* 271–98.

Torres, Sergio. "Hacia una teología del Tercer Mundo." *Selecciones de Teología,* 70 (1979) 157–62.

———. "La vida espiritual en las comunidades religiosas." *Diakonía,* 17 (1981) 9–22.

———, and Eagleson, John, eds. *The Challenge of Basic Christian Communities* (papers from the International Ecumenical Congress of Theology, São Paulo, Brazil, Feb.–March 1980). Maryknoll, N.Y., Orbis, 1981.

———, and Fabella, Virginia, eds. *The Emergent Gospel: Theology from the Underside of History.* Maryknoll, N.Y./London, Orbis/Chapman, 1978.

Ureña, Enrique. "Teología europea y teología latinoamericana." *Razón y Fe* (Madrid), 203 (1981), 351–67.

Vargas Machuca, Antonio, ed. *Jesucristo en la historia y en la fe: Semana Internacional de Teología.* Salamanca, Fundación Juan, March, 1977.

———, ed. *Teología y mundo contemporáneo: Homenaje a Karl Rahner.* Madrid, Cristiandad, 1975.

Vidales, Raúl. *Cristianismo anti-burgués: Teología de la vida, teología de la muerte.* San José, Costa Rica, DEI, 1978.

———. "Logros y tareas de la teología de la liberación." *Concilium,* 96 (1974) 423–30.

———. "Perfil teológico de Gustavo Gutiérrez." *Servir,* 82 (1979) 466–76.

———. "El sujeto histórico de la teología de la liberación," in Pixley and Bastian, *Praxis,* 17–30.

———. *Desde la tradición de los pobres.* Mexico City, CRT, 1978.

———. "Vida-trabajo, binomio central del bien común en la tradición cristiana," in Tamez and Trinidad, *Capitalismo,* vol. 2.

Vives, Josep. "¿Como aparece Dios en la experiencia del mal y la injusticia?" *Sal Terrae,* 6 (1982) 407–15.

Wright, G. Ernest. *El Dios que actúa.* Madrid, Fax, 1974. English original, *God Who Acts: Biblical Theology as Recital* (London, SCM, 1966).